Stratford-Upon-Avon Studies
second series

General Editor: Jeremy Hawthorn
Professor of Modern British Literature,
University of Trondheim, Norway

Criticism and Critical Theory

Editor: Jeremy Hawthorn

Edward Arnold

© Edward Arnold (Publishers) Ltd 1984

First published in Great Britain 1984 by
Edward Arnold (Publishers) Ltd, 41 Bedford Square, London WC1B 3DQ

Edward Arnold (Australia) Pty Ltd, 80 Waverley Road, Caulfield East, Victoria 3145, Australia

Edward Arnold, 300 North Charles Street, Baltimore, Maryland 21201, USA

British Library Cataloguing in Publication Data

Criticism and critical theory.—(Stratford upon Avon studies, second series)
   1. Criticism
   I. Hawthorn, Jeremy   II. Series
   801'.95   PN81

   ISBN 0–7131–6414–X

Text set in 9/10 pt Garamond Compugraphic
by Colset Private Ltd, Singapore
Printed in Great Britain by
Biddles Ltd, Guildford, Surrey

Contents

Acknowledgements

The publishers wish to thank the following for permission to reproduce copyright material:

Crossroad Publishing Company for material from *Truth and Method* by Hans Georg Gadamer, copyright © 1975 by Sheed and Ward Ltd, used by permission of The Crossroad Publishing Company; *Diacritics* for material from de Man, 'Semiology and Rhetoric' in Josué V. Harari, ed., *Textual Strategies: Perspectives in Post-Structuralist Criticism*; Harcourt Brace Jovanovich Inc, the author's Literary Estate and The Hogarth Press for material from *A Room of One's Own* by Virginia Woolf, copyright 1929 by Harcourt Brace Jovanovich Inc; renewed 1957 by Leonard Woolf (reprinted by permission of the publisher); *Studies in English Literature* for material from 'Recent Studies in the Renaissance' by Patrick Cullen, *SEL* 22 (winter 1982), pp. 157–85.

Preface

In 1970, when *Contemporary Criticism* was published as a volume in the Stratford-upon-Avon Studies series, many teachers of literature such as myself responded to its appearance much as a parched traveller in the desert might have been expected to react to the offer of a glass of water. Those of us who had been students of literature in the 1960s had spent so much of our time arguing about criticism, agreeing upon the need for more theoretical discussion about its province, function, and value. And yet at that time so little overt discussion of such matters was available in textbook form, and much that was available was not up to date with recent developments. The received opinion of an older generation often appeared to be that one learned about criticism by doing it; our feeling that we were none too happy about 'doing it' before we had a clearer idea of what exactly it was that we were supposed to be doing seemed to be treated either as evidence that we were unfit to enter the noble profession of Letters, or as the sad but inevitable result of opening up university education to excessively large numbers of young people.

Our paranoia was doubtless exaggerated: after all, those who contributed to *Contemporary Criticism* were certainly not all of our generation. But anyone who was involved in a struggle to introduce a syllabus on literary criticism (or, worse still, on critical theory) in the late 1960s or 1970s will know that it was not just a question of paranoid exaggeration.

A volume entitled *Criticism and Critical Theory* published in 1984 risks being welcomed more as that same glass of water might be reacted to by a drowning hydrophobic. In the last 14 years more than one bookshop has set aside a special shelf for works of critical theory, and this shelf may today contain more books than shelves set aside, say, for studies of the eighteenth-century novel or of similar traditional areas. For some this signals a very dangerous trend – a movement away from a concern with actual literary (or other) work, and towards a dilettante interest in theory for its own sake: self-indulgent and self-enclosed.

This stereotype will not survive comparison with the evidence of the present volume. Three of the contributions are primarily concerned with single texts, and the others are very far from a disregard of specific textual material. Moreover, few areas of intellectual debate are less self-enclosed than most of those now concerned with criticism and critical theory. Of course, there *is* criticism that is élitist, self-indulgent and self-fixated, just as there is theoretical discussion of the same characteristics.

But consider what E.D. Hirsch has agreed is ' "one of the most significant" critical movements of recent years' – the feminist movement in criticism.[1] Excellent as the *Contemporary Criticism* volume is, a present-day reader of it cannot but be struck by the fact that all of its contributors are men. 'Cannot but be struck' because the nature of critical debate over the past decade or so has forced us to be aware of such matters. It is clear that the feminist movement in criticism did not originate in literary criticism. It was part of a larger movement of struggle in society at large. Nevertheless, without the work of feminist literary critics that movement would not automatically have influenced the way we read and criticize literature. Furthermore, there is no doubt at all that works of feminist literary criticism have had effects that go far beyond the reading and criticizing of literature (or film, or other works of art). As Cheri Register has put it, feminist criticism is ultimately cultural criticism[2] – a point reiterated by Barbara Hill Rigney in her discussion of Virginia Woolf's *A Room of One's Own* in this collection. And to the extent that it is cultural criticism, feminist criticism can hardly be accused of being self-enclosed.

We know from the New Critics, however, that it could be – certainly would, in the past, have been – criticized for something else: for treating literature not 'as literature', but as symptom of or evidence for something else. If the contributors to the present volume do not spend much time agonizing about the difference between 'literary' and 'non-literary' readings of literature, this does not mean that they are uninterested in the issue of how much, and what, knowledge needs to be brought to the reading of a literary (or other) text. Indeed, the concern of many contributors with central problems of reading and interpretation actually highlights this issue.

. In a very important article in *Contemporary Criticism* Ian Gregor argued for the need to progress beyond the New Critical treatment of the literary work as object ('Verbal Icon' or 'Well-wrought Urn') and instead to pay more attention to what in his opinion we obtained from E.M. Forster's discussions of character and plot in *Aspects of the Novel*: 'the feeling of what it is actually like to read a novel'.[3]

---

[1] Hirsch's comments are based on a statement of Jonathan Culler's, and are to be found in a review of Culler's *On Deconstruction: Theory and Criticism after Structuralism* (Ithaca, Cornell U.P., 1982). See E.D. Hirsch Jr, 'Derrida's Axioms', *London Review of Books*, V, 13 (1983), p. 18.

[2] Cheri Register, 'American Feminist Literary Criticism: A Bibliographical Introduction', in Josephine Donovan, ed., *Feminist Literary Criticism: Explorations in Theory* (Lexington, U.P. of Kentucky, 1975), p. 10.

[3] Ian Gregor, 'Criticism as an Individual Activity: The Approach through Reading', in Malcolm Bradbury and David Palmer, eds., *Contemporary Criticism* (London, Edward Arnold, 1970), p. 199.

In its concern with the reading experience Gregor's article was prophetic of one of the dominant shifts of critical concern over the past decade and a half: that shift away from concern with the text as thing-in-itself towards concern with the reading of the text. But whereas Gregor pays no attention to the differential and even contradictory readings given by different individuals to the same work, focusing rather upon a generalized 'reading process', much criticism since 1970 has preferred to grapple with solutions to what Jonathan Culler has dubbed the single most salient and puzzling fact about literature: 'that a literary work can have a range of meanings, but not just any meaning'.[4] In contrast, the veteran New Critic W.K. Wimsatt, in his own contribution to *Contemporary Criticism*, listed six possible alternative focuses for literary study without using the words 'reader' or 'reading' once.

In the present volume the contributions from Robert Crosman and R.A. Sharpe confront problems associated with reading and interpretation directly. So too does John Corner's essay, taking the discussion beyond the limits of literary interpretation and meaning. But the contributions by P.D. Juhl and Iain Wright are also concerned with problems which become more demanding once one turns one's attention from texts towards the reading of texts. The title of Robert Crosman's essay asks a question almost unthinkable in literary-critical circles 14 years ago. What all of these essays tackle – directly or indirectly – is the question of differential readings. Do literary (or other) texts have one meaning which is related to the author's intention, as P.D. Juhl argues? What is the connection between meaning and interpretation: does the latter follow a correct perception of the former (as R.A. Sharpe argues), or does the latter rather produce the former? Has what Terry Eagleton has dubbed the 'Reader's Liberation Front' really liberated readers, or has it misled its naïve adherents?

Such questions have to a certain extent been crystallized by the extension of such debates to film and television. In Britain over the past decade and a half what we can call academic–institutional politics have had an interesting involvement in the intellectual debates around such questions. Whereas the study of film has very often emerged out of literary studies, and has (to risk a very large generalization) in consequence followed a somewhat text-biased path of development, the study of television has more often been associated with sociological traditions of work which have been far more biased in favour of research into audiences, institutions, and agencies of production and control. The contrast between these two different traditions has been very fruitful: it has pointed to different sorts of weakness on both sides, and has led to serious consideration of the ways in which the strengths of both could be brought together. And the juxtaposition of theoretical work in the different fields of study has often

[4]Jonathan Culler, 'Prolegomena to a Theory of Reading', in Susan R. Suleiman and Inge Crosman, eds., *The Reader in the Text: Essays on Audience and Interpretation* (Princeton, Princeton U.P., 1980), p. 51.

been extremely thought-provoking. As an example one could cite the issue of the political implications of different theories of 'reading'. Extreme pluralist/individualist theories of reading associated with literature (forms of deconstruction, for instance) have frequently claimed for themselves a very radical or Leftist status;[5] in contrast, the pluralist/ individualist theories which have been labelled 'Uses and Gratifications' in mass-media studies are often overtly anti-Marxist, and are rather characterized by their adherents as liberal–humanist in inclination.

The inclusion of essays concerned with film and broadcasting in this volume bears testimony to the growth of interdisciplinary work in institutions of higher education in the 1970s and 1980s – in Britain especially in the polytechnics. Such interdisciplinarity is not only intellectually fruitful: it also serves to remind us that many seemingly abstract and technical issues in critical theory do have very important (and, sometimes, immediate) connections with issues of pressing social and political importance. In his introduction to *Contemporary Criticism* Malcolm Bradbury remarked wryly that the judge in the British 'Lady Chatterley' trial might be thought of as a crypto-New Critic in the light of his refusal to listen to evidence about Lawrence's intention or about his achievement in other works. Students of literature today are likely to be aware that a discussion of 'intention' links not just to debates about the meaning of *Paradise Lost*, but also to questions about the ideological determinants of television news reporting.

Colin Mercer's isolation of four main problems in critical theory at the start of his contribution focuses attention on to the way in which the political and the critical (whether or not literary) have been yoked together (sometimes with violence) with increasing regularity in the past decade or so. To take but one of the problems Mercer looks at – that of ideology – we can recognize that whatever the excesses attributable to participants in debates around this subject, the debates themselves have had a fruitful effect on the discussion of literature, film and television. And as a result, larger questions concerning crucial issues of knowledge and consciousness in history have been highlighted.

The dimension of history is mentioned by Mercer as the site of other, wide-reaching problems, a fundamental premise which is implicitly accepted by Iain Wright in his article. Many different academic and intellectual disciplines have been much preoccupied by debates around the vexed issue of the relationship between formal and historical approaches. Like the partners in a tempestuous sexual relationship, both of these make periodic attempts to survive on their own, but such attempts are usually short-lived. Here it is perhaps important to distinguish between formal and formalistic approaches: a criticism that has no sensitivity to formal issues is unlikely to have any real understanding of history, whilst an ahistorical criticism will be likely to perceive formal matters in an

---

[5]See, for instance, the highly loaded usage of the word 'radical' throughout Christopher Norris's book *Deconstruction: Theory and Practice* (London, Methuen, 1982).

unhelpfully mechanical and absolute manner. Thus although different varieties of Structuralism have on occasions managed to dehistoricize many areas of intellectual inquiry – even managing to win victories in the heart of enemy territory and to establish bridgeheads in Marxism – their victories have not been lasting.

Ahistorical or anti-historical critical theories tend to flourish in two rather different situations: firstly when periods of stability and steady expansion in society are such as to allow people to forget that things do change, and secondly when things change so rapidly and unpleasantly that a refuge in purely formal speculations can offer the illusion of an escape from history. If the New Criticism (at least in the time of its post-war hegemony) prospered in the former situation, more recent attempts to dispense with history have mushroomed in the latter one.

With history we come full-circle back to the problem of interpretation. Robert Weimann's epochal article 'Past Significance and Present Meaning in Literary History' neatly illustrates a complex of problematic issues in its title.[6] Arguments about meaning and interpretation often involve consideration of the relationship between past and present, a relationship both causal and interpretative.

Many of the critical debates which have dominated literary-critical discussion over the past decade and a half can be reduced to a core problem: 'How do we reach agreement?' Few retain any confidence that a quiet discussion of objective evidence followed by the reasoned question 'This is so, isn't it?' will result in general accord. 'Reaching agreement' dominates our world and not just our literary criticism, of course. From negotiations about nuclear weaponry to much less pressing considerations of the means whereby opposing views can be reconciled the reaching of agreement – even where it is an agreement upon how we cope with our disagreements – is, justifiably, the obsession of our age. In their preface to *Contemporary Criticism* Malcolm Bradbury and David Palmer stated that their aim in collecting the essays in the volume together was a double one: 'to look at the state and function of criticism at the present time, and to offer an exploration of the various methods of critical procedure that are now prevalent.' The emphasis here is more on mapping the field than on resolving boundary disputes, and this I think is an accurate representation of the mood of the time: three years after *Contemporary Criticism* the journal *Cultural Studies* published an article entitled 'Literature/Society: Mapping the Field'.[7] Perhaps the fact that Robert Crosman can refer both to Nixon and Reagan whilst discussing how we deal with the fact that different readers interpret the same text differently is an indication of the extent to which public events over the last decade and a half have made all

---

[6]Weimann's article was first published in *New Literary History*, but has been reprinted in a number of volumes, including Robert Weimann, *Structure and Society in Literary History* (London, Lawrence and Wishart, 1977).

[7]No author given, 'Literature/Society: Mapping the Field', *Cultural Studies* IV (spring 1973), p. 21.

of us more conscious that we need to devote more attention to learning ways of reaching agreement – or at least living with disagreement.

Susan Horton has seen the 'neatly antithetical critical positions' of E.D. Hirsch and Stanley Fish to be helpful to all of us in clarifying the way in which we approach texts and interpretation: the former recommending that we discriminate between a determinate, singular and univocal meaning on the one hand and a multiple significance that can vary from reader to reader on the other, and the latter maintaining that meaning can never be univocal or singular, 'since it is always generated out of particular readers' encounters with a text'.[8]

The New Critical confidence that as we are all dealing with the same text we should be able to reach agreement about it has given way to an agreement (and it is worth stressing that Hirsch and Fish and their respective adherents *do* seem to agree on this) that if meaning is left to individual readers then agreement on a single meaning will not be possible. It would seem that contemporary history has convinced many or most of us that human beings do not, generally, agree with one another. Hirsch solves this problem by granting supreme authority to the single intending author (which raises problems for our pursuit of the meaning of texts without such a simple genetic origin: a folk song, a television programme, or even perhaps the *Iliad*). Fish seemed to counsel us to learn to live with a plurality of meanings, without being too helpful on the specific problems faced by those who mark essays or grade exams.

Does all this remove criticism from a proper concern with individual texts to an ethereal realm of pure critical problems? As I have already suggested, not on the evidence of this volume. In addition to those contributions centrally concerned with a single literary text, Christopher Butler's essay addresses the question of whether new forms of literature require, or produce, new forms of critical explanation (or, rather, whether the pleasure which they give does so). Certainly, the flourishing of interest in the reading process cannot be divorced from the nature of that modernist and post-modernist literature and art that foregrounds the 'reading' process in a self-conscious manner. And far from their critical or theoretical concerns actually cutting off either Terry Lovell or Maud Ellmann from the texts about which they are writing, the opposite can be seen to be the case: a determination to tackle certain critical or theoretical issues can make the critic's relation to and interaction with a text more intimate and more rigorous.

The aim of this volume, then, is not just to indicate the range of methods, approaches, and theories that are important in literary (and other) studies today. It is also to draw attention to tensions, points of conflict, contradictions and disagreements within literary studies and in contiguous areas – not to celebrate or luxuriate in these, but to further the

[8]Susan R. Horton, *Interpreting Interpreting: Interpreting Dickens's 'Dombey'* (Baltimore and London, Johns Hopkins U.P., 1979), p. vii.

task of confronting them and their implications. If there is more criticism and critical theory on today's bookshelves than there was, the need for criticism to be self-aware and theoretically alert and alive has not diminished.

Jeremy Hawthorn

Note

All criticism that I know about is concerned with questions of interpretation and meaning. Thus 'reader response criticism' is badly named, because it implies that such criticism is solely or primarily concerned with the emotions of readers. In fact, what 'reader-response critics' have in common is the premise that since texts are known only through reading, the atom of literary study is not a text in isolation, but a text-plus-reader, and thus some attention to the reader is necessary. 'Reader-response criticism' is such a silly name for this premise that many critics deny they belong at all to the movement, and thus the debate over whether or not a particular critic is or is not a 'reader-response critic' can waste much valuable time. 'Reader critic' might be a better shorthand term.

Harold Bloom achieves the position that texts are different when read by different readers in what seems to me a roundabout way. First he posits that there is such a thing as 'reading', which ordinary readers do, but that great poets 'misread' their predecessors in order to justify their own poetic programme: 'In order to become a strong poet, the poet reader begins with a trope or defense that *is* a misreading. . . . A poet interpreting his precursor . . . must *falsify* by his reading.' Next, however, Bloom invites ordinary readers to do what he describes 'strong' poets as doing: 'I hope by urging a more antithetical criticism, one that constantly sets poet against poet, to persuade the reader that he too must take on his share of the poet's own agon, so that the reader also may make of his own belatedness a strength rather than an affliction.' (*Misreading*, see note 4, p. 80.) For Bloom, '*mis*reading' is individual, active, creative, valuable, while 'reading' is collective, passive, sterile, dull. Thus, although preserving the old reading/misreading polarity, Bloom valorizes the second term, leaving one to wonder why he keeps the pejorative prefix 'mis'. Perhaps it is simply there to attract attention (no small virtue).

Avoiding the simple polarity of readers/misreaders, Stanley Fish divides readers into 'interpretive communities'. Within each community interpretive rules are in force that enable members to determine what constitutes right reading, and what is misreading. What the nature of these communities is, how a reader discovers what one he is in, and whether he is free to leave, are questions that Fish does not answer (see note 7). A recent attempt to name and describe an actual 'interpretive community' (the profession of college and university literature teachers), Steven Mailloux's *Interpretive Conventions: The Reader in the Study of American Fiction* (Ithaca, Cornell U.P., 1982) seems to me to have very limited success: even within the supposed community, each interpretive crux turns out to be a dispute about which rules to apply, and so the communities multiply by dividing. Building consensus (if that is our goal) seems to me a matter both of conventions and of negotiation, and I have the indispensible notion of 'negotiated' meaning from David Bleich, *Subjective Criticism* (Baltimore, Johns Hopkins U.P., 1978).

Norman Holland is very good at showing how actual readers' psychological makeup influences their interpretation of literary texts: see *Poems in Persons* (New York, Norton, 1973) and *5 Readers Reading* (New Haven, Yale U.P., 1975). Two recent collections of a spectrum of approaches to reader criticism are Jane P. Tompkins, ed., *Reader Response Criticism: From Formalism to Post-Structuralism* (Baltimore, Johns Hopkins U.P., 1981) and Suleiman & Crosman, cited in note 3. Both contain extensive annotated bibliographies of criticism that because it considers the role of the reader in the interpretation of literary texts can if one chooses be called 'reader criticism'.

1

Is There Such a Thing as Misreading?

Robert Crosman

Once upon a time, and a very good time many think it was, no one in his right mind, at least no one in the academy, would seriously have asked this question, certainly not in print. 'Misreading', after all, is a province of 'misunderstanding', and the project of understanding – the task of *not misunderstanding* – is a vital and perpetual human enterprise. Misunderstanding, international relations experts assure us, is what threatens to blow the world up. Talk, communication, *understanding* is our only hope for human survival on this planet. And in our personal lives, too, only understanding makes it possible for us to love our mates and our children, work with our colleagues, and judge the issues of the day as responsible citizens. Misunderstanding, and hence misreading, is as manifest as it is deplorable.

Besides, we have direct *experience* of misreading. If there were no such thing as misreading, how could any of us ever have followed a road-map incorrectly, or have driven the wrong way down a one-way street, or inadvertently swallowed something in our medicine chests marked 'For External Use Only'? Each of us has direct experience that confirms the commonsensical reply: 'Yes, indeed, there *is* such a thing as misreading.'

And yet the concept of misreading, like its golden twin 'right reading', has in the past dozen years achieved the key status in intellectual discourse of an essentially contested concept. In this, as in much else, our age is unique. In all the history of literacy, when readers agreed on nothing else, they nonetheless agreed on the existence of the *category* of misreading, however that category might be filled.

In literary studies – in Anglo-American literary studies, anyway – the first hint of that category's weakening was in the doctrines of New Criticism, particularly in the concept of 'the intentional fallacy', which asserted that in interpreting a text it was misguided or futile to look beyond that text for its author's private intentions. 'If the poet succeeded in doing it', William K. Wimsatt and Monroe Beardsley wrote, 'then the poem itself shows what he was trying to do. And if the poet did not succeed, then the poem is not adequate evidence, and the critic must go outside the poem – for evidence of an intention that did not become

1

effective in the poem'.[1] New Critics did not absolutely abandon the category of 'misreading', but by separating a text's meaning from its author's intention, they discarded the principal tool of earlier generations for discovering what that category contained. The criteria for judging an interpretation of a text became for New Criticism the interpretation's 'richness', 'subtlety', or 'satisfyingness'. It was hard to think of these vague or emotional qualities as objective. Misreading thus became a problematic concept. Which of several readings was the most 'successful' might be settled by a rhetorical free-for-all, but the criteria for deciding 'right readings' were not clear.

E.D. Hirsch noticed this fact and argued it eloquently in his 1967 book, *Validity in Interpretation*. Stripped of its authorial intention, Hirsch argued, the word 'meaning' ceases to mean anything, and there is no misreading:

> When disagreements occur, how are they to be resolved? Under the theory of semantic autonomy they cannot be resolved, since the meaning is not what the author meant, but 'what the poem means to different sensitive readers' [T.S. Eliot]. One interpretation is as valid as another, so long as it is 'sensitive' or 'plausible'. . . . If the meaning of a text is not the author's, then no interpretation can possibly correspond to *the* meaning of the text, since the text can have no determinate nor determinable meaning.[2]

Just a whiff of Hirsch's powder cleared the boulevards. Within a few years, no one could be found who would confess to being a New Critic. Yet Hirsch failed to achieve his real objective: a return to the Gold Standard of authorial intention, whose inaccessibility, ambiguity, and frequent irrelevance Wimsatt and Beardsley had demonstrated about as well as Hirsch had demolished the New Critical substitutes.[3] Or perhaps it is not quite true to say that Hirsch's counter-revolution failed; it might be truer to say that he helped fragment the field of literary study further. In Renaissance literary studies, for example, the 70s saw a decline in New Critical 'readings' of texts, and a return to work of a generally more historical nature, though less often biographical than contextual in method (*Paradise Lost* in the context of a 'tradition' of Protestant poetics, etc.). Yet critical high-flyers, especially those influenced by French thinkers like Claude Lévi-Strauss, Michel Foucault, Jacques Lacan, and Jacques Derrida, abandoned even the genteel pretence of looking for the *meaning* of the text, and began, in the name of freedom and critical

[1]William K. Wimsatt and Monroe Beardsley, 'The Intentional Fallacy', in *The Verbal Icon: Studies in the Meaning of Poetry* (Lexington, Kentucky U.P., 1954). The essay was first published in *The Sewanee Review* in 1946.
[2]E.D. Hirsch, *Validity in Interpretation* (New Haven, Yale U.P., 1967), pp. 4–5.
[3]Authorial intention as a workable objective criterion of judging meaning is demolished yet once more in my essay 'Do Readers Make Meaning?', in S. Suleiman and I. Crosman, eds., *The Reader in the Text: Essays on Audience and Interpretation* (Princeton, Princeton U.P., 1980), pp. 149–64.

creativity, to *boast* that they were misreading!

In the United States, Harold Bloom was the specimen case. In his 1975 book, *A Map of Misreading*, and in the books that followed it, he gave misreading an entirely new status. Ordinary readers – huddled together in interpretative communities, sustained by logic, reason, historical knowledge, generic conventions, hermeneutic traditions – *read*. Extraordinary readers *misread*. Bloom's paradigm was William Blake. Blake, a revolutionary and visionary poet looking for a precursor for his daring revisions of Christian theology, thought he had found that spiritual father in John Milton. 'Milton', he wrote, 'was a true poet, and of the Devil's party without knowing it'. Thus Satan was, Blake believed, the true hero of *Paradise Lost*, and (in William Empson's phrase) 'the poem is so good because it makes God look so bad'. Legions of lesser readers have been battling that interpretation for nearly two centuries now, but though it is contained, it will not die. Such power there is in creative misreading.[4]

Bloom, though he does not like to be thought of as such, is essentially a second-growth New Critic, a younger Yale colleague of Wimsatt, Cleanth Brooks, and Robert Penn Warren, the Founding Fathers, in America, of the New Criticism. 'Father' is of course an anxious word for Bloom. In terms of his own system, he has fought these fathers to a stand-off (*A Map of Misreading*, p. 80) by taking the skeleton of misreading out of the family closet and displaying it proudly over the mantelpiece. The point is, though, that Bloom is largely a home-grown American product: Emerson is frequently on his lips, and de Man is quoted as a sort of sibling-rival, with whom Bloom is in friendly competition. Other champions of misreading fly the French flag. Lévi-Strauss, Lacan, Foucault, and Derrida resist being lumped together, whether under the name of 'structuralism', 'deconstruction', or any other title. There are large differences between them, and indeed they make a habit of attacking each other, but for all of them literature, or discourse generally, is constructed out of opposites ('binary oppositions' for Lévi-Strauss) that make reading, as it was for the New Critics, a process of negotiating tensions, ambiguities, ironies, and paradoxes. New Critics, after giving free play to these contradictions, liked finally to try to resolve them. Even Bloom, for all the freedom he apparently allows 'strong' readers to misread, ultimately grounds all sincere and valuable misreading in a kind of Freudian *Zeitgeist*, and thus turns all writing and all reading into a lament over belatedness. For Jacques Derrida, currently the most influential of French thinkers on American literary academics, the glory of great texts is their 'undecidability'. Writing, for Derrida, implies the absence, not the presence, of an author, a necessarily incomplete record of his thoughts and purposes, which must be inhabited by the *reader's* intentions before it becomes interpretable. 'The reader writes the text', Derrida boldly proclaims, but since the reader is himself not a stable entity, being instead a succession of contexts and purposes which change almost from moment to moment, even that text is

[4] Harold Bloom, *A Map of Misreading* (New York, Oxford U.P., 1975).

'undecidable', a blur. When Derrida visited Providence in 1975, I asked him about his puzzling dictum:

> Me: Is the text the reader writes different from the text the author wrote?
> Derrida: *Oui*.
> Me: Do the two texts have anything in common?
> Derrida: *Oui*.

What, under these conditions, is the status of 'misreading'?

Bloom, though he seems to preserve the distinction between 'right reading' and misreading, actually blurs that distinction. Since *mis*reading, at least when performed by strong, creative minds, can yield better, more interesting results than 'right reading', misreading can be preferable, and in that sense 'right'. Derrida, and deconstructionists generally, tends to go on to obliterate the distinction between misreading and right reading entirely. If every text is merely the trace of an author's intention, if all language is inherently ambiguous, so that the reader must appropriate it, suppress its 'minority voice', and make it say what *he* wants it to say, then *all* reading has that wrenched, arbitrary, 'undisinterested' quality we once associated with *mis*reading. All reading is misreading, then – which is as good as saying that there is no such thing as misreading.

As I argued in a previous article, 'Do Readers Make Meaning?', reading is a contextualizing procedure, a matter of fitting the present text into a context of other texts, traditions, concerns that one has in mind before encountering this particular text, and of translating *this* text into 'one's own words', using the strategies derived from the context we apply.[5] We may misapply that context – as when a scholar of numerological bent, convinced that the middle line of *Paradise Lost* would have special significance, miscounted and thus ascribed centrality to the wrong line – but generally our readings differ because we apply different contexts and strategies. To say that there is no such thing as misreading, then, is generally to say that there is no way of prescribing the context in which a particular work is to be read.

Before testing this still provocative dictum, let us pause to observe that 'misreading' can have at least two senses, corresponding to the distinction between 'subjective' and 'objective'. The *strong* sense of misreading is that there are objective standards (authorial intention, binding conventions of reading) by which to judge interpretations, and to judge some interpretations to be impossible, wrong. The *weak* sense of 'misreading' posits no such objective standards, but admits that no mind can accept every possible interpretation of a particular text. When someone shares with us his interpretation of a text, we may disagree so strongly with it that we say not simply that we disagree, but that he's misreading. We are using

[5]See footnote 3, above.

the word in its weak sense. If we can *prove*, by logical application of binding rules of interpretation (as is sometimes possible in a court of law, though over time even legal rules are themselves subject to slow change), that his interpretation is wrong, then he is misreading in the strong sense. No such universals are available in the anarchic realm of literary interpretation, however, though E.D. Hirsch tried to install authorial intention in that privileged position, and devised a kind of judiciary process to enforce it, which he called 'adjudication'.

Most professional students of literature are sceptical of the one, and dissatisfied with the other sense of 'misreading'. It doesn't seem possible to point to, much less agree on, any single, universal standard of interpretation, nor does it seem enough to make reading entirely a matter of personal conscience. We rely instead on a hypothetical majority rule – 'majority of informed opinion' – and on the rhetorical skill or political power of the individual interpreter in swaying that opinion. Unlike both the strong and the weak definitions of 'misreading', however, which are matters of principle, this 'semi-strong' definition of misreading relies essentially on *politics*: the 'majority of informed opinion', itself a product of hierarchical social institutions like the structure of the profession of literary teachers, imposes its interpretations, and its standards of interpretation, upon the minority who disagree. In fact, since the 'majority' is not determined by a nose-count, but by a weighted suffrage of authority, prestige, and power, 'right reading' may belong to a minority only, and the actual majority may be, secretly at least, 'misreaders'. It is in this sense, I take it, that deconstructionists cheerfully admit to misreading – not that they believe in objective standards of interpretation, but that they know they are breaking conventions of reading which the majority recognizes, or that the powers-that-be wish to enforce. Until deconstruction, the admission that one was misreading could only mean that one had now changed one's mind about the text; by *persisting* in error, deconstructionists imply that there is no such thing as error!

It is my view that like the strong sense this third, the 'semi-strong' sense of misreading, is illegitimate. It frequently claims, like E.D. Hirsch, to rest on the strong sense, the notion of an automatic, binding criterion for meaning. Unlike Hirsch, however, it doesn't specify what that criterion is, because to do so would (as Hirsch's example illustrates) elicit disproofs of that criterion's inevitability. Nor does it arise naturally from a consensus of readers whose weak senses of misreading all happen to agree. If they did spontaneously agree then there would be no dissent, and no need to invoke a more 'objective' criterion to silence dissent. Rather, it is a 'winner take all' arrangement, much like the American two-party system, which in the interests of uniformity and co-operation imposes a certain outward conformity on our *public* acts of interpretation, even while it allows us – behind the scenes, as it were – to politick for and persuade others, if we can, of the need for changing the rules of interpretation. Under this system, the category of misreading can change contents from year to year, as we have seen it do over the past decade, but it can never be allowed to disappear. Nor is the weak meaning of 'misreading' – the personal inability to see from what standards of interpretation someone else's reading arises, or an unwillingness to *agree* with those standards – sufficient, since it might not produce a working consensus. Only the strong meaning, or in its absence the semi-strong, is adequate to this purpose of silencing dissent.

With this much of the recent history, and a little of the theory of misreading on the table, let's turn to an example, and see if we can decide whether there is such a thing as misreading. Or rather, since we've already seen that readers do spontaneously apply the word in several senses, let us see if one of those senses suits us better than the others. In order to test the criterion of authorial intention, I will have to use something of my own composition, and since I have published no fiction, drama, or verse, I will, in order to find an entirely disinterested reader of my own work, have to use a review of my critical book *Reading Paradise Lost*. This review, by Patrick Cullen, has the virtues of being brief – it appeared in an omnibus review of 'Recent Studies in the Renaissance' – and extremely candid. It takes a very definite stance towards my book, and only at the end does it try to back off from a judgement that it has already clearly pronounced. Cullen begins by bracketing my book with another 'introduction to *Paradise Lost*', by G.K. Hunter, but I pick the review up only when Cullen turns to mine:

> Although both Crosman and Hunter talk about 'the reader' or 'readers' in the course of their discussion, their sense of that (sometimes useful) fiction is very different. Hunter's readers are those who need some learned and sophisticated guidance in order to become part of Milton's 'fit audience . . . though few'. That genial autocracy would not please Crosman; for he is very much the partisan of the response of a common reader who can jolly well do without all the weighty baggage of learning that the scholars have tried to foist on him. Crosman is a member of the school-of-perpetual-virgin reader-response criticism, in which the reader always seems to be experiencing the work for the first time. Crosman contends that we need a sequential reading that reflects the common readers' initial experience of the poem (unlike the reading of 'the critic', who assumes his readers can see the whole text at once, having read it). Rejecting various formulations of 'the reader' as closet autocracies, Crosman acknowledges that 'if response is a key aspect of literary experience but is inescapably subjective, then a key aspect of literary criticism can have nothing to say about it. All responses are equally valid, and there is no "reader" of *Paradise Lost*, or of any other poem – there are only readers' (p. 14). There is a way out of that bind, however: 'Instead of prescribing responses we can *describe* them' (pp. 14–15). (Crosman claims Fish as his chief mentor–antagonist, but surely this is closer to Norman Holland, whom Crosman nowhere men-

tions.) One may well wonder what makes the description of personal responses an escape hatch from critical relativity, but Crosman has an answer for that: 'This is possible because of art's universality, and because of the common humanity all readers share' (p. 15). With this (to me) astonishing claim, I realized that Crosman and I do not inhabit the same universe, certainly not the same century. The author then claims that, in the ensuing chapters, he 'will try to describe not what the reader should feel but some – a little – of what he *does* feel as he reads *Paradise Lost*' (p. 17). I bristled at this statement: I did not want, nor did I need, this stranger to articulate what I feel. 'You presume, Sir', I thought. In his next chapter, on 'Milton's Great Oxymoron', Crosman began telling me how confused I was as I began reading the poem; and, finally, on page 35 I read: 'Repeatedly Milton's text asks the reader to choose between antithetical contexts, epic and Christian. Will responsible readers be able to make the right choice? My belief is that they will not.' And it was on page 35 that I closed the book. This does not necessarily mean that *Reading Paradise Lost* is a bad book. Though it is as theoretically naïve as reader-response criticism can get, it is obviously an extremely well-intentioned work, written by someone who likes the poem and who wants to share his own pleasures and problems with it. I also think he cares for his own audience, and one does not always find that in academic criticism; and so, rather than pronounce a final, harsh judgment on the book, I should conclude with the obvious: I am clearly not the reader for whom it is intended.[6]

Let's start with the strongest of the strong notions of misreading, and ask if Cullen has been true to authorial intention. Clearly he hasn't. I did not intend my reader to quit on page 35 in disgust. I didn't mean to presume, or to be perceived as presuming: I meant, rather, to disarm with sweet reasonableness. I did not say (or mean to imply) that the reader of *Paradise Lost* was or ought to be a 'perpetual virgin', though I did say that the poem was written to be read front-to-back, that our understanding of it changes and progresses as we read farther, and that when we reread Book I, our memories of Book III or Book X are far less vivid than the present scene once again unfolding before our eyes. The 'perpetual virgin' remark seems to me like a cruel caricature of these (not very eccentric) ideas, as does the out-of-context quotation that buttresses it, often selected to avoid the saner portion of my remarks (Cullen's idea that 'the reader' is a 'sometimes useful fiction', for example, was a point that I myself made at some length in the few pages that Cullen actually read).

But Cullen, I take it, need not be concerned with my *feelings* about his reading, nor even with my more intellectual intentions, *except as they are communicated by the book*. The authorial intention that is relevant to this discussion is not my wounded feelings, or even my state of mind as I wrote

[6]Patrick Cullen, 'Recent Studies in the Renaissance', *Studies in English Literature* XXII (1982), pp. 182–3.

the book, but certain conventions operative both *within* the book and within the interpretive community of those who read it.[7] To make certain he has dealt properly with the book's intentionality, a reader must do at least two things: he must read attentively, and must read *the whole text*. Cullen ignored the latter rule, and I think the former as well. Thus he misquotes me at lines 16–17, adding the phrase 'a key aspect of literary' where it does not appear in my text, and he also says that I 'nowhere mention' Norman Holland, whose name appears on page two, and two of whose books are cited in a note to that page. His indignation at my presuming to 'articulate what I [i.e. Cullen] feel' ignores an extensive and explicit qualification and disclaimer that I attached directly to the sentence that so annoyed him (see lines 29–31). The rest of the paragraph modifies considerably the impression that sentence alone might make on a reader:

> In the pages that follow I will try to describe not what the reader should feel, but some – a little – of what he *does* feel as he reads *Paradise Lost*. Some of my readers [i.e. Cullen] will nonetheless object that behind my 'is' lurks an 'ought'. Those who read my interpretation in that spirit will defeat its purpose, however, for my aim is not to bring forth one more (at best) ingenious and sensitive 'reading' of Milton's epic, but to provide a mimesis of how a reader (myself) reads a poem. My aim is not to foist *my* interpretation onto other readers, but to show other readers that they are, inevitably, collaborating with Milton when they read, and that they could enhance their pleasure and comprehension by doing so with more vigor and self-confidence. The 'reading' itself is provisional – every one of my readers will find it untrue of himself in some respects, as will I myself in five years' time. There is not one of my readers, I hope, who will not be able to improve upon it, not only from his own point of view, but from mine.[8]

In order to convict me of 'presumption', Cullen had to ignore the loopholes I gave myself in this paragraph. He could do this because he had already exposed the notion of the 'reader' as a fiction, a point I can hardly refute, since I made it myself in the very chapter Cullen is quoting. My reader *is* a fiction, an hypothesis I am asking my readers, Cullen included, to adopt, at least provisionally, and if he chooses not to adopt it, he is perfectly within his rights. My 'universal' reader is a constitutive fiction, an *enabling* fiction, the move that sets my machinery in motion, like Milton's claim to be telling us Man's story when he tells us Adam's. If we can't entertain, even temporarily, that hypothesis, then we can't – at least with any pleasure or profit – read on. This is why Cullen quit reading.

It will do me no good, however, to tear my hair (though I *did* tear my

---

[7] I have borrowed the notions of 'reading strategy' and 'interpretive community' from Stanley Fish, *Is There a Text in This Class?* (Cambridge, Mass., Harvard U.P., 1980), chs. 6–16.
[8] *Reading Paradise Lost* (Bloomington, Indiana U.P., 1980), p. 17.

hair) at Cullen's 'misreading' of my intentions, or my book's intentions. He was simply doing what *all* readers do on occasion: he was refusing to grant my premises. My assumption was that, beneath their scholarly learning and literary sophistication, readers are much the same *at base*. Pretty clearly, this was the assumption that Cullen refused to make. His resistance to that premise is embodied in the entire structure of oppositions in his review. On the one hand we have common readers, perpetual virgins, free of the 'weighty baggage' of learning and scholarship, and therefore ignorant, 'naïve' – and finally fictitious; on the other hand we have the 'autocracy' (I think he means 'aristocracy') of learned and sophisticated 'fit' readers, scholars and critics, who need no one to describe what they feel. No one *could* describe what they feel, in fact, for they are unique individuals, not part of a herd. Concern for 'common readers' is given some faint credit for being 'well-intentioned' and caring (lines 41–3), but the aristocratic virtues of excellence and hauteur ('You presume, Sir') are clearly in the ascendant over the democratic, which Cullen reacts to as if a sweaty plebean were clutching him by the lapels and puffing garlic in his face.

It is tempting to amalgamate a notion of authorial intention incorporated *in* the book with a sense of the conventions of the reading community for which I wrote (admittedly academic, professors and students; no one else reads *Paradise Lost*, or at least no one else reads commentaries on it) and say that Cullen erred in not granting my premise, and interpreted that premise in as discreditable a sense as possible in order to exempt himself from the tedious chore of having to read the rest of my book. Indeed, I do think that something like this happened: to justify to himself his breaking of book-reviewing's cardinal rule (one must read the book before reviewing it) Cullen misrepresented my first chapter as *so* foolish that no sensible reader would waste his time on it.

Tempting as it is to convict Cullen of misreading in this strong and seemingly absolute sense, however, the argument simply won't hold up. No reader can or should grant an author *any* premise the author wishes to make. Most conceivable premises, as a matter of fact, are proscribed. No author can ask me seriously to entertain, for example, the premise that *Paradise Lost* was actually written by James Whitcomb Reilly, or that it is an allegory of nuclear disarmament, or that it contains no verbs. More generally, any author who assumes as the basis for argument that Jews, blacks, or women are evil or inferior doesn't command a fair, unbiased hearing, and the potential list of offensive, imbecilic, or downright criminal premises an author *might* adopt is inexhaustible. Trotsky's dictum that within the revolution all is permitted, but outside the revolution nothing is permitted, is true of all interpretative communities without exception: the price of a hearing is assent to certain constitutive, unquestioned assumptions of that community. What is really at stake between Cullen and me is the legitimacy of my assumption within an interpretive community to which we both belong – that of professional students of literature.

Neither the innate authority of authorial intentions, nor the immutable, binding nature of reading conventions define the *a priori* content of misreading. Misreading is an empty category until we, individually or collectively, decide what to put in it. As teacher and scholar Cullen is a member of, and as reviewer he addresses *other* members of a hierarchical profession that has a stake in the notion of a hierarchy of readers, not common and not equal. His conviction is that, like him, other members of that profession will recognize my premise of a 'universal reader' as subversive of the profession, but (after rigging the evidence as strongly in his favour as possible) he finally leaves it for them to decide whether it is subversive, rather than 'pronounce a final, harsh judgement' – that is, he pronounces a judgement, but leaves it to the professional community to confirm it.

The issue really is: is the 'universal' reader an admissible hypothesis in the academic community? I think it is; Cullen thinks it isn't. Cullen would doubtless point to the expertise painfully acquired over years by the Ph.D. scholar, and ask what on earth that scholar was doing if he wasn't learning to read better? He might go on to hint that the status of the profession, both *vis-à-vis* other, solider disciplines, and with respect to our students, rests on the superiority of the trained literary mind over the untrained. E.D. Hirsch, in his charmingly ingenuous way, blurts out this concern directly when he says:

> the teacher of literature who adheres to Eliot's theory [that one interpretation is as valid as another] is also the preserver of a heritage and the conveyor of knowledge. On what ground does he claim that his 'reading' is more valid than that of any pupil? On no very firm ground. (*Validity*, p. 4)

Note here that Hirsch is talking about the pragmatics of power. If the profession of literary study surrenders its claims to a kind of absolute authority over literature, then pupils, administrators, and the public at large may decide that their services can be dispensed with.

My sense of the politics involved is exactly contrary, however. A literary education has nothing very tangible to offer in the way of material rewards. A college graduate with a B.A. in literature is looking at a job market that at best may be willing to train him or her in commercial and administrative skills for which a social-science or even a technical background would seem more appropriate. Literary study, it seems to me, has three enticements: first, it's fun to read great literature; second, reading great works of literature can, over time, make us wiser than we were; and third, a literary education can teach independent habits of mind and an ability to communicate the fruits of those habits in conversation and in writing. The effect upon students drawn for these reasons to literature of a dogmatic, condescending teacher, convinced of his students' unfitness to read, is only too apparent. Far from being truly aristocratic, which I take to be the serene conviction of one's own abilities and value to others, as expressed in a willingness to use those abilities where they are needed, hauteur and arrogance are the marks of parvenu defensiveness and insecurity. No field today – certainly not the natural sciences, where an attitude of doubt, humility, and receptivity to new ideas is the hallmark of the superior mind – is characterized by certainty and infallibility. To pretend to such authority in literary matters is to seem not competent but ridiculous.

We might ponder a few analogies in the political arena. Strong Presidents, like Washington, Lincoln, and F.D. Roosevelt, spent little or no time ministering to their own sense of dignity, or trying to appear in control. 'Strong' was not a word that was frequently on their lips; they *were* strong, and saw no need to assure themselves, and everybody else, of that fact. It was a deeply insecure and guilt-ridden figure – Nixon – who dressed the White House guard in imperial livery, who went to state dinners amid a flourish of trumpets, and who spent much time brooding on what a strong man in his position would do. Similarly, the Reagan administration's wish to increase armaments, if it proceeds from anything more than political debts owed to financial backers in the defence industry, arises not from a sense of strength but of weakness. Since it is aimed at a Soviet régime that, although armed to the teeth, itself feels (with much reason) weak, we can hardly doubt that another ruinous round of armament is on the way. The more 'strength' the two sides reach for, the weaker they become, since true security consists of mutual respect of the rights of others, not of aggressive behaviour that invites retaliation. My ultimate objection to Cullen is not to his principles of interpretation, which have much to recommend them, but to the intolerant, aggressive way he asserts them, as if they were the *only* viable standards, and as if whoever did not observe them were a fool.

There is (to return to this essay's opening remarks) no longer any such thing as a 'working majority' in literary studies, and perhaps the time when there was such a thing was not such a very good time after all. Marxists, Freudians, Jungians, Semioticians, Structuralists, Formalists, myth critics, deconstructionists, Lacanians, Foucauldians, Neo-Aristotelians, feminists, subjectivists, historical critics, rhetorical critics, old New Critics, and humanists of every kind and stripe, have laid before us a smorgasbord of interpretations and interpretive principles that if we are wise we can pick and choose from to reach *our own* critical method. And all these schools would benefit themselves, and us, if they wrote and spoke a lingo that addressed itself not only to other initiates but to the literate general reader, and if they said 'it seems to me' once in a while, rather than pretending to an 'objectivity' in which no one really believes any more.

According to the view of reading communities that, following Fish, I have been elaborating, there is no such thing as 'objectivity' in literary interpretation, and there never was. Rather, a certain set of interpretive standards was kept in place by the majority, or by the dominant minority, of interpreters, and all other standards were prohibited. If that day is now at an end, as I think and profoundly hope, then we need not abandon our notion of misreading, but we do need to soften its claims. Both sides of the controversy are partly wrong, which is to say both are partly right. Derrida is right: 'misreading' is too powerful a charge to level against an opponent; it consigns him to a paradise of fools where his motives and concerns cannot be understood, or addressed, because they are, quite simply, *wrong*. Yet Derrida's opponents are right too: the category of misreading will never disappear; it is too useful, necessary even, for us personally and in our negotiations. Certain readers will none the less accept that it is not an inevitable category, and that at times it must be denied, or transcended.

For in a curious way, harmony in the realm of text interpretation derives not from the apparent *strength* of our notion of misreading, but from its *weakness*. In the absence of absolute standards, which if they exist at all seem forever unattainable, since no one can convincingly identify them, and in the absence even of a 'working majority', whose sway depends upon both a professional hierarchy and on the illusion of absolute standards that cannot be specified, there is no useful notion of 'misreading' left except the weak one of personal standards. Cullen is misreading my book, I feel, because as a reader myself I can find a better meaning for my words than the one Cullen ascribes to them. But 'better' from whose point of view? From my own, of course! If he were here, I'd tell him, as I've told you, what *my* interpretation of those words is, and try to get him to agree with me, while listening carefully to the counter-interpretations he would offer. We'd be negotiating a new meaning for the text, different in some respects from what either had previously had in mind.

Perfect agreement? I dream not of it – in such a case, anyway, where what each is asking of the other is to change a long-held, deeply cherished value. But we'd enrich each other's conceptions of the text, and of its context; we would part amicably, and live in peace. Paradoxically, by a process Milton understood very well, a war on misunderstanding – in the sense of an attempt to blame *others* for it, and to try to wipe it out by compelling them to relent – only aggravates it ('evil upon itself shall back recoil'). Only when we tolerate misunderstanding in others, and try to examine ourselves for an unconscious complicity, can we reach understanding and peace.

There is still, alas, such a thing in the world as misreading. But the less we war against it, the sooner it will disappear.

Note

The debate about interpretation has largely been set in terms of the controversy over relativism. Is there a correct interpretation of a work of art, and is that correct interpretation to be identified with the authorial intention or with what the text determines? Or are the interpretations available multifarious? Here and elsewhere I have tried to steer a middle course between these alternatives, assuming that interpretation in the performing arts and in literature has roughly the same characteristics.

M.C. Beardsley, *The Possibility of Criticism* (Detroit, Wayne State U.P., 1970)
Jonathan Culler, *Structuralist Poetics*, (London, Routledge and Kegan Paul, 1975)
E.D. Hirsch, *Validity in Interpretation* (New Haven, Yale U.P., 1967)
    The Aims of Interpretation (Chicago, Univ. of Chicago Press, 1976)
Joseph Margolis, *Art and Philosophy* (Brighton, Harvester, 1980)
S.H. Olsen, *The Structure of Literary Understanding* (London, Cambridge U.P., 1978)
R. Wollheim, *The Sheep and the Ceremony* (London, Cambridge U.P., 1979)

2

The Private Reader and the Listening Public[1]

R.A. Sharpe

I

There is a well-known passage in 'Linguistics and Poetics' in which Roman Jakobson spells out the general features of linguistic communication:

> The *addresser* sends a *message* to the *addressee*. To be operative the message requires a *context* referred to, seizable by the addressee, and either verbal or capable of being verbalized; a *code*, fully, or at least partially, common to the addresser and the addressee; and finally, a *contact*, a physical channel and psychological connection between the addresser and the addressee, enabling them both to enter and stay in communication.[2]

One natural reaction to this would be that it is so banal as to be remarkable that anyone should feel it worth saying, much less quoting. However banality does not preclude falsity. Jakobson regards this general account of communication as applying to poetry given the additional proviso that poetry focuses on the message for its own sake. About the latter clause I shall have little to say. However an explanation of why an apparently trivial description of the nature of communication so utterly misses the nature of art in general and poetry in particular leads to the heart of the matter. For it makes us ask fundamental questions about the role of inter-pretation in art. I shall briefly recapitulate a theory about this, a theory which I have spelt out in greater detail elsewhere,[3] and then I shall raise more general questions about the role interpretation plays in the literary arts as against the performing arts. The conclusion I shall draw is that, roughly speaking, the reader has a more active role than a concert-goer or

---

[1] This paper has developed in answer to an objection made by Professor Eva Schaper to an earlier paper of mine, 'Interpreting Art', in the *Proceedings of the Aristotelian Society*, supp. vol. 60 (1981). Her reply has the same title and is in the same volume.

[2] R. Jakobson, 'Linguistics and Poetics', in T. Sebeok, ed., *Style in Language* (Cambridge, Mass., MIT Press, 1960), p. 353. (Original italics.)

[3] See also my *Contemporary Aesthetics: A Philosophical Analysis* (Brighton, Harvester, 1983).

play-goer and that this underlines the private as opposed to the public place of reading in our society.

Jakobson thinks of literature, and this includes poetry and drama, as forms of communication. Of course, some works that are studied for their literary virtues are communications in which an identifiable message which can be cast in the form of propositions is being sent from writer to reader. Swift, Lamb or Orwell are just a few of the writers who fall into this category. However, what makes them of literary interest, I submit, is rather what is left after the identifiable message is subtracted.

I say this because of what I believe literature shares with the performing arts. Both are objects for interpretation. The reader interprets the poem, novel or play: the actor interprets the role he is assigned and the instrumentalist or conductor interprets the music. It is conceivable, I suppose, that the two usages involve homonyms rather than synonyms and that we have here two forms such that it is inadvisable to treat the word as univocal. On this view the two senses of interpretation are as different as Barclays Bank is from the bank on which the wild thyme grows. What argues against this assumption are the common factors in the relation of reader to work and of performer to work. The common factor which is most significant is the degree of freedom the interpreter possesses within the constraints imposed by the text. Interpreting is not describing; it is not a matter of simply recording facts about the text such as that it is in iambic hexameters or sonata form; the interpreter also exhibits imagination, sensibility, and, at best, originality and creativity. What Leavis says about *Hard Times* or *The Europeans* and the way Solomon plays Beethoven equally reveal the art of the interpreter.

In interpretation the critic or performer offers a general view of a work which is based on certain episodes which present themselves as of particular importance or significance. I have used the active voice advisedly. The foregrounding of these episodes, as the fashionable jargon goes, is only to a certain extent within our control. These are passages that 'strike us'. They seize our interest and involve us; they may or may not give us pleasure. In the case of the horrible or sublime they may fascinate us. The point is that they stand in a causal relationship to our experience. The critic then weaves these elements into a discursive view of the work and, by judicious quotation, simultaneously exemplifies and supports the general account he offers. Characteristically he will identify pervasive themes which are present in the individual passages he cites. In the same way the performer will 'bring out' certain sections of the work he performs and thereby both exemplify and support the general character which he thinks the work has. Thus he may attend to one of the inner parts, voicing it in such a way as to bring to our attention a feature which other interpreters overlook. Or he may take a passage whose importance is universally recognized and play it or speak it in a way which imparts to it a novel character. If I am right about this then the process of interpretation in both literature and the visual arts on the one hand and the performing arts on the other makes much the same demands on the interpreter and reveals much the same sort of structure. The conclusion we should draw is that communication is a very poor model for the relationship between artist and interpreter. though, as we shall see, it is a good model for the relationship between the interpreter and *his* public. For the point about interpretation *vis à vis* the work is that the interpreter is free within constraints to present one of a number of possible views of the text. Of course the range of 'meanings' which can be ascribed to a literary text is not unconfined. They are dependent on the prior meaning of the individual words, sentences, phrases and images which comprise the text and that sense is the sense which they could have had for a contemporary audience. We cannot wreak destruction on the work of art by permitting its meaning to vary in time according to the whim of its public.[4] We can discover, by scholarship, what 'nice', 'presently' or 'sleave' meant at the time Shakespeare wrote, and this imposes the first constraint on how we interpret. There are also, of course, works whose 'message' is obvious to a greater or lesser extent; for instance, *Animal Farm*, *The Fable of the Bees*, or *Gulliver's Travels*; once we have discovered the author's target, then the critic takes that as understood and attends to those features of the work which do require his interpretative gifts. We advance the starting point for critical interpretation. The fact that Orwell was attacking the evils of Stalinism is, after all, hardly a matter for aesthetic investigation. If then a work allows, as most works do, a variety of interpretations, some of which will be mutually inconsistent, and no one of which can be said to be the right one, what room is left for the idea of communication? The only remaining possibility is the possibility of communicating a disjunction of as many interpretations as are possible. But such indefiniteness seems to me a *reductio ad absurdum* of the idea of communication.

Significantly, many of the features we admire in an interpretation mirror the features we admire in a work of art. We admire an interpretation which presents detail in such a way that it coheres with the overall interpretation. Take a famous crucis, the length of the fermata in the opening bars of Beethoven's Fifth Symphony; if a conductor opts for a long pause at this point, the signs are that his overall interpretation will be epic rather than dramatic – that the performance will be characterized by broad tempi and a spacious overall effect rather than fast tempi and sharp contrasts. Moreover, we value an interpretation which will make sense of all the detail. A great pianist, it is often said, 'makes all the notes count', though without reducing major thematic material to the level of visibility of passage work, of course. Essentially, we look for unity in an interpretation; we do not expect the character of the performance to change

---

[4]·Some ascription of meaning is required before interpretation can begin, otherwise we cannot compare rival interpretations as in fact we do. To do this we need a text and a text consists of words with meanings. Getting a grasp of the basic meaning of a text may not be easy and I do not think that there is a sharp dividing line between understanding the meaning of the text, which may require understanding a metaphor, and the broader process of interpretation. But my sympathies lie closer to Hirsch and Beardsley than to the deconstructionalists on this highly controversial matter.

dramatically in mid stream without some reason. The sorts of reasons which might count in favour of a sudden switch would themselves be embedded in other features of the interpretation, of course; if such a change were effective it would not provide a counter example to the general thesis.

No doubt there are other features that good interpretations possess. We must remember, too, that these prescriptions are very broad. They are not sufficiently precise to act as recipes for the production of adequate interpretations. If, indeed, recipes for the production of interpretations could be swapped as easily as recipes for tea bread, then we would lose another feature which we admire in interpretation, namely individuality or uniqueness. Let me expatiate on this a little. Obviously interpretations are passed from one performer to another, most evidently through teaching, and interpretations are likewise passed from one teacher of literature to another or to his pupils. But great critics and great interpreters think out their own response to a work. Interpretations which are a mere reflection of somebody else's interpretation are indeed copies of interpretations and not interpretations in their own right, much as copies of works of art are not themselves works of art. In these ways, the merits of interpretations mirror the merits of works of art. What makes for a rather attractive architectonic is the fact that we admire especially just those works of art that can nourish a variety of interpretations, interpretations that have, in turn, virtues comparable with those we admire in art. Over and above all this, there is another aspect on which I have yet to touch. Both art and its interpretation are sometimes said to have 'depth' and depth is much prized. What is depth?

One of the few analyses of 'depth' in art is to be found in Anthony Savile's recent book *The Test of Time*;[5] Savile says nothing, however, about the related question of depth in interpretation. He proposes a number of 'truisms' which any analysis must respect. Firstly, depth is propositional in form, secondly that what is deep is constant and has permanent hold on our affections, and thirdly that depth and truth are intimately linked.

One immediate difficulty with the first and the third claims is that they rule out either music or its interpretation being counted as deep. According to his pupils, Dvorak rarely talked about the music he played; however on one occasion he was examining the Hammerklavier, and, coming to the 13th and 14th bars of the Adagio, he raised his voice and said: 'That is something! That is profundity! That is an abyss.'[6] What are we to make of this? It does answer to the feeling of musicians, of course, that if anything in music is deep or profound (and for the present, I take the words to be synonymous), it is this. But no propositions are being asserted and there is nothing here which is true of false. Perhaps we can see why we feel the way

---

[5.]A. Savile, *The Test of Time: Essays in Philosophical Aesthetics* (Oxford, Clarendon Press, 1982).
[6.]John Chapman, *Dvorak* (Newton Abbot, David and Charles, 1979), p. 173.

we do about the music if we think of somebody stumbling on some illuminating truth. This hesitant progress is surely mirrored in the movement to that dramatic modulation. It is as though something can only just be said. In music there is usually no gap between profundity of manner and profundity of matter for nothing is being said. One form of depth lies in the appearance of saying something deep. We could describe such depth as belonging to the expressive surface of the work.

Of course, music might display a mock profundity. The slow movement of Mahler's First symphony comes to mind with its parody of a funeral march, though it is noteworthy that the contrast between matter and manner here depends upon the fact that the thematic material has established associations in other contexts. The funeral march in question is a minor version of the nursery rhyme familiar to us as 'Frère Jacques'. The gap which here opens between matter and manner is possible because of an oblique reference to other music.

Profundity in literature appears less problematic because depth can be cashed in terms of the truths which are being asserted, truths most commonly about human nature. But what makes a truth deep, as opposed to superficial? What can we say about this contrast? The surface-depth contrast is, of course, ubiquitous in modern culture. It appears in the Freudian contrast between latent and manifest, in music in the difference between the Ur-linie and its transformations, or in the deep structure of grammar and its superficial formations. Consider, for example, *Macbeth*. On the surface it is a play about murder and the struggle for power. More profoundly, argues Mahood, it is a play about fertility and barrenness.[7] Mahood points out that one leitmotiv in *Macbeth* is 'children'. If this is indeed a deep theme then we would expect it to recur in different forms, and so it does. The heath is blasted, the witches are infertile, and Lady Macbeth is willing to dash her own child to death. The point about deep interpretation, whether it is illuminating or not, is that it purports to uncover a theme which is not evident on the surface of the play. The surface of the play, and by the surface I mean the text and plot understood with the minimum of licence, can be viewed as a transformation of ultimate themes. This process of revealing the deep themes will involve selective quotation, the interpretation of the material in terms of concealed ideas, the juxtaposition of material from different parts of the play to show that the same ideas are present in different guises etc. I would not claim that a clear and precise distinction can be drawn between the meaning of the surface and the underlying themes. Such a distinction is bound to be more or less a matter of degree because understanding what is apparently the surface may involve the difficult task of construing a metaphor. However, the deep themes of a work are necessarily more general and pervasive.

Can we parallel this in music? Why do we think that, for example,

---

7. M.M. Mahood, 'From Shakespeare's Wordplay', in John Wain, ed., *Macbeth*, Casebook series (London, Macmillan, 1969), p. 207.

Solomon's performance of the Hammerklavier sonata is deep or profound, for instance? An answer which parallels the literary account I have just given is to be found in the type of thematic analysis given by Reti and Schenker and their disciples. The idea that a work of music may be unified by an underlying Ur-linie or melodic figure which does not necessarily appear in the surface texture of the music gives a clue as to how we may understand depth in music. But, just because such an underlying theme may not appear in the audible or visible text, it presents us, and the performer, with a problem as to how this can be presented in performance. If the unifying thread, of which other important themes are transformations, is audible *in toto*, of course the problem is less extreme. The performer must then phrase the music to draw attention to this and then accent or otherwise foreground the elements in other themes which are drawn from this basic idea. This form of interpretation bears an obvious analogy to the interpretation in performance of a play. The relevant selection and integration is there. Where the unifying thread is not produced *in toto* then all that the performer can do, other than explain verbally in musical or dramatic criticism, is to stress the requisite elements and trust that the audience catches on. By stressing certain segments of a theme, or by giving it a certain expressive character, the musician can convey the sense of a whole from parts which are not contiguous, that whole being the deep structural element of the work.

An example, obvious perhaps but nonetheless apposite, of this second form of depth occurs in the *op*. 109 piano sonata of Beethoven. The first movement consists of rapid broken chords alternating with an expressive adagio section. At bars 87–8 the pianist must, in order to bring out the melody, look for a stepwise theme obtained by treating the bars as though there is an upper voice. By doing this, the interpreter picks out a phrase whose tail is entirely characteristic of this work, a little melodic fragment which occurs again and again. It is possible to miss it, though Tovey says in his notes that nobody would be foolish enough not to phrase it in this way.[8] The point is that by judicial accenting a phrase may be made to appear which has a structural function.

For this to count as an example we must accept that the theme is not complete in itself but that an inference, whether conscious or unconscious, needs to be drawn by the listener. The result of this inference is that he then hears the relationship of this fragment to those other elements with which it forms a totality.

One thing which comes out of our discussion is the possibility that a distinction is to be made between depth and profundity. Tovey says that the right way to interpret the Beethoven is 'obvious' and if it is obvious it can hardly be profound. I hedged my bets on this earlier, when I allowed that a distinction might have to be drawn here, even though it was not clear that these two words make the distinction we want. The distinction allows that an interpretation might be deep without its being original,

8. Associated Board editions

unobvious, revelatory or moving in any way, and that is a possibility I wish to permit.

The sort of account I have presented comes close to that which Savile describes as Nietzschean: 'A deep thought is simply one that holds a key position in a structure of beliefs' (p. 127). Savile objects to this analysis on the grounds that the links with truth and consistency which are required for depth disappear. He objects that a belief could be superficial and profound relative to different systems and that it need not be true. Neither objection is of any weight. Firstly, a thought may be deep relative to a given work of art and part of the surface of another. Consider, for example, the famous opening of *Anna Karenina*. It might well be the case that the conclusion that happy families are alike in their happiness whilst the misery of unhappy families differs might be reached only after considerable interpretative analysis in a novel, say, by Jane Austen. Secondly, the truth of art is a very problematic requirement anyway. It cannot apply to music and, unless 'deep' is construed as merely honorific, the Nietzschean alternative seems the most likely.

II

I have given reasons for rejecting the idea that art communicates a message to us. But the model of communication does, I think, fit the relation of interpreter to his public. It makes sense to consider the interpreter as communicating. On the one hand the critic obviously presents us with a set of statements which in one way or another are 'about' the text even if it is not clear that it makes much sense to consider them as true or false. For if one interpretation is true, then it follows that those inconsistent with it are false and this seems a hard line. The strength of a work like *Ulysses* or *Hamlet* may well be its capacity to sustain a number of mutually incompatible interpretations.

At this point recall the special case of music. If it were not for the performer the music would remain inaccessible. Whereas the text of a poem or a novel is available to anybody who can read, the presence of a musical score is not sufficient. The work has to be performed and in the course of performing it the musician cannot avoid interpretation because the notation which is before him is less than completely specific. The notation underdetermines the performance. This remains so despite the penchant of composers for increasingly precise directions as to tempo and dynamics. Indeed it is noteworthy that even a very fully notated work such as one of the Mahler symphonies leaves a great deal of scope for the interpreter; consequently successful interpretations seem to vary at least to as great an extent as do successful performances of the less fully notated Viennese classics. Mahler himself once remarked that the conductor must play the notes which are not written.

One way, then, of regarding the performer's task is to see him as communicating the work to the audience. We cannot equate the work with the performance, of course, for then we would be forced to allow that the work ceased to exist when not being performed, ascribing to it a unique kind of intermittent existence. Another reason for rejecting such an equation is the fact that no single performance is identical with the work. What I hear tonight may be Karajan's interpretation of the Eroica, but it will not be the Eroica in *eo ipso*. There are one or two analogies we may find helpful here. First of all it may help to think of a score as a sort of recipe in accordance with which the audible music is produced. Just as the individual cook may produce a dish in accordance with the traditional recipe yet, in the course of it, make his own contribution, so the interpreter of a Beethoven sonata may add his own unique insight to the playing of the work. The notation is a guide to the production of the sound and the precision of these guides has increased. In pre-classical music we may not even know what instruments are intended: in a Mahler symphony there are very detailed dynamics for different parts, hair-pins and accenting. Yet the notation is no more a presentation of that sound than the configuration of the groove a presentation of the music.

A second and perhaps more apt analogy is to think of the performer as expressing the music in his interpretation. Here the notion of communication returns. Consider how a person expresses a state of anger. The expression of anger also satisfies a criterion for the existence of the anger. We know that the man is angry because his behaviour expresses that anger. It might be possible, of course, for a man to express anger without really feeling it; he simulates anger for a special purpose. Equally, it is easy to conceive of a man concealing the genuine anger he feels.

Turning now to the work of music, the performance of the work shows the existence of the work in a rather stronger way. Whereas I can dissemble anger, I cannot express in performance a work that does not exist. My performance of it guarantees its existence. A much closer parallel than the expression of emotion is the expression of an idea or a theory. Here the expression of the theory or idea guarantees the existence of that theory or idea. Furthermore it can be expressed with greater or lesser animation and intelligence. All these features are also to be found in the interpretation of a play or a piece of music. In certain cases one interpreter may better convey the structure of the work, another convey more immediately an overall impression of the work, and so on. It seems natural to take the interpretation *in performance* as an expression of the work; the performing arts are close, in this respect, to the relationship in which a particular treatise, lecture or article stands to the theory which it expresses.

So far, then, we have compared two forms of interpretation. The first occurs where a critic writes about a work of literature. If I read first the critic and then the poem, then what I take it to mean may well be influenced by what the critic has said. He would be disappointed if I were not. But it is possible for me to read it 'cold' with just my general knowledge and my knowledge of the state of the language at the time it was written. In the second case, however, there is no way in which I can hear a piece of music cold; it is always mediated through the performer's interpretation. I could form an impression of the work through reading the score, as I may form an impression of a play through reading the text. Indeed critics presumably quite often form their understanding of a work without having heard a performance, though this can be a chancy business: scores may look poor on paper but sound surprisingly well. Anybody would prefer to have heard the work or seen the play just as an art critic would prefer not to have to rely on illustrations of a painting. One important barrier to an understanding of the work has been removed.

Consequently there is an incomplete parallel between the performing and the non-performing arts; there is a two-term relationship in the case of literature between work and reader, and a three-term relationship in the case of the performing arts between work, interpretation and audience. Even if my reading of a poem is deeply influenced by a critic's interpretation of a poem, my reading is not mediated via what the critic says in the way in which my hearing a work of music is mediated via the performer's actions. The critic's remarks are a further causal factor affecting my understanding of the poem; it may affect what I notice about it, my understanding of various allusions, metaphors and similes for instance. But they do not present the work of art to me. The interpretation I make of Andrew Marvell's Mower poems remains an act of mine in a way in which the interpretation of a Brahms capriccio is not mine but Stephen Bishop-Kovacevic's.

Is it possible for the listener or for a member of the audience at a play to make a further act of interpretation whose object is the interpretation of the music or the play? In a limited way, perhaps. Let me sketch how I think this might be possible. Any work offers a range of possibilities for an interpreter. He can bring out inner parts, stressing structural relations; he has to decide where the climax should be placed and how the various sections are to be weighted. The decisions are multifarious. Now certainly the listener may fail to catch on through no fault of the interpreter. But can he notice things about the performance which the interpreter did not notice himself? If he can, is the interpretation then different, perhaps better than the interpreter himself recognizes? I think both are possible but either will still be a case where the listener registers the nature of the interpretation. For the listener to go beyond this and interpret the performance it is necessary that he pick out features of the interpretation and fit these into a whole governed by an overall characterization of the interpretation. But in a performed work he is now doing what will already have been done competently or incompetently. Only if a 'neutral' performance were possible could there be the basis for an interpretation of the performance. Even then the interpreting listener merely provides a recipe for a particular interpretation which might have been embodied in a performance.

At this point, I ought to enter a caveat. The situation may be complex and subtly different when we consider a play whose text has become familiar. Our experience of a Shakespeare play must be affected by our previous understanding of the text, a text which we have read privately as well as seen enacted. Consequently our stance is ambiguous between that of the private reader and that of a member of the play-going public who attends to the interpretative acts of the director and players. Am I alone in finding dramatic performances of Shakespeare too swift for the poetry to be relished? The phenomenology of our experience of dramatic poems is unique.

In the cases I have considered so far we have assumed that the performer does not fail in his attempt at getting across the details as well as the general character of the work. No doubt many interpretations fail to make the detail count in the way required to produce the general character at which the interpreter aims, with the consequence that either the work as performed seems to have no clear general features at all or the character does not seem consistent. An example of the latter might be where a performer radically changes for no good reasons the shaping and dynamics of a theme in the recapitulation of a sonata form movement, thus causing the unity of the movement to come adrift. Not only may there be some misconception in the interpretation which could account for the sort of failing listed above, but there may be mishaps. Through loss of concentration, technical shortcomings or accidents like the breaking of a string, the interpreter may fail to embody his conception of the work in performance.

However this may be, our main concern is with the ways in which the listener's grasp of the performance fails to accord with the performer's even when the performer embodies his interpretation more or less to his own satisfaction. He plays it roughly as he intends to play it. We need now to consider whether this parallels the variety of ways in which a poem can be read.

Although there are a variety of second order interpretations of a performance possible, they vary in their relative failure to grasp the nature of the interpretation. Whereas various interpretations of a Mozart piano concerto may represent equally valid readings of that work, the listener's various readings of an interpretation vary in the extent to which they fall short; the variety is a measure of comparative failure and not comparative richness, as it is for the readers of a poem, or the performers of the work. Through no fault of the interpreter, the listener may fail to see what the interpreter is driving at and, indeed, luxuriate in features of the performance which the interpreter did not intend to be in the forefront of his attention. The irritation of musicians with their public, though hardly excusable, usually stems from the latter's failure to see what the interpretative point is, even though they may enjoy the music none the less. This no doubt lies at the back of Schnabel's sour remark 'The audience applauds, even when it is good'.

There are a number of ways in which the interpretation may not be grasped by the audience. Firstly, the interpreter might attempt an overall effect through certain nuances in the detail; the detail might register but the overall point be missed. The second and converse is perhaps less bothersome to the interpreter; he will expect that the amateur listener will miss some of the detail but if the overall nature of the interpretation is grasped the performer will be reasonably satisfied even if the response falls short of the ideal. The ideal would, of course, be a response in which the listener is both sensitive in registering the overall character the interpreter gives to the performance and intelligent in that the listener registers the exactitude of the skill in the playing of detail which creates the total effect.

Although it is no demerit in a work for it to under-determine an interpretation, it will be a demerit in an *interpretation* if it under-determines a listener's or a reader's response in a parallel way. A consequence of the view I have just put forward is that we are right to regard the audience at a performance as passive as compared with the reader of a poem or of a work of fiction. The audience's active role consists in sizing up the nature of the interpretation and the relation between detail and general character; we may also ask ourselves whether the interpretation is adequate to the work itself. Is this a performance which is a valid view of the work? Can you play Bartok's Third Piano concerto in such an aggressive and down-to-earth fashion, or does some of the essential poetry disappear? But this marks the limit of the listener's participation. His judgement of the performer's interpretation is, after all, right or wrong, true or false. It is not a creative act comparable with that of reading a poem, directing a play or personally performing the music.

In the opening essay of the collection *On Difficulty*,[9] George Steiner remarks on the fact that music has become the central art in our culture. One reason for this is, in his view, that music is a participatory art whereas reading is private. Steiner does not define the opposition between public and private. I shall take it that the privacy of reading lies in the singularity of the reader's response and the publicity of the performing arts in our sharing the insights of the interpreter with whom we communicate. It will, I think, be obvious that my arguments tend to Steiner's conclusion. The listener is in a more passive, though not totally quiescent position, *vis-à-vis* the work, than is the reader. Exceptionally, of course, the listener may object to the interpretation on the basis of an imagined ideal performance, but few listeners are in this position. Although we may frequently think that that way of playing it is not how it should go, only rarely are we able to put precisely the alternative detail which would make a more coherent and convincing rival account. The listener is at some distance from the reader, who places his own construction on the text. The listener is part of a public, even if he listens to the music alone at home in the dark, to the radio or to a recording. The reader, in contrast, does not simultaneously encounter work and interpretation as the listener does.

Perhaps this is a somewhat rosy picture of the reader. It makes him more reflective than he really is. Normally, as a rather careless reader, I simply register the outline of the plot or the general drift of the poem, excited perhaps by some particularly striking description or particularly memorable image. Occasionally I put a book down and think about what I have read for ten minutes or so, but I am capable of reading entire novels or poems at this somewhat superficial level and, aside from those who are

[9] Steiner, *On Difficulty and other essays* (Oxford, Oxford U.P., 1978)

professionally concerned with literature, I doubt whether I am untypical. It might be argued that this is no better than the listener who absorbs the music, admiring the cascades of liquid notes in Chopin, or Beethoven's tempestuous virility, without thinking of the particular qualities or deficiencies of the performance.

No doubt this is true, but the difference remains, for aesthetic distinctions are fixed by the ideal case. The most the interpreter expects of his audience is that they see the general effect and its dependence on the detail. The best the poet expects is that the reader draw his own conclusions about theme and tone and the way the textual detail supports it. There is a famous remark by Coleridge in which he says of Shakespeare that he makes his reader, for a moment, 'an active creative being'. This is true of the perceptive reader, but not, I think, of even the intelligent listener.

Note

Below, I indicate some of the more immediately useful books and journals relating to the area of work examined by the paper. In addition, the footnotes contain details of further relevant work.

Cultural Studies and Cultural Analysis

Chapter 2 of Raymond Williams's *The Long Revolution* (London, Chatto and Windus, 1961), 'The Analysis of Culture', is an important early discussion of the prospects for a criticism-based cultural research. Volume I of Richard Hoggart's essay collection, *Speaking to Each Other: About Society* (London, Chatto and Windus, 1970), contains many relevant reviews and lectures written during the author's Directorship of the Centre for Contemporary Cultural Studies at Birmingham University. During the 1970s the Centre published its own journal, *Working Papers in Cultural Studies*, and the 10 issues of this hold a wide range of substantive cultural analyses, including 'readings' of media output, as well as many valuable discussion papers.

Textual readings of Broadcasting and the Press

Apart from the pioneering studies in the *Working Papers* of the Birmingham Centre, the journals *Screen* and *Screen Education* (Society for Education in Film and Television) have published detailed analyses of television form. A number of examples of the cultural reading of television also appear in John Fiske and John Hartley, *Reading Television* (London, Methuen, 1979). In my view, the most impressive interpretative study of television journalistic form is Charlotte Brunsdon and David Morley's *Everyday Television: 'Nationwide'* (London, British Film Institute, 1978). David Morley's *The 'Nationwide' Audience* (London, British Film Institute, 1980) follows this through into the kind of audience enquiries which my paper argues are necessary.

On the press, A.C.H. Smith's *Paper Voices* (London, Chatto and Windus, 1975) offers the most extensive study of press texts so far published, focusing on popular newspapers and social change during the period 1935–65. Linguistic approaches to press analysis are to be found in Roger Fowler *et al.*, *Language and Control* (London, Routledge and Kegan Paul, 1979).

An important sociological, and interpretatively restrained, line of enquiry into news texts has been developed by the Glasgow University Media Group in *Bad News* (London, Routledge and Kegan Paul, 1976) and *More Bad News* (London, Routledge and Kegan Paul, 1980). More recently, sociological, linguistic and 'cultural studies' strands of work on broadcasting, the press and advertising are represented in Howard Davis and Paul Walton, eds., *Language, Image, Media* (Oxford, Blackwell, 1983).

3

Criticism as Sociology: Reading the Media

John Corner

What kind of knowledge does criticism produce and how does it relate to enquiries which seek to promote historical or sociological rather than linguistic or aesthetic understanding? Posing these terms as alternatives might appear to ignore the ways in which concepts like culture and discourse have been employed to reject such distinctions. But how successful has this employment been at the level of research method?

In what follows, I want to pursue questions about criticism and social inquiry by looking at how critically-based approaches have been used to 'read' mass communications as part of 'reading culture'. I shall start by considering some conventional aims of literary analysis and by examining the assumptions of the first group of critics to take a close interest in media output. Following this, I want to discuss some methodological aspects of 'Cultural Studies' as it became formed from a line of socio-literary investigations then being importantly developed in the writings of Richard Hoggart and Raymond Williams.[1]. In particular, I am interested in the problems involved, first, in attempting to read 'through' media material to originating conditions and contexts and then in attempting to read, as it were, 'ahead' of it, in such a way as to calculate its social influence.

The Critical Approach: Some Assumptions and Intentions

When those self-conscious practices of interpretation which inform critical analysis are applied to texts defined as literary, the aim is most often that of heightening understanding, awareness and appreciation of the work's properties among a primarily academic readership. It is the work's own qualities as representation – cognitive and aesthetic – which provide the focus and object, as well as the primary ground, for exploration.

Despite the increase in recent years of more directly historical, social and political kinds of criticism, a majority of published studies and undergraduate programmes in literature are still based on a relationship to texts

[1]Particularly Richard Hoggart, *The Uses of Literacy* (London, Chatto and Windus, 1957) and Raymond Williams, *The Long Revolution* (London, Chatto and Windus, 1961).

consonant with this broad goal of appreciation. In teaching, a strong implication of curriculum philosophy is that as well as there being literary pleasures to enjoy and much to learn *about* literature, there is also much to learn *from* it, and that such knowledge of this kind accrues to the reader by virtue of the distinctive properties of authorial mind and sensibility evinced by the works themselves. In that regard, critical modes of knowing often operate partly within the terms of literary modes of knowing, this leading, understandably, to relations of reading in which there is a considerable deference exercised towards 'what the text knows and how it speaks' no matter what points of disapproval or disagreement are then taken up. Such an attitude may well be authentically the result of critical respect, though the very institutionalization of the stance, and particularly its use in education, can serve to promote it as an obligatory formal/professional reading position. Many teachers of English will know how authoritarian appropriations and renderings of 'the canon' can push this through into what is finally a politically complicit narrowing of student reading possibilities and of attitudes to literary and social values.

Furthermore, one consequence of the related convention – that close interpretative analysis is an activity performable properly only on works considered to display distinguished qualities of mind (poor works being occasionally used to throw these qualities into relief) – is the automatic dismissal of critical attention to journalistic, broadcasting and popular cultural texts. This position remains powerful in many English departments, frequently blocking or marginalizing work on popular fiction and on film and putting most of mass communication output beyond the pale altogether.

Now prejudice of this type is based on a mistaken sense of what most critically-informed work on the media is trying to do; assessments are made from too limited an idea of the aims of close reading. However, the way in which enquiries were carried out by those academics who contributed to the first major phase of critical interest in mass communication did not offer much by way of clear alternatives.

The most important of early critical engagements with modern media processes in Britain was that conducted during the 1930s by critics involved in the *Scrutiny* project, notably of course the Leavises.[2] Close readings here, when offered at all, were mostly used as illustrations to support the general argument about mass culture. These readings provided what was really a secondary documentation of 'obvious' symptoms within what we may call a pathology of the modern. The primary evidence adduced to support the diagnosis (chronic debasement of public sensibility) consisted of generalized accounts of contemporary values and a selective and fanciful version of national cultural history.

With surprisingly little concern for differentiation, the output of the

---

[2]See the general discussion and references in Francis Mulhern, *The Moment of Scrutiny* (London, New Left Books, 1979). A key text is F.R. Leavis and Denys Thompson, *Culture and Environment* (London, Chatto and Windus, 1932).

media was 'read off' against the aesthetic and moral criteria used in the appraisal of literature and not only found to be wanting but to constitute a threat to the values which literature (and criticism) stood for. It was not then thought necessary either to argue for this judgement with any sustained local emphasis or, indeed, given the judgement, to press further any specific enquiries into just how media forms and styles worked, in what ways they were read and what their registered pleasures might actually be. The critics are clearly aware of the way in which media language selectively assumes and advances particular social relationships and evaluations, but the connection with the cultural is made immediately, and then sustained, at the level of generalized adverse judgement. This stops the often penetrating sense of the increasing social centrality and commodification of media usages (particularly those of advertising) from being taken through into any kind of controlled social enquiry.

Here is an example of a suggestion for further work taken from Leavis and Thompson's *Culture and Environment*, published in 1933:

> Work out the life of a person who responds to the advertisements he or she reads. Compare it with the lives of the villagers in *Change in the Village* and of the Dodsons in *The Mill on the Floss*.[3]

At its worst, as this might imply, the *Scrutiny* perspective on the processes of the media carried an assumption about the practical consciousness of audiences and readerships so simplistic and brusquely unsympathetic (Q.D. Leavis's phrase 'the herd' remains disturbingly memorable)[4] as to preclude utterly the asking of the kinds of question I have indicated above.

My interest here is not in taking up those important issues of cultural formation and change which the work of this group of critics raises but in noting the extent to which what was undertaken by them was primarily an evaluative polemic about the media and not an enquiry, least of all a detailed textual enquiry, into how media meanings were made. The one partial exception to this that I know of, though it concerns itself with popular fiction rather than 'the media' as such, is Q.D. Leavis's *Fiction and the Reading Public*.[5] Significantly, this too fails to enquire into the forms which popular readings of popular fiction take and instead assumes that the limitations detected in the texts answer to, or are reproduced as, limitations in the imagination of the readership.

Although from the 1930s onwards literary critics regularly commented on the character of media journalism and entertainment (sometimes with the doubtful aid of invented examples, so as to bring out what it was argued were the typical features of the kind of work under discussion) it was not until Birmingham University set up the Centre for Contemporary Cultural Studies in 1964 under the Directorship of Richard Hoggart that a

---

[3]Leavis and Thompson, p. 113.
[4]Q.D. Leavis, *Fiction and the Reading Public* (London, Chatto and Windus, 1932). See p. 67 for example.
[5]Full reference above.

more thorough debate about critical aims and methods began. Within the terms of the 'Cultural Studies' enterprise the idea of an enquiry into media texts became clearer and more easily separable from those principles and assumptions informing most of the work being done in literature departments. Although, as in the *Scrutiny* approach, the starting point was an anxiety about the increasing centrality of the media to modern society, the need for more fully descriptive and explanatory accounts replaced the earlier desire to set up as a sort of cultural magistrates' court through which the maximum number of decadent texts might receive a summary, critical come-uppance. It involved giving critical reading and the interpretative wholes which are its products ('readings') a much more developed sociological function.

Content Analysis and the 'Cultural Reading'

When the literary-trained researchers of the Centre's first phase of activity considered what inroads Sociology had so far made on the analysis of such material as newspapers, broadcast programmes and advertising copy they were not too impressed. In Britain, very little detailed attention had been given to media forms, styles and themes – the concentration of studies was in the social psychology of media influence – and most of the work that had been published followed the American social science tradition of 'content analysis'. This term refers to various procedures of textual study, all of which are based on the systematic categorization and counting of content elements in a given media item.[6] The procedures permit a high degree of control over subjective impressionism at points in the analysis (though the initial phase of category formulation is clearly a vulnerable one), but their classifications are often unable to register the nuances of meaning at work in a given strip of imagery or verbal discourse. The breaking-up and classifying-out of texts into content categories works against any apprehension of the formal structures of the item, its local language use and the 'positionality', or significance in relation to one another and to the text as a whole, of the meanings generated.

What was abstracted from texts as either 'manifest' or (more trickily) as 'latent' content in these kinds of study, revealing though it might be about certain recurring thematic features in the material, seemed very far from those various sequences and organizations of significance which would be active in the assumptions and intentions of media producers and in the watching or reading experiences of audiences. In some research contexts, the very idea of 'content' study tended to under-rate or deny the idea of significant form, a tendency noticeable in the ease with which studies worked across formally quite different kinds of media material

[6]A critical and well-referenced account of early work is given in George Gerbner, 'On Content Analysis and Critical Research in Mass Communication', in Lewis Dexter and David White, eds., *People, Society and Mass Communications* (New York, The Free Press, 1963), pp. 476–500.

with an apparent confidence in the analytic constancy of the content categories employed.

Such limitations were regarded by many intending readers of culture not just as local problems of method but as aspects of a general conceptual inadequacy in the investigation of cultural practices by social scientists. The degree of reifying crudity, unimaginativeness and positivistic zeal ('sociological reductionism') frequently attributed to content studies seems exaggerated if the empirical boldness of many of the projects is allowed for, together with their nature as attempts to locate media items within existing, if unfortunately often functionalist, frameworks of social explanation.[7] Polemics of this kind also run the risk of downgrading the research benefits which highly explicit procedures of analysis can bring through replicability – that is to say, other people can check your findings.[8]

Nevertheless, many of the methods of content study then in use had been devised to advance the researching of a mass communication process modelled in diagrams as the sending of 'messages' to the public via the 'carriers' of different 'channels' and 'formats'. This whole paradigm was rather disposed to regard the operation of the media within society as essentially the basic telegraph circuit writ large! Certainly, literary critics of whatever persuasion would have seen techniques so developed as unlikely to come up with anything about *Hamlet* they would find interesting. Cultural researchers had this at least in common with them, that they thought there was a good deal more going on in the images and the language they were looking at than any typology or system of classification had yet been able to account for.

Just such an attitude was clearly expressed by Alan Shuttleworth in one of the Centre's earliest discussion papers:

> This much is, I think, agreed within the Centre: that in order to undertake a sociology of literature, or a sociology of popular culture or the mass media, or a sociology of the history of taste, then only 'content analysis' of the same subtlety and discrimination is adequate as would warrant a literary critical judgement. Here, clearly, is a task for the Centre: to train sociologists in literary criticism.[9]

Shuttleworth's main aim is to re-work Leavis's ideas about a 'humane

---

[7] A good case for the strengths of content analysis is made out in James Curran 'Content and Structuralist Analysis of Mass Communication', a paper prepared for Project Two of Course D305: Social Psychology (Milton Keynes, The Open University, 1976).

[8] For a discussion of how computer processing can be used to obtain inter-observer reliability see Alan Beardsworth, 'Analysing Press Content: Some Technical and Methodological Issues', in Harry Christian, ed., *The Sociology of Journalism and The Press* (University of Keele, Sociological Review Monograph 29, 1980), pp. 371–95. Much of the force of evidence in the Glasgow University Media Group's *Bad News* (London, Routledge and Kegan Paul, 1976) comes from procedures of this kind.

[9] Alan Shuttleworth, 'A Humane Centre', in *Occasional Papers Two* (University of Birmingham, 1966), reprinted in Peter Davison *et al.*, eds., *Literary Taste, Culture and Mass Communication* XIV (Cambridge, Chadwyck-Healey, 1980), pp. 43–66.

centre' of studies[10] (importantly, studies whose primary if not exclusive method would be that of carrying out 'readings') so as to inform the more sociologically inclined enquiries underway at Birmingham. Given these new emphases though, how was that 'dense contact with particular material' (?) which his paper claims criticism affords (and which contrasts with, but potentially complements, sociology's 'generalizing modes of thought') to produce social knowledge? The initial answer followed on from a developing vein of work in literary studies by claiming that it provided the possibility of a sort of cultural 'depth analysis'. Unlike the abstracted categorizations of content analysis, a critical reading well done – closeness permitting depth – could, it was argued, interpret and diagnose back down the line of semantic links and shifts connecting textual rhetorics and their components with the matrices of meaning in cultural and social organization.

Reading as Cultural Archaeology

It might be useful here to consider three comments by Richard Hoggart in order to bring out some general principles of this 'depth analysis' and to aid a discussion of the problems which attend an extension of critical concerns in this direction. The first comes from *The Uses of Literacy* (1957), the other two from a book review written in 1967:

> [We] have to try to see beyond the habits to what the habits stand for, to see through the statements to what the statements really mean (which may be the opposite of the statements themselves), to detect the differing pressures of emotion behind idiomatic phrases and ritualistic observances.[11]

> That method [of the book under review] is primarily to look at the texts themselves and work out their cultural meanings, the degree to which they express the consciousness of the age below the explicit level, at the level where the strains show.[12]

> We are making, in a sense very difficult to define satisfactorily, a reading for values, one which brings to the surface the complex patterns of values embodied in, carried by, the prose.[13]

While all three of these comments might be regarded as being about the same broad socially interpretative project, I think it is interesting to note how the first one differs in emphasis from the other two. They all suggest a

---

[10]See the arguments in F.R. Leavis, *Education and The University* (London, Cambridge U.P., second edition 1979).

[11]Hoggart, *The Uses of Literacy*, p. 18. Quoted by Stuart Hall in the Introduction to *Working Papers in Cultural Studies 1* (Birmingham University, Centre for Contemporary Cultural Studies, 1971), p. 7.

[12]Richard Hoggart, 'On Cultural Analysis', in *Speaking to Each Other*, vol. I: *About Society* (London, Penguin, 1973), p. 120.

[13]Hoggart, 'On Cultural Analysis', p. 121.

kind of reading work which is diagnostic rather than reconstructive (in the sense that they want to get from their texts something other than what these texts appear to be saying 'officially') but the first formulation proposes this primarily as an activity of contextualization. It is more a kind of broad reading than a close reading that is proposed. Here, the interpretative work of the analyst/reader is directed towards locating the items within hypothesized or assumed schemes of social significance, thus rendering them diagnosable. These schemes have to be already analytically available (at least in provisional ways) in order that recognition and correlation (what stands for what, what is really being said, etc.) can be accomplished. What can then be observed about the utterances or behaviours lies 'beyond', 'through' or 'behind' the signifying forms themselves and, indeed, is presumably not routinely perceivable via the kinds of interpretations that would be performed on them in everyday life. It is worth pointing out here though that, of course, unless the analyst has access to the schemes used to produce such quotidian interpretations, any inferences as to 'real' significance are likely to be impaired by an inadequate construing of the 'apparent'.

The other two quotations appear to pose the relationship between analyst/reader, text and interpretative context rather differently. Here, in addition to that narrative or informational sense which is the first objective of reconstructive reading (literary readings may also reconstruct an implied propositional sense which, as a characteristic of art discourse, is deemed 'official'), the texts are seen to be carrying or 'embodying' certain social meanings and values. It is the analyst/reader's job to make these explicit by an intimate apprehension of forms and tones (they have to be brought 'to the surface'). However, despite this emphasis on the texts as sources (and, as such, the points of focus of what are viewed as enquiries primarily conducted upon and within texts), connections with the earlier kind of reading outlined are present. In the second quotation a key part of the project is the calculation of the extent to which the works examined express 'the consciousness of the age'. This phrase, an odd one to find in Hoggart's critical vocabulary, is clearly something of a throwback to the grand monolithic abstractions of one kind of literary history. Be that as it may, the putative historical entity it refers to is something which the analyst must be expected to have knowledge of prior to the analysis if he or she is to assess the text's expression of it. While this does not by itself condemn the procedure described to circularity, a dialectical movement between generalities and the particular being necessary to all knowledge production, it does suggest, as I think do the differences across the three formulations, certain difficulties presented by 'deep reading' as a method no matter what kind of material is under scrutiny. Cultural analysts have themselves registered these difficulties[14] and in recent years the employ-

---

[14] An interesting account of methodological issues attending the 'deep reading' of literature is given in Andrew Tolson, 'Reading Literature as Culture', *Working Papers in Cultural Studies 4* (1974), pp. 51–68.

ment of semiotic concepts, replacing Hoggart's tentative phrasings with theories about the operation of socio-textual codes, has posed them in new ways. However, they remain as problems for any reading-based enquiry and have been particularly apparent in studies of the media, notwithstanding the many illuminating investigations of discursive form which have been carried out.

They follow, I believe, from the relations existing in any piece of 'cultural reading' between what can be referred to, developing my remarks on the quotations, as its textualist and contextualist phases, and from the nature of these phases as produced in the analysis.

In the textualist phase, the material (news item, advertisement, television programme etc.) seems to be located within the analysis as some multi-levelled *repository* of meaning, having a deep level or 'deep structures' (Chomsky's phrase does extensive duty here) to which the reading can penetrate. These meanings are perceived to be properties of the texts even though they do not form part of its 'official' discourse and may not be registered in the settings of lay interpretation (e.g. reading the paper, watching television, seeing the hoarding from the bus). To use a phrase from one kind of deterministic account, they are 'inscribed' within the textual form, an impress of its sociality as a product, and can be retrieved by sensitive analysis. The line of historical and social enquiry thus lies 'down and through' the text.

In the contextualist phase, which in many media analyses is given prefatory and/or concluding functions and occupies a relatively small part of the account, the researcher frames and situates the texts (as read, or about to be read, 'closely') thus making them mean within the terms of what are consciously applied, and perhaps explicitly argued for, orders of significance. This is most clearly seen to occur at very general levels of diagnostic reading (e.g. certain editions of *Picture Post* located within the contexts both of photo-journalism's development and British social history[15]). What is 'read off' here is registered (as it would have to be in Hoggart's first example above) not as a property of the texts but as a product of the descriptive/explanatory orders themselves as they engage with and organize into significance symptomatic features of the material under analysis. These orders may, of course, be held to identify and account for factors (assumptions, inferences, elements of what Williams, in a still useful if troublesome phrase, terms 'structures of feeling') which are active in the production practices of media employees and in the interpretations made by audiences, whether consciously in use here or not.

Now the separability of the actual processes from which these two phases are constructed seems to me to be less clear a matter than cultural readings customarily require in order to provide warrant for the propositions they wish to make from textual study. Indeed, the textualist phase

[15]The example is drawn from Stuart Hall, 'The Social Eye of the Picture Post', *Working Papers in Cultural Studies 2* (1972), pp. 71–120. This study is a very general contextualizing account with suggestions for more detailed textual analyses.

can be viewed as involving an analytically convenient objectification, a complex semantic entity being produced from the physical fact and separateness of units of image, speech and notation – that programme, this article. However temporarily, it threatens to leave out of account the constitutive function of interpretative schemes – whether reconstructive or diagnostic, lay or academic in intention – for all realization of significance from notational form. Newspaper articles, advertisements, documentaries, comedy shows – like novels, poems and plays – gain what referential and expressive stability they have by virtue of those conventions of significance within which image and notation become meaning and by virtue of the alignments between these conventions across social groupings, situations and time. This much is a grounding principle of cultural analysis. It is precisely to those conventions less directly entailed by the more determinate language features, to conventions of assumption, implication and connotation, including those involving sense-making from still and moving images, layout styles and narrative sequences, that 'deep readings' of the media most often seek to address themselves. To do this by posing the text as somehow a 'frozen moment' in the circulation of public values and significance, a held layering of meanings indexical to the culture at large and susceptible of semantic excavation, is to ignore interpretative contingency in the interests of securing a handy data base.

One typical result of this is the reproduction in the sphere of cultural analysis of familiar critical arguments about textual 'presence'.[16] One researcher finds evidence ('traces' perhaps) in the text of, say, conflicting production aims or certain (possibly historically distant) ideological themes or reportorial assumptions which cannot be 'found' by other researchers. We might, for instance, have an argument about what was 'in' and what was 'not in' television coverage of the Falklands War. Many contested characteristics (e.g. omissions and recurrences of names, phrases, explanations, descriptions and shots; formal features of the discourse) might be confidently established purely by textual reference. But a whole range of propositions which it would be important for cultural analysts to make about active assumptions and meanings could not be sustained, as might well be attempted, by textual reference alone, however tightly theorized the readings. An 'is it there or not?' framing (which in literary studies can be made to fit in happily with the idea of the text as kaleidoscopic promoter of possibilities) is a misplaced and potentially over-assertive way of handling an enquiry where the question is not 'how can this text be read?' but 'what were the organizing values, inferences and assumptions within which it was produced?'.

Clearly, the status and relationships of texts and readings confront every

[16]Some of these problems are documented in Graham Murdock and Peter Golding, 'Ideology and the Mass Media: The Question of Determination', in Michèle Barratt *et al.*, eds., *Ideology and Cultural Production* (London, Croom Helm, 1979), pp. 198–224. See also D. Anderson and W. Sharrock, 'Biassing the News: Technical Issues in Media Studies', *Sociology* XIII, iii (1979), pp. 368–85 and the subsequent responses in issues XIV, iii and XIV, iv (1980).

student of expressive forms with difficult problems of conceptualization. Nevertheless, the kind of enquiry which the last question above points to – properly one part of a pragmatics of media discourse – can only be conducted by the linking of an analytic focus upon textual forms with a much wider range of inter-textual, ethnographic and historical investigations into public orders of significance. The schemes of interpretation at work at different phases of the production and circulation of media texts would here be a central point of concern, one which included sharper reflexive awareness of schemes brought into play by the analyst.

This is not to allot texts a merely relative importance as simply projections of interpretative schemes. Questions of textual notation and the kinds of significance that can be generated from this cannot be handled in terms of a single, unitary 'meaning' of which either the text or the reader must then be identified as the real source.[17] Nor is it to suggest that some sort of reversal of 'deep reading' emphases is what is required were it achievable, texts (old radio comedy programmes, for instance) somehow being realized into their full, 'deep' social indexicality when externally researched interpretative schemes were applied.

Indeed, no easy prescriptions for research can be made, but more use of oral history methods, interviews, related non-media texts and cross-textual comparisons could, it seems to me, provide 'thicker' interpretative accounts to connect both with analytic readings and with institutional studies. Such an extended programme of work would present the researcher with new kinds of interpretative and correlational opportunities, a lot more of them than at present in media institutions and on production phases.

In fact, an early Birmingham Centre study of the popular press and social change, published in 1974 as *Paper Voices*,[18] is brilliantly suggestive about the connections that can be made between a variously sourced history of particular public attitudes and feelings and the specific shifts in a newspaper's mode of address and editorial position. Disappointingly, it remains itself under-documented outside of its main sections of textual commentary.

I have suggested, then, that contrary to the ambitions of textual depth analysis, the social character of what the media produce is not something to which 'readings' can give privileged access. This applies equally to those projects which have concerned themselves less with matters of origin and formation than with questions of influence.

Reading and Cultural Influence

In attempting to go 'through' texts to local and general conditions of production, media readings are close in approaches and problems (specif-

[17]Useful discussions of these matters as they affect literary studies are collected in S. Suleiman and I. Crosman, eds., *The Reader in the Text* (Princeton, Princeton U.P., 1980).
[18]A.C.H. Smith, *Paper Voices* (London, Chatto and Windus, 1975). See particularly the Introduction by Stuart Hall.

ically, those following from assumptions about textual stability and held meanings) to that kind of literary historiography suggested by Raymond Williams in his early and influential outline study of the 1840s.[19] However, the second objective which analytic reading was given within cultural research on the media has no parallel in literary studies at all. This involved the carrying forward of a textual interpretation into arguments about the significance media items had for contemporary media publics and about their influential powers.

In literary studies, the discursive protocols of criticism certainly do not require that offered interpretations be capable of being shared by or attributable to readers at large, let alone be indicative of influence exerted upon them. This is because literary studies are addressed to a professional community of skilled readers within which originality of personal interpretation, plausibly argued from consensually agreeable textual properties, is what a reading conventionally delivers. Of course, some of the texts which form the corpus of literary study are read, if at all, by only a very few people outside the framings and requirements of academic work, so that questions about their public meanings and their effects upon general consciousness are unlikely to be raised. But even where the works enjoy a wider circulation, their general readership is not considered of much importance to the pursuit of critical knowledge. *Wuthering Heights*, for instance, is read widely in library editions and paperback form outside of schools, colleges and universities but the collections of essays and the conference papers which analyse it have little place for any study or attempted survey of its particular significances, pleasures and appeals within the broader sphere of its public existence. Research of this kind might even be regarded as evidencing some new manifestation of the affective fallacy. The interpretations, then, which the book receives from non-professional readers in settings other than a syllabus do not count in a critical enterprise which holds the text as provisionally free of any specific production or reception determinants in order to promote readings linking textual potential with highly distinctive kinds of, as it were, 'creative insight'.

Some studies of media work, particularly those on film and on broadcast drama, have reproduced this critical stance almost without modification, although in film studies there has lately been discussion about the extent to which a form of cultural analysis rather than a form of criticism should be the main business in hand.[20]

Certainly, as we have already seen, the social research objectives of the cultural reading make its interpretative task a different one. Here once again, but now with respect to what happens 'in front' of the text, it is precisely not originality that is sought but a descriptive reconstruction of the kinds of meanings, evaluations and ideological clusterings which make

---

[19]Williams, *The Long Revolution*, chapter 2.
[20]An excellent, polemical discussion is John Hill's 'Ideology, Economy and the British Cinema', in Barrett, *Ideology and Cultural Production*, pp. 112–34.

their reinforcing or modifying entry into the sphere of public discourse with each particular media narrative, news item, magazine article, television commercial and so on.

This returns the researcher to a similar set of problems, of textualism and contextualism, to those which I have outlined above. For just as texts themselves do not have an independent deep semantics sufficient to provide primary data for the reconstruction of a history and a context, neither can their variable public realizations by different viewers and readers in different settings be established through close analysis.

As one moves further away from the more socially objective significance of descriptive language, through conventions of cultural inference and on to the imaginings of character and action elicited by visual and verbal narratives (all unhelpfully subsumed into 'the text's meaning' by some commentators) so the analyst's own textual realizations become increasingly inadequate as bases for general accounts. This is so whether the readings are somehow consciously 'offset' to try and allow for the interpretative tendencies of kinds of ideal typical reader or projected straight from the analyst's version on to an undifferentiated public understanding and response, as in the accounts given by the *Scrutiny* group. The differentiating factors of class, education, gender, age and personal biography work to multiply the public existences of a text (whether *Coronation Street*, *Boys from the Black Stuff*, the editorials of the *Daily Mirror* or *News at Ten*) out of the comprehensive possession of any attempted 'normative' reading.

Among the variations of registered significance there is clearly much common interpretative and imaginative activity going on. As well as being constructed within broadly available conventions of language, imagery and cultural association, media texts are constructed within the terms of social power relations. Particular established and developing ways of organizing social perception, dominant ways of framing and explaining social structure and action are at work. We can say of these that they are implicit in the texts (as 'preferred readings', to use an influential research notion) but the prepositional metaphor of this phrasing should not be allowed to lead to assumptions about their presence there – awaiting the analyst's discovery – somehow independent of the reading work by which they come to mean. Perhaps ideas of completeness attaching to the widely used notion 'cultural product' are unhelpful here.

Many of the most interesting readings of contemporary media material have worked because they offer detailed descriptions of the reading or viewing experience – commentaries on their own realizations – 'read off' from the social sense of an analyst sufficiently inside common interpretative frames for the account to seem to answer to a much wider sustaining of meanings.[21] This kind of phenomenological study necessarily remains suggestive and highly variable, however, as a means for assessing

[21]For instance, on popular television, Richard Dyer, 'The Meaning of Tom Jones', *Working Papers in Cultural Studies 1* (1971), pp. 53–64. A similar success principle may be at work in Roland Barthes, *Mythologies* (tr. A. Lavers, London, Cape, 1972).

the public 'take up' of media productions. Further enquiry here, as in the study of production contexts, can only proceed through a more comprehensive attention to the heterogeneity of interpretative schemes and practices in social use. And this is to raise only the question of understood meanings and significance, in relation to which any questions of influence and attitude formation would have to be carefully posed.

Again, as I suggested earlier, the need is for ethnographic data on audiences and readerships to place alongside and to support and inform the textual studies. Methodologically bold though this work may have to be initially, the availability of more accounts and transcripts concerning what sense media publics make of what they see and hear and how they make it is a necessity for the development of a textual sociology.

The most important work so far undertaken in this area is undoubtedly that by David Morley, on audiences for the early evening television news magazine *Nationwide*.[22] This complements an analytic reading of the programme by detailed discussion with members of different audience groups. One of the many difficulties of method it encounters is that of getting adequate access to the primary work of audience interpretation as this follows the programme's sequence of face-to-camera presentation, links, interviews and voiced-over filmed reports. Study of the subsequent expressions of viewer reaction, including those of disagreement with propositional content, is no substitute for more fundamental examination of the processes by which the media significations are construed. There are signs that Morley's initiative is now getting the critical attention and development which it deserves and that attempts to follow through empirical enquiries into the interacting levels of sense-making from media items will be one part of this.[23]

Proper analytic address to the schemes of significance and to the contingencies upon which the social existence of media meanings depend must involve more wide-ranging and developed types of work on interpretational settings. These might include working across the phases of production and reception of a single item or programme, carrying out more extensive intertextual studies, and doing interview surveys around public issues which are receiving a variety of media treatments in different genres and forms.[24]

This is a large undertaking, and interpretative or linguistic readings will play an important analytical role in it. They will not, however, constitute an attempt to derive from textual criticism some kind of social hermeneutics. The cultural cannot be reconstructed by extrapolation either backwards or forwards out of the textual because it is just what is at issue in deciding what texts are and mean.

[22]David Morley, *The 'Nationwide' Audience* (London, British Film Institute, 1980).
[23]See Justin Wren-Lewis, 'The Encoding/Decoding Model: Criticisms and Redevelopments for Research on Decoding', *Media, Culture and Society* v, ii (1983), pp. 179–97.
[24]Some elements of this broader approach are impressively present in Phillip Elliott, Graham Murdock and Philip Schlesinger, ' "Terrorism" and The State: A Case Study of the Discourses of Television', *Media, Culture and Society* v, ii (1983), pp. 155–77.

Note

This essay attempts not so much to reconcile Marxism and Structuralism as to side-step some of their inbuilt antagonisms. To this end I have found it necessary to resort to certain theoretical texts and propositions which both pre- and post-date the problem. Exemplary among these is the combined *oeuvre* of Voloshinov/Bakhtin. I have used this formula since it is now generally acknowledged that those works under the name of V.N. Voloshinov, *Marxism and the Philosophy of Language* (London, Seminar Press, 1973) and *Freudianism: A Marxist Critique* (London, Academic Press, 1976) were, in fact, written by Bakhtin who, under political pressure at the time of their writing (in the 1920s), felt it safer to remain invisible. Under his own name though, Bakhtin has published two applications of his 'dialogic' theory of the literary utterance, *Rabelais and His World*, (Cambridge, Mass., MIT Press, 1968) and *Problems of Dostoyevsky's Poetics*, (Ann Arbor, Ardis, 1973). Apart from Julia Kristeva's useful commentary on Bakhtin in the introduction to the French edition of *Rabelais*, the implications of the work seem to have been ignored by 'mainstream' Structuralism. For a concise and useful account in English though, see Tony Bennett, *Formalism and Marxism* (London, Methuen, 1979).

A similar project concerned with a theory of the utterance and the conditions of production of discourse is now being developed by French theorists in, for example, Michel Pechêux, *Les vérités de la palice* (Paris, Maspero, 1975), Régine Robin, *Histoire et linguistique* (Paris, Colin, 1973) and Françoise Gadet and Michel Pechêux, *La langue introuvable* (Paris, Maspero, 1981). Compatible with this project and similarly influenced by the work of Louis Althusser is the work by Renée Balibar and her associates on the question of the 'national language'. See *Les français fictifs: le rapport des styles littéraires au français national* (Paris, Hachette, 1974) and R. Balibar and D. Laporte, *Le français national: politique et pratique de la langue nationale sur la Révolution* (Paris, Hachette, 1974).

Two recent works have significantly influenced my own arguments about necessary realignments of literature and history. These are Franco Moretti, *Signs Taken for Wonders* (London, NLB/Verso, 1983) and Benedict Anderson, *Imagined Communities* (London, NLB/Verso, 1983). Anderson's analysis of the *national* context of literature's purview and Moretti's reintroduction of the techniques of 'Rhetoric' into literary analysis along with the associated conceptions of consent and pact enabled me to attempt to form a bridge with the work of Antonio Gramsci and the concept of hegemony.

4

Paris Match: Marxism, Structuralism and the Problem of Literature

Colin Mercer

> The starting point of critical elaboration is the consciousness of what one really is, and is 'knowing thyself' as a product of the historical process to date which has deposited in you an infinity of traces without leaving an inventory.
> Antonio Gramsci

This piece of advice, dating from around 1935, might be taken as announcing, *avant la lettre*, the agenda for what has now come to be termed 'critical theory'. But it also announces four of its major problems; the central points of friction which emerged a few years back in the encounter, the match (in both meanings of the term) between Marxism and Structuralism. These four problems, or we might call them 'stakes' can be designated as follows. First, the problem of self, of identity or of subject ('knowing thyself'). Second, the problem of history ('the historical process to date'). Third, the problem of culture or of ideology ('an infinity of traces'). Fourth, the problem of knowledge, interpretation or science ('an inventory'). These are not, of course, new problems. Neither are they specific to Marxism and Structuralism, but they have come together, or returned, as manifestations or symptoms of a distinctive and recurring disorder. Like the dream images in Freudian analysis, it's not so much that they are there but the ways in which they are recounted which is important: the language used, the omissions, the slippages, the frictions between one image and another which is the point of analysis. To continue the analogy further, the encounter has been marked by its symptomatic repressions and cathexes. With a dominance of history, the question of self or 'subject' tends to be either repressed or marginalized. And vice versa. With the 'infinity of traces' of culture, language or ideology to the fore, the question of knowledge or of interpretation has been relegated.

Examining some of the terms, the tensions and the fragmentary results of this encounter, specifically as they turn around the question – the problem – of literature, I want to assess some of the points of more productive compromise which might enable us to hold together the four major stakes provisionally or at least for long enough to allow some sort of 'compromise equilibrium'. This seems to me to be essential for the grounding and elaboration of any critical theory whilst being modestly aware, as Franco Moretti has recently put it, that 'the historical project lies almost entirely in the future.'[1]

A few provisos of a cautious methodological nature are needed before proceeding. Neither Structuralism, nor, more scandalously perhaps, Marxism, are unified, consistent and 'complete' bodies of theory. Structuralism as a term and as a practice has been defended by some of its main protagonists (the early Barthes, Levi Strauss) and rejected as a useless label by others (Foucault, Lacan). It is a methodology covering a range of disciplines from anthropology to mathematics. It emerged in a recognizable form with a set of broadly contiguous aims in the Paris of the early 1960s. Its context and history have been recounted a thousand times and this is not the place to elaborate further on that. But there is a central and overriding theme of Structuralism which I want to hang on to for the purposes of this essay: that is, the core of all structuralisms in the *linguistic analogy*. As Barthes puts it in an early essay, 'It is probably in the serious recourse to the lexicon of signification . . . that we must finally see the spoken sign of structuralism.'[2] We will ultimately have recourse to the old advice about trusting the tale and not the teller, but that will do for the present.

There are of course no Structuralist governments in the world. No blood has been spilt over the legitimacy or otherwise of Structuralism. No Structuralists have been tortured for their beliefs. This is perhaps a clumsy and banal point and it is not meant to posit 'authenticity' against 'intellectualism'. It is meant to signal a basic asymmetry between the genealogies of Structuralism and Marxism. Marxism, in the face of Structuralism, has been able to lay claim to a certain 'pedigree of the real' on precisely this basis. It has been able to hang on to that famous thesis on Feuerbach inscribed in stone at Highgate Cemetery about changing the world and not just interpreting it. But, and this is something which has been demonstrated with some precision over recent years, the claim to an authentic and demonstrable unity of theory and practice is not a claim to the unity of theory *per se*. Best, perhaps, to take the old man's word for it that there is a lot that he would have liked to have covered but simply didn't have time for. In the context of these declared lacunae and of the mutual recognition of limitations, literature, as yet undefined, might have something to say.

An Infinity of Traces: the Linguistic Analogy

Language, according to a sketchy formulation by Marx in *The German Ideology*, is the curse of the 'spirit', burdening it with 'matter'. The tone is ironic, critical, because in reality, 'language *is* practical consciousness that exists also for other men, and for that reason alone it really exists for

[1]Franco Moretti, *Signs Taken for Wonders* (London, NLB/Verso, 1983), p. 27.
[2]Roland Barthes, *Essais critiques* (Paris, Seuil, 1964).

me personally as well.'[3] This is the problem for idealism when confronted with language; that the letter killeth whilst the spirit giveth life. Language, quite simply, gets in the way of pristine consciousness: it burdens it with its second-hand character. Even Mallarmé who went the furthest 'away' from language, finally had to admit that a throw of the dice would never abolish chance and to reconcile himself to the fact that *'enoncer signifie produire'* – to utter means to produce.

With a few exceptions language has constituted something of either a mental block or a peripheral concern for Marxists in the Western tradition. There are lots of reasons for this, both practical and theoretical, which are not intrinsic to Marxism itself. But there is one abiding symptom which presents itself as generalizable across the range of application of Marxism: that is, the problem of *articulation*. This is another of those usefully ambiguous terms which embodies two meanings: to connect, or hold together (as in a lorry) and to express, as in speech. Marxism has, on the whole, tended to be quite hot on the first of these meanings – how things, relations, etc. hold together, what their conditions of existence are and what their determinate effects. It has not, on the whole, been as sharp as it could have been on the second of the meanings – how these things, relationships, etc. are expressed, how they become, to use an old-fashioned term, meaningful. Skilled in the analysis of the circuit of distribution within the mode of production, it has tended to theoretically marginalize the circuit of distribution of representations (political or otherwise). It is in this sense that the analysis of literature can attempt to modify some of these gaps but on condition that we allow literature the power, among other cultural forms, not just of 'expressing' but also of 'connecting' and holding together.

Comparing the text of the French and English translations of Juri Tynianov's 'On Literary Evolution' one notices some quite significant slippages around the question of literature's 'orientation' to that which is not literature. Here is the English version of one crucial passage: 'This interrelationship is realized through language. That is, literature in relation to social conventions has a verbal function.'[4] And here is the French version: *'Cette corrélation entre la série littéraire et la série sociale s'établit à travers l'activité linguistique, la littérature a une fonction verbale par rapport à la vie sociale.'*[5] A little later we have, in English, 'The orientation of a literary work then proves to be its verbal function, its interrelationship with the social conventions.'[6] And in French, *'L'orientation de l'oeuvre (et de la série) littéraire sera sa fonction*

[3]Karl Marx and Frederick Engels, *Selected Works* (3 vols., Moscow, Progress Publishers, 1973), p. 32.
[4]Jurij Tynianov, 'On Literary Evolution', in L. Matejka and K. Pomorska, eds., *Readings in Russian Poetics* (Ann Arbor, Michigan U.P., 1978), p. 73.
[5]Tynianov, 'De l'évolution littéraire', in T. Todorov, ed., *Theorie de la littérature* (Paris, Seuil, 1965), p. 132.
[6]Tynianov, 'On Literary Evolution', p. 74.

verbale, *sa corrélation avec la vie sociale.*[7] I can't say which is the more accurate. But just on the basis of this comparison, I can say that there is something significantly missing from the English version – the notion of *series*. There are no references to this in the English version. There are seven in the French which must, I suppose, give it something of the status of a concept. But what does this concept and the associated idea of *orientation* entail? From Tynianov, as from other Formalists of his generation, this is not entirely clear. We know that the orientation is linguistic, that it is through language that literature 'connects' with the outside world. This, at least, is an advance since we know that it is not through the 'spirit' of the author, or of the age, and we can surmise, given the complexity of language as a system, that we are not dealing with issues of reflection and expression. But there is no answer at this point: against 'literariness' we have what . . . otherness? The notion – or concept – of the *series* provides us with a minimal clue. It suggests that literature is, in the English-language version, an 'order' *alongside of* (and, again, there's not much suggestion of a hierarchy in this ordering) *other orders*. Thus far and no further with Tynianov and his associates, except, of course, that there is an 'orientation' between the orders or series.

This question, posed in passing form in the interstices of two translations, has been one of the central sticking points in the encounter between Marxism and Structuralism. The terms of the opposition are well enough known. If Structuralism, after Formalism, follows the trace of the signifier, then Marxism's true domain is that of the real or the referent. Kant's dilemma of fact and judgement, of the 'knowability of the thing in itself' is here reproduced. Given the relationship between Structuralism, in its 'classical' variety at least, and Saussure's distinction between *langue* and *parole*, this is not surprising. What emerges from this distinction is an essential separation between the categories of individual and society. The problem is that the dimension of *parole* is effectively untheorizable. It is *enabled* by the system of *langue*, it takes place within that structure, that structure *speaks* it, but 'it' remains just that – a sort of linguistic Robinson Crusoe in the sense of Marx's metaphor.[8]

Not that this problem has not been perceived within structural linguistics itself. Jakobson's work on personal pronouns or 'shifters' and Benveniste's insistence on the importance of the 'correlation of subjectivity'[9] in the production of discourse has attempted to modify the shortcomings of the Saussurian dilemma but without, for all their value, modifying the basic terms of the problematic. Making the utterance *inter-subjective* is not the same as developing a theory of subjectivity at which point the Marxist theory of ideology and the linguistic analogy might come together.

[7]Tynianov, 'De l'évolution littéraire', p. 132.
[8]Karl Marx, *Capital* (London, Pelican, 1976) I, p. 169 *et passim*, As Marx observes, 'political economists are fond of Robinson Crusoe stories'.
[9]Cf. Emile Benveniste, *Problèmes de linguistique générale* (Paris, Gallimard, 1966) I, p. 232.

Literature, Barthes says, is the 'institutionalisation of subjectivity'. This, it might be added, is the point of its power from which all other resilient and historically embedded notions – taste, value, discrimination, beauty, harmony, truth – radiate. The classic form of the linguistic analogy has not been able to accommodate this problem. And the problem is this: that although Structuralist analyses of literature have been able to identify, as it were, the 'weapons' being used, and possibly even the 'factories' in which they were made, they have not been able to say anything about the *strategies* in which they are deployed. And vice versa for Marxism: with an eye to the long term strategies and intentions, it has used rather blunt tools to understand the weapons. Via the linguistic analogy, the problem has been that the concentration on linguistic specificity in either its Formalist or Structuralist variant in literary forms does not give you any necessary purchase on literature's specific mode of signification. The literary 'object', and here we have to confront the problem that literature is not just a discourse like any other, disappears within the general categories of language.

What then is literature's specific mode of signification? To approach this question we have to transform the terms of the linguistic analogy. If, for linguistics, language is a system of signs, for literature it must be understood as a practice in which we have to account for the ways in which subjects specifically redistribute those signs. The first stage – and it is only a necessary preliminary step – is to see literature as Kristeva puts it, 'seized in the space of the subject, its topology, history and ideology'.[10] I emphasize that this is only a *first* stage because it is not, contrary to fashionable theories of deconstruction, *only* about that.

Know Thyself?

We need, in effect, a linguistic analogy which can encompass – and explain – the notions of orientation, of series, raised by Tynianov. We need to know the nature and the contours of literature's specific form of mediation. The notion of the subject, of subjectivity is, as I have argued above, a starting point. But an important additional notion here is that of a *pact*: the nature of the contact or, more correctly, *contract* between the subject and its 'topology, history and ideology' in literature. The sort of pact I am thinking of here is like that suggested by Oswald Ducrot when he writes that 'Independently of all information, the simple play of language establishes between individuals certain relations of collaboration, struggle, domination and dependence.'[11] This seems to me to come closer to a form of 'discourse theory' more compatible with the most incisive moments of Marx's analysis and critique of political economy in *Capital*. The functioning of the linguistic phenomena in literature is not integrally linguistic. It is not, after all, a raw material which makes a commodity.

[10]Introduction to Bakhtine, *La Poétique de Dostoievski* (Paris, Seuil), p. 7.
[11]Cited in Régine Robin, *Histoire et linguistique* (Paris, Armand Colin, 1973), p. 26.

The linguistic analogy can only be of use to the analysis of literature if it is defined by reference to the processes of the positioning of the 'protago- nists' or the 'heroes' within it. In other words we need to know not just the taxonomy of the literary discourse but also its conditions of production.

What are the conditions of production of a literary discourse, a 'work' of literature? They can, of course, be enumerated sociologically as levels of literacy, of cultural achievement, of market access, institutional distribu- tion and so on. But before reaching those broader questions we have to approach the question on its own terms. We have to stick for the moment to the linguistic analogy and ask, quite simply, how does the language *work* in this context? This is not a question about 'literariness', about the intrinsic qualities or devices of a literary text measured in terms of syntax, rhythm, metre, realism or whatever. It is a question about something prior to that: a question of what Voloshinov/Bakhtin calls the 'co-creation of contemplators'.[12] This, according to Voloshinov is the *only kind* of objecti- fication required by a work of art. What does this mean? Voloshinov gives the example of a conversation consisting of a single word – 'well'. The situation, or context, is two people sitting silently in a room prior to one of them uttering this word. How should we proceed to analyse this? Clearly a syntactic, or morphological or semantic analysis won't do. The 'purely verbal' part of the utterance gives us nothing to work on. We need to know that 'something else' which makes this word have a meaning for the locu- tor, in Voloshinov's terms, the 'extraverbal context'. This, he argues, is comprised of three components: (i) the *common spatial purview* of the interlocutors' – the fact that they are sitting in a room with a shared view of the window; (ii) their *common knowledge and understanding of the situation* and (iii) 'their *common evaluation* of that situation.'[13] The cause of the conversation was that they had both looked up at the window and noticed that it had begun to snow in May. Thus,

> On this 'jointly seen' (snowflakes outside the window), 'jointly known' (the time of the year – May), 'unanimously evaluated' (winter wearied of, spring looked forward to) – on all this the utterance *directly depends*, all this is seized in its actual, living import – is its very sustenance.[14]

Yet all of this, Voloshinov stresses, 'remains without verbal specification or articulation'. We can effectively only understand the 'meaning' of this conversation when we have some clue as to the 'shared spatial and ideational purview' of the verbal scenario.[15] Here, clearly the situation is a limited one and says nothing as such about literature. But this does pro- vide the opportunity for an important theoretical statement: 'their dis- course does not at all reflect the extraverbal situation in the way a mirror

[12]V.N. Voloshinov, 'Discourse in Life and Discourse in Art', in *Freudianism: A Marxist Critique* (London, Academic Press, 1976), p. 98.
[13]Voloshinov, 'Discourse', p. 99.
[14]Ibid.
[15]Ibid.

reflects an object . . . the discourse *resolves the situation*, bringing it to an *evaluative conclusion*, as it were.'[16]

The utterance is therefore comprised of two broad components: the actualization of the utterance in words and what Voloshinov calls the 'enthymeme' or the assumed part. Broadening the scope now, Voloshinov argues that this 'assumed' part may be '*that of the family, clan, nation, class and may encompass days or years or whole epochs.*'[17] This is a theory of utterance quite distinct from Saussurian linguistics. Whereas for the latter the utterance or *parole* is strictly related phonemically, syntactically, and morphologically to the system of *langue*, the question of the 'assumed' in the utterance is contingent. What Voloshinov calls in another work the 'specific variability of the utterance' or the 'multi-accentuality' of the sign has no role to play here.[18] The question, in other words, of 'social value judgements' inscribed within the utterance can only be tacked on and remain theoretically subordinate. True, there have been some masterful attempts to hold together these two domains within Structuralism such as in Barthes's *S/Z* where the first two codes – the hermeneutic and the proairetic – relate to the actualization of the utterance, and the other three – the cultural, the semic and the symbolic – relate to the 'assumed', but the alliance remains an uneasy one precisely because the notion of 'code' itself tends to hold apart the 'real' and the 'fictive'. For Voloshinov, this separation is not a problem since it is not so much a question of coding as of *inscription*: 'Life . . . penetrates and exerts an influence on an utterance from within, as that unity and com-monness of being surrounding the speakers'.[19] *Intonation* is the term used by Voloshinov to designate the nature of the transaction between the 'utterance' and the 'assumed'. This intonation takes the form of a silent contract between three participants: the '*speaker* (author), the *listener* (reader), and the *topic* (the who or what) *of speech* (the hero).'[20] The title of Voloshinov's essay, 'Discourse in Life and Discourse in Art' gives us some clue as to the nature of the connections, the orientations between 'art' and 'life', literature and history, fiction and the real and they give us a clue also to Tynianov's rather cloudy notion of series. We are looking for connections at the level of *discourse*. In other terms, the connections are to be established not between text, subject and 'world' but in the 'symbolic' forms which construct and hold these entities together. Thus, in Balzac we can continue to look for the arrangement of objects and 'commodities', in Lawrence we can continue to trace the oppositions of 'vitalism' and 'mechanicism', in Conrad 'organicism' and so on, but only as a first (taxonomic) stage in the analysis. What is much more important in order, crudely, to relate that 'structure' to its range of 'functions', is to examine

---

[16]Voloshinov, 'Discourse', p. 106.
[17]Ibid.
[18]Cf. V.N. Voloshinov, *Marxism and the Philosophy of Language* (London. Seminar Press, 1973), *passim*.
[19]Voloshinov, 'Discourse', p. 106.
[20]Voloshinov, 'Discourse', p. 105.

the intercourse, the dialogue, the terms of the agreements, between the literary 'series' and other forms of discourse. It is now fairly clear, for example, that the very notion of 'literature' in its English usage, is unthinkable outside of its articulation with discourses on literacy and improvement in the nineteenth century. It is clear that the very notion of 'English Literature', now naturalized across a thousand curricula, is a particular constellation of political and ideological values. It is a notion which has embedded within it a whole 'spatial and ideational purview': a preferred 'author', a preferred 'reader' and a preferred 'hero'. It is, or should be, impossible to read any text outside of or ignorant of, those general points of co-ordination. From Voloshinov's monosyllabic discourse we move to the broadest points of contact between 'text and world'. We begin to examine why, for example, the notion of 'rounded character' (Eliot rather than Dickens) plays such an important role not just in 'literary appreciation' but in countless film reviews and casual discussions on *The Book Programme* or *Bookshelf* or *The South Bank Show* or *Aquarius*: not because, as a sort of Marxist common sense would have it, this reflects an externally realized preference for bourgeois individualism, but because that topic or hero is *part of the contract*. It is a question of what we might call theoretical chronology.

The Historical Process to Date: from Dialectics to Dialogics

Chronology – time in general – is, of course, an abstract concept. It constructs certain points of co-ordination – today, yesterday, the past, the future, the nineteenth century and so on – partly in order to secure and stablize a presence *now*. It is not less 'real' because it is abstract. We experience the difference in real terms between today and tomorrow through the punctuation of sleep, or work schedules and so on. The existence, pertinence and 'appreciation' of a cultural form like a novel has assumed something of this mode of being. We know that it was not written today, but in the past, either immediate or distant. When we open a book we expect it to tell us something about that past, among other things. But we know also, through a sedimented common sense, that yesterday came before today, that 'history' is prior to the experience of reading the novel. We know that, in some cases, history is the referent against which the 'signifier' of the book is measured for adequacy, or access, or compatibility. In some senses, this is a peculiarly 'British' problem. Because, as Perry Anderson puts it, 'history is both the process and the discipline which seeks to understand it', the word 'history' functions ambiguously as a condenser of both the 'real' and of a 'realism' in the approach to that real. Marxist historiography in Britain has shown how powerful and effective that condenser can be. In France there is a loophole in the notion of history: the word *histoire* means both history as a process and 'narrative' or 'story'.[21] Indeed, in colloquial French, *'cette histoire'*

---

[21]On the theoretical implications of this conception of history see J.P. Faye, *Théorie du récit* (Paris, Hermann, 1974).

frequently refers to an elaborately constructed and sceptically received account of a personal experience: a demotion of the concept unthinkable in English and also a loosening-up of the chronological hierarchy. This loophole is one of the points at which a Structuralist methodology has been able to insert itself. If history is also a narrative or a story, then its mode of existence must be susceptible to the forms of textual or mythic analysis on which Structuralism sharpens its tools. History too is susceptible to the linguistic analogy, and indeed, something of this type of analysis has been developed in France through the work of the *Annales* group of historians.[22]

How does this loosen the chronological hierarchy with respect to a literary form? To approach this tangentially, we can borrow an example from one of the *Annales* historians, Emmanuel Le Roy Ladurie's work on *Carnival* set in the context of an uprising at Romans, in the south of France, in 1579-80. The carnival is, of course, a cultural and symbolic form. It is a system of meanings and of practices and rituals. Le Roy Ladurie's approach to this phenomenom consists in taking the carnival itself not as evidence of 'something else' in history, but as the very matrix of the negotiation, the sharp conflict between classes at this moment. He does not, as it were, read off something 'more real' from the existence of the cultural form. The cultural form is an articulation of that reality itself. It is not an 'ideological product' or an 'object' against history, but is part of the symbolic pact constituting that history.

Literature, it must be said, transacted through the judgemental categories of literary criticism and curricular 'appreciation', has resisted this sort of approach. History is there *post facto*. Vice versa for historians, literature is another form of evidence. Sometimes there is a compromise: literature does such and such 'because of' certain historical conditions outside of itself or in order, like Balzac or Dickens, to be 'saved' for a progressive tradition, 'in spite of' prevailing social relations. The silent chronology still prevails in whichever variant: history first, literature second, yesterday then today, cause then effect.

What if we were to say quite simply that literature is part of the historical process: that as a symbolic system it partakes in the *dialogue* of history? That literature is by definition what Voloshinov/Bakhtin calls a 'dialogic' form? Franco Moretti has recently put this point quite cogently:

> What is at issue once more is the orientation of the historian's gaze: whether one should look only at what is *behind* the masterpiece, unilaterally emphasizing a break, a rupture of the historical tissue – or whether, by showing the consequences of every great work, one should accentuate its function as a genuine producer of historical 'stability'.[23]

It is not just that literature 'speaks of' history. It also *speaks* that *histoire*.

[22]See especially Emmanuel Le Roy Ladurie, *Carnival: A People's Uprising at Romans 1579-1580* (London, Scolar Press, 1980).
[23]Moretti, p. 13.

We return, finally, to the questions of orientation and series which, in different terms, have been the central points of friction between Marxism and Structuralism. The question we can ask of the first of these terms is not what is the orientation of this literary text or corpus towards history? but rather what is the nature of the orientation – or intonation – of *this* manner of speaking history? Who is involved in this dialogue? What sort of pact is being established within and by this dialogue? A certain complicity is 'always already' established between, as it were, contracting parties as a condition of existence of the meaning of a discourse. Literature can and does 'innovate' within this set of constraints, but only so far. And not, of course, on its own.

This brings us to the second notion – that of the series. If literature is oriented towards other series through language or its 'verbal function' then this means that those other series are not just 'life' or the 'real' or social conventions, but are themselves symbolically constituted through other forms of language. The series is a matrix of different signifying practices providing a structure of *forms* of signification in a given conjuncture. Within this matrix, it is not the object 'literature' which is the point of analysis, but the relationships *between* literature as a 'symbolic form' and other forms of signification: political, scholastic, ideological and so on. To use the notion of series in this context then is to insist on the place of literature within a general 'sociology of symbolic forms, a history of cultural conventions' as Moretti puts it.[24] This has profound implications for the hierarchy in which literature is at present situated.

Compiling the Inventory

The most rigorous form of 'intrinsic' literary criticism, whether it be Formalist, Structuralist, Marxist or New Critical, can only ultimately achieve the dissatisfaction of an unnamed 'pseudo-scholar' in E.M. Forster's *Aspects of the Novel* who 'classified novels by their dates, their length, their locality, their sex, their point of view, till no more seemed possible.' But, Forster adds, 'he still had the weather up his sleeve, and when he brought it out, it had nine heads.' Even this left the critic dissatisfied and he had to add 'one more thing, and that was genius'. Even then he had to add that this was useless without considering the tone of the novel – 'personal and impersonal'. And that this was useless in itself without, correspondingly, the notion of genius.[25] We might call this the literary 'Munchhaüsen effect' referring, after Pechêux, to the legendary Baron Munchhaüsen who managed to lift himself up into the air by pulling his own hair. This is an ideological effect, a metaphor to designate the way in which the human subject sees him/herself as 'determinant and not determined'.[26] It means, in this case, that literary criticism, that

[24]Moretti, p. 19.
[25]E.M. Forster, *Aspects of the Novel* (London, Penguin, 1962), pp. 19–20.
[26]See Michel Pêcheux, *Les vérités de la palice* (Paris, Maspero, 1975), p. 142.

'accompaniment to reading' provides no purchase, no point of analysis beyond its own existence. An industry, a whole cultural and educational and ideological series has been built upon this 'effect'. If there is dialogue, it is between author and reader: there are no other determinations effective within this monovalent transaction.

The question now is, to return to Voloshinov/Bakhtin's more theoretical statements, how to reconstruct the co-ordinates of the dialogue or how to position the participants of author, listener and hero. How to understand the 'shared spatial and ideational purview' within the language itself, in the structure of the utterance. This may, as in Voloshinov/ Bakhtin's example, simply be a room with a view or it may be a much wider *assumed* than that. Let's go as wide as we can and say that this purview is the nation.

'And the Bible, which preaches this word, will forever remain, as Goethe called it, not only a national book, but the Book of Nations.' Thus Matthew Arnold in the preface to his own blueprint for a national culture, *Culture and Anarchy*. The nation is perhaps one of the most deeply embedded and ideologically powerful of all 'assumeds' in modern culture. It is easy to forget what a modern innovation this is: how comparatively recent was its formation into what Poulantzas calls a 'temporal and spatial matrix'. This is partly because, sharply condensed in the present, the nation as an effective metaphor draws its resources predominantly from the past: from a sense of profound continuity and tradition. Deploying powerful images it projects and inflects composite forms like 'national traditions', 'national culture', 'national character' and even 'national landscape' on an apparently seamless 360 degree screen converging on 'us' as its focal point from all angles.

If we are to return to something like an historical analysis of subjectivity in literature: if we are to concern ourselves with the forms of its institutionalization, then this seems to me to provide a necessary, though not sufficient, basis for reconstructing some of the basic co-ordinates of the 'spatial and ideational purview' which is inscribed into its texture. The nation, that 'imagined community' as Benedict Anderson has recently termed it,[27] seems to me to provide both the great 'assumed' and the great unexamined of *British* writing since the seventeenth century. For my present purposes this example provides some historical specification and some theoretical modifications to the analysis of literature with which I want to conclude.

Much has been said about the change in world-view or 'episteme' from the medieval to the post-Renaissance but, with a few exceptions, little has been said about two of the fundamental 'cultural' co-ordinates involved in this – language and the nation. Against the background of a growth of what Anderson calls 'print-literacy' and its economic companion 'print-capitalism' there is, in seventeenth-century Britain, a whole panic over the question of language and a proliferation of volumes and treatises on

[27]See Benedict Anderson, *Imagined Communities* (London, NLB/Verso, 1983).

everything from the invention of forms of shorthand to correct pronunciation and usage. In the works of Francis Bacon, Samuel Hartlib, Cave Beck and Jan Comenius, language becomes simultaneously a new 'theoretical object' and the vector for political and ideological concern later to be consolidated and institutionalized in the formation of the Royal Society. This, we can argue, was not merely an academic or purely linguistic concern: there are broader points of connection. As Gramsci puts it: 'Each time that in one way or another the question of language comes to the fore, that signifies that a series of other problems is about to emerge; the formation and enlarging of the ruling class, the necessity to establish more and more "intimate", more and more sure relations between the ruling groups and the national-popular masses, that is, the reorganization of cultural hegemony.'[28]

Adequate forms of *representation* in order to secure a 'sturdy civil society' is how Hobbes put it (and we can't ignore that in Hobbes, as later in Locke, there is a strong concern with language, the connection between 'words' and 'things'). This is where we should begin to look for the bases of a new set of *pacts*, a new 'enthymeme' in the symbolic system in the seventeenth century. And hegemony here is one of the terms from Marxism which might be coupled with a sufficiently developed form of textual analysis derived in part from Structuralism in order to understand not just the role of the text 'in' history but also, across the whole range of writing and symbolic forms, from Hobbes to Marvell, from Harrington's *Oceana* (1656) to Cave Beck's *The Universal Character* (1657). The new connections – between language and instruction, language and perspicacity, language and adequacy, language and common sense give us some clues as to the nature and direction of the transactions involved in the shift away from 'seeing language as a 'mode of access' to the divine, towards language as *doxa*. As Barthes put it, 'each jargon (each fiction) fights for hegemony; if power is on its side, it spreads everywhere in the general and daily occurrences of daily life, it becomes *doxa*, nature. . . . A ruthless *topic* rules the life of language; language always comes from some place, it is a warrior *topos*.[29]

Is it possible to detect something in the way of this struggle, something of the flavour of these 'more and more "intimate", more and more sure' relations in literature in a way which is not purely contextual or historically contingent? On condition that we broaden the horizon of theoretical enquiry and simultaneously resist the centripetal power of the notion of 'Literature' or of 'Tradition'. This might, in the first instance be a step as small as looking not just at Daniel Defoe's acknowledged 'greats' – *Robinson Crusoe, Moll Flanders, A Journal of the Plague Year* – but also looking at his *Essay on Projects* which established certain proposals: 'a blueprint for a young capitalist society which must admit the temperings of government direction and control . . . the

[28]Antonio Gramsci, *Quaderni del Carcere* (Turin, Einaudi, 1975), p. 2346.
[29]Roland Barthes, *The Pleasure of the Text* (London, Cape, 1975), p. 28.

establishment of a central bank, income tax . . . the direction of labour, the building of national highways . . . an academy for the correction and refinement of the English tongue, the emancipation of women.'[30] But then the problem is how to establish the connections. OK, Defoe, they say, did this *as well*, but this is, strictly speaking, political and not literary. But is it not possible here to establish certain important connections at the level of language which are consistent across the range of his writing? Defoe, as we know, was a 'reporter' and proud of it, a person who not only describes but *relates* = constructs and holds things together. (Again, the French have a word for it: *rapporter* means both to 'report' and to 'relate'!)

The *Journal of the Plague Year* is certainly a report in both of these senses. It is a work which articulates the primary figures of a new type of purview, both ideational and spatial, of city and nation: a certain conception of the transparency and social interchangeability of language, an assuredness – and in part a construction – of the perspicacity of the listener, and then, of course, the 'third term' – the topic or hero. In Defoe's *Journal* this is not, in the first instance, a person but rather a 'hero community' implemented through a sense of connection of elements within the heterogeneous time and space of the city. It is a space where the succession of plurals – of events, streets, quarters, people, disfigured corpses, buildings and dates – provides the bearings for a distinctively new conception of community. It is heterogeneous but it has a solidity, a realism and the incipiently documentary and grainy authenticity brought on by the 'Great Leveller' of the plague. It creates, as Benedict Anderson puts it, 'that remarkable confidence of community in anonymity which is the hallmark of modern nations.'[31] We could go further and say that the plague here functions as the necessary metaphor for the establishment of that new conception of community: that given the *tabula rasa* brought on by the plague, *this* is where we begin to establish and negotiate the new relationships, the new connections.

On its own, of course, this won't do. Other connections need to be made not just with other works by the same author, but also at those points where we can detect, other similar convergences, other discursive 'regularities', other points of contact with the cultural, political and symbolic forms of the period. What is sure though is that in this theoretical horizon, within this conception of language, literature, or what we retrospectively understand by that term, is necessarily *demoted* from its assumed hierarchical prominence to take its place among other systems concerned with the production of *sense*, common or otherwise.

But having said that, having demoted literature's *ontological* position and placed it elsewhere we still have to acknowledge the *methodologically* important place which literature holds within the general

---

[30]Introduction by Anthony Burgess to the Penguin edition of *A Journal of the Plague Year*, (London, 1976), p. 10.
[31]Anderson, p. 40.

conspectus of language and discourse. This is because, as Gramsci cryptically puts it, of the 'quantity and quality of implications involved.' Franco Moretti has recently put this in more elaborate terms: 'Heterogeneity of connections . . . is *in the nature of literature itself*. Literature is perhaps the most omnivorous of social institutions, the most ductile in satisfying disparate social demands, the most ambitious in not recognizing limits to its own sphere of representation.'[32] We should hang on to that 'perhaps' since in the context of the development of film and television studies in recent years there are other forms which might, at some stage, want to lay claim to omnivorousness, but as an historical observation, in terms of duration and ideological effects, it is certainly true.

There is perhaps no more significant testimony to this than the role played by literature in other periods when the question of intimate and sure relations was again firmly at the head of the agenda: in post-Revolutionary France and in late-nineteenth-century England. The example of France has been extensively analysed in the work of Renoe Balibar and Dominique Laporte in two works, *Les français fictifs* and *Le français national*. Of these works it could be said that it is the 'omnipresence' of literature which is the catalyst for analysis, but the *theoretical* starting point is the recognition that the 'literary text is a privileged operator in the concrete relations between the individual and ideology in bourgeois society'.[33] Selected and privileged texts, consolidated by criticism and *explication* as 'Literature' played a fundamental role in the 'politics of language' of the emergent settlement during the nineteenth century. A politics directed towards a universalizing of language away from the pre-capitalist 'formalisms' of Grammar, Rhetoric and Scholasticism and towards a more diffuse and 'societalized' form of language which would correspond, at another level, to the universalization of the 'citizen' and the values of taste, clarity and precision which would be preferred at that point. Literature is not evidence of this social contract, nor is it simply the basis for it, but it is an important vector within this field of force relations.

These points of contact – with the formation of the national language, the role of that in the formation of hegemony, seem to me to provide the necessary, if not sufficient, conditions for embarking upon that 'sociology of symbolic forms' but on condition that the general theoretical framework suggested by the concept of hegemony is not just some more subtle way of talking about ideological domination. Inserting a concept like hegemony within an historiography does not just mean 'softening up' the analysis, insisting on the 'mediated' nature of class structure and so on. It also means shifting the focus somewhat towards a different set of co-ordinates: towards the points of equilibrium (however unstable) in a given conjuncture, towards the points of negotiation,

[32]Moretti, p. 26.
[33]Pierre Macherey and Etienne Balibar, 'Présentation', in R. Balibar and D. Laporte, eds., *Les français fictifs* (Paris, Hachette, 1974), p. 46.

towards the points of resistance as well as the points of domination, towards, as Voloshinov puts it, the 'competing value judgements' in every 'ideological sign'. This is where the theoretical structure and directions of a theory of the utterance as suggested above, and a *possible* theoretical structure from within Marxism itself might begin to come fruitfully together.

There seems to be emerging now a more general recognition of this possibility which for the moment at least is going under the name of Rhetoric. Both Franco Moretti and Terry Eagleton have, in their most recent works, revisited this discarded notion. Defined by Eagleton, 'Rhetoric in its major phase was neither a "humanism", concerned in some intuitive way with people's experience of language, nor a "formalism" preoccupied simply with analysing linguistic devices. It looked at such devices in terms of concrete performance – they were means of pleading, persuading, inciting and so on – and at people's responses to discourse in terms of linguistic structures and the material situations in which they functioned.'[34] The study of Rhetoric was, in other words, a 'formal' way of either consolidating or of analysing certain broad ideological and discursive agreements. The formulation was, of course, pre-Kantian, which meant that it didn't have any problems with the dilemma which still stalks the analysis of literature and, for that matter, any cultural form, of 'fact' and 'judgement'. This helps because, for Moretti, Rhetoric provides the 'way in' to a much needed realignment of 'literature' and 'history' and a co-ordination of their modes of analysis. For Moretti, rhetorical figures show themselves to be 'unrivalled mechanisms for welding into an indivisible whole description and evaluation, "judgements of fact" and "judgements of value" '.[35] An analysis informed by such a procedure would thereby study the structure of the utterance, the assumed or 'preconstructed' of the utterance, and the whole structure of persons or 'subjects' contracted in to it. And furthermore, it does this simultaneously. Not first history then text, first fact then judgement, but within a single, albeit complex, theoretical topology.

It is something of an historical irony that, in order to compile our inventory, we might have to go back to one of the first principles of the analysis of language, to a concept which pre-dates the problem!

---

[34]Terry Eagleton, *Literary Theory* (Oxford, Blackwell, 1983), p. 206.
[35]Moretti, *Signs Taken for Wonders*, p. 4.

Note

Deconstruction has become a very influential – and prolific – movement in recent years: the following are some of the more important and representative texts of or about this movement.

M.H. Abrams, 'The Deconstructive Angel', *Critical Inquiry* III (1977), pp. 425–38.

Roland Barthes, *Essais critiques* (Paris, Seuil, 1964); English tr.: *Critical Essays* (Evanston, Northwestern U.P., 1972).

Image, Music, Text (New York, Hill and Wang, 1977).

Le Plaisir du texte (Paris, Seuil, 1973); English tr.: *The Pleasure of the Text* (New York, Hill and Wang, 1974).

S/Z (Paris, Seuil, 1979). English tr.: *S/Z* (New York, Hill and Wang, 1974).

Harold Bloom, *A Map of Misreading* (New York, Oxford U.P., 1975).

et al, Deconstruction and Criticism (New York, Seabury Press, 1979) (essays by Bloom, de Man, Derrida, Hartman, and Miller).

Jonathan Culler, *On Deconstruction: Theory and Criticism after Structuralism* (Ithaca, Cornell U.P., 1982).

Paul De Man, *Allegories of Reading: Figural Language in Rousseau, Nietzsche, Rilke, and Proust* (New Haven and London, Yale U.P., 1979).

Blindness and Insight: Essays in the Rhetoric of Contemporary Criticism (New York, Oxford U.P., 1971).

'The Epistemology of Metaphor', *Critical Inquiry* V (1978), pp. 15–30.

'The Rhetoric of Temporality', in Charles Singleton, ed., *Interpretation: Theory and Practice* (Baltimore, Johns Hopkins U.P., 1969), pp. 173–209.

Jacques Derrida, *De la grammatologie* (Paris, Minuit, 1967); English tr.: *Of Grammatology* (Baltimore, Johns Hopkins U.P., 1976).

L'Ecriture et la différence (Paris, Seuil, 1967); English tr.: *Writing and Difference* (Chicago, Univ. of Chicago Press, 1978).

'The White Mythology: Metaphor in the Text of Philosophy', *New Literary History* VI (1974), pp. 5–74.

'Signature Event Context', *Glyph* I (1977), pp. 172–97.

'Limited Inc abc', *Glyph* II (1977), pp. 162–254.

Michel Foucault, *Language, Counter-Memory, Practice* (Ithaca, Cornell U.P., 1977).

Josué V. Harari, ed., *Textual Strategies: Perspectives in Post-Structuralist Criticism* (Ithaca, Cornell U.P., 1979).

Geoffrey H. Hartman, *Saving the Text: Literature/Derrida/Philosophy* (Baltimore, Johns Hopkins U.P., 1981).

Barbara Johnson, *The Critical Difference: Essays in the Contemporary Rhetoric of Reading* (Baltimore, Johns Hopkins U.P., 1981).

J. Hillis Miller, *Fiction and Repetition: Seven English Novels* (Cambridge, Mass., Harvard U.P., 1982).

Christopher Norris, *Deconstruction: Theory and Practice* (London and New York, Methuen, 1982).

John Searle, 'Reiterating the Difference: A Reply to Derrida', *Glyph* I (1977), pp. 198–208 (a reply to Derrida 'Signature Event Context', followed by Derrida,' Limited Inc abc').

5

Playing with Texts: Can Deconstruction Account for Critical Practice?

P.D. Juhl

I Introduction

In the following, I shall present a few considerations against deconstructionist theory in general and Paul de Man's version of that theory in particular.

The general view which I would like to challenge goes something like this:

A text does not have a meaning in the sense of something that is 'signified', that is meant, by the configuration of words of which it consists. Instead the text is said to practise 'the infinite deferral of the signified'.[1] This does not mean that it refers in some way to something inexpressible, rather it means that the text is a play of signifiers. It is like a piece of language, 'structured, but decentered, without closure'.[2] Its irreducible plurality of meaning is the result of the text's 'associations, contiguities, and cross-references'[3] with an indefinitely large number of other texts, 'intertexts',[4] among which it is located. It is 'woven' with 'quotations without quotation marks', 'references and echoes' which 'traverse the text from one end to the other in a vast stereophony',[5] so that no two readings can ever be the same and any particular text dissolves into many texts.

It is obvious that on this view the author is utterly dispensable. The text 'is read without the father's signature' and hence the author becomes 'a "paper author" '.[6] The question of the author's sincerity turns out to be a pseudo-problem, since 'the I that writes the text is never, itself, anything more than a paper I'.[7]

Since there is no meaning to be discovered, only the play of signifiers,

---

[1]Roland Barthes, 'From Work to Text', in Josué V. Harari, ed., *Textual Strategies: Perspectives in Post-Structuralist Criticism* (Ithaca, Cornell U.P., 1979), p. 76.
[2]*Ibid.*
[3]*Ibid.*
[4]Barthes, p. 77.
[5]*Ibid.*
[6]Barthes, p. 78.
[7]Barthes, p. 79.

the text requires the reader to play along, as it were, to collaborate with it 'in a single signifying process'.[8] Furthermore, as the text 'is the space in which no one language has a hold over any other, in which all languages circulate freely',[9] it 'allows no enunciative subject to hold the position of judge, teacher, analyst, confessor or decoder'[10] – presumably because for any such potential position in a text there will be a layer of meaning which undermines, deconstructs that position.

Now if this theory of the text is even roughly correct, it is clear that anything like a speech act model of literary interpretation cannot be right. Conversely, if there is such a thing as understanding a text and if that is essentially like understanding a person's speech act and hence necessarily involves reference to the speaker's intentions, then not much remains of the theory of the text sketched above.

I shall first consider two general objections to the claim that if there is a logical connection between the meaning of a text and the author's intention, then the play of signifiers will come to an end at some definite point, and we can, at least in principle, determine what a text means. Since the kind of theory I am concerned with and which, I take it, deconstruction purports among other things to provide, is essentially an attempt to account for the practice of criticism in terms of the relationship between the central concepts involved in that practice, I shall then examine a few representative examples of Paul de Man's interpretive practice. I shall try to show that underlying the practice – in sharp contrast to the metacritical pronouncements – of even so radical a defender of deconstruction as de Man, who has been described as 'its foremost American exponent',[11] is a concept of the meaning of a work such that what a work means is logically tied to what the author intended.

II Is It Possible to Determine What an Author Intended?

Even if the meaning of a text is logically tied to the author's intention, it is not immediately obvious that the play of signifiers can be shown to come to a halt somewhere, that we can then even in principle, let alone in fact, determine what the text signifies. For it is possible that what an author means is not in principle determinable. It might be, as Gadamer has maintained,[12] that the author's intention is simply an empty place marker which is filled by whatever we take the text to mean.

But surely it is not the case that for any interpretation I might dream up, the author of the work in question can plausibly be said to have intended

[8]*Ibid.*
[9]Barthes, p. 80.
[10]Barthes, p. 81.
[11]Christopher Norris, *Deconstruction: Theory and Practice* (London and New York, Methuen, 1982), p. 17.
[12]*Wahrheit und Methode: Grundzüge einer philosophischen Hermeneutik* (Tübingen, J.C.B. Mohr, 1965), p. 373. (*Truth and Method* [New York, The Seabury Press, 1975], p. 357).

that interpretation. Milton, for example, could not have alluded to a certain passage or formulation in Eliot. Nor for that matter could he be thought to have parodied, say, Blake, or 'expressed' certain feelings about the Franco-Prussian war – though what he did 'say' or 'express' might conceivably be applicable or relevant to the latter. These examples are admittedly crude, but they do serve to show that the asserted connection between meaning and intention is by no means vacuous.[13]

But even if we can, in a sense, determine what an author intended, we might still not be able to arrest the play of signifiers and arrive at the signified. And in this case, the reason may be that however we formulate our interpretation, that formulation will necessarily involve metaphorical statements. For we may then ask what exactly that formulation (that set of interpretive statements) means. And if any answer to that question necessarily involves metaphorical statements as well, we end up with an infinite regress. No matter how we answer the question as to what the new formulation means, we can always and indefinitely continue to ask what the answer means. Hence we can never arrive at the signified. All we get is yet another set of signifiers.

In a way this argument seems irrefutable. Yet one has the uncomfortable feeling that something is amiss: namely, that a criterion as to what is involved in knowing what we mean is being invoked which is unduly rigid and extreme. After all, we do seem in general to know what our interpretations mean; we seem in general to be pretty clear as to what our interpretations commit us to in terms of the author's knowledge, beliefs, feelings, tendencies, and so on. Are we simply deceiving ourselves in believing that we know what we mean? Or is this one of those cases in which an absolute demand has been imposed on a concept, in this case the concept of meaning, or of knowing what we mean, such that by its very nature our language is incapable of satisfying this demand?

Consider cases in daily life where we determine what someone intended. The jury in a homicide trial, for example, may decide that the defendant did not act in self-defence but committed murder. And the difference is a difference in intent.

Any evidence that the man committed murder will be evidence of his intent and will be evidence that he committed murder in virtue of being evidence of intent. Now if it is in principle impossible to determine what a man intended, then a great many more men have been unjustifiably convicted of murder than anyone suspected. And if it is possible to determine what a man intended in this kind of case in ordinary life, then why not in literary interpretation?

It is hard to see that there is any difference in principle between the two cases. Of course, we cannot be certain of what a man intended. The man accused of murder may have been hallucinating at the time and have

[13]For a more detailed discussion, see Juhl, *Interpretation* (Princeton, Princeton U.P., 1980) and 'Stanley Fish's interpretive communities and the status of critical interpretations', *Comparative Criticism* v (Cambridge, Cambridge U.P., 1983), pp. 47–58.

imagined that the man he killed was attacking him. This may be unlikely, depending on the circumstances, but it is not impossible. In any case, we have a pretty good idea of what we are ascribing to him when we claim that he committed murder, rather than acted in self-defence. Consequently, if there is a logical connection between the meaning of a text and the author's intention, then we have good reason to suppose that there is a definite point at which the play of signifiers ends and the signified is reached.

III De Man on the 'Vertiginous Possibilities of Referential Aberration'

Now Paul de Man has claimed that 'poetic writing is the most advanced and refined mode of deconstruction: it may differ from critical or discursive writing in the economy of its articulation, but it is not different in kind'. Like any other text, then, a 'literary text simultaneously asserts and denies the authority of its own rhetorical mode'.[14]

One of de Man's examples to illustrate this claim is the following: when his wife asks him whether he wants his bowling shoes laced over or laced under, Archie Bunker replies: 'What's the difference?' And she proceeds to explain to him what the difference is, not realizing that what he meant was 'I don't give a damn'. De Man concludes that the utterance has two mutually exclusive meanings,

> one which asserts and the other which denies its own illocutionary mode. It is not that there are simply two meanings, one literal and the other figural, and that we have to decide which one of these meanings is the right one in this particular situation. The confusion can only be cleared up by the intervention of an extratextual intention, such as Archie Bunker setting his wife straight; but the very anger he displays is indicative of more than impatience: it reveals his despair when confronted with a structure of linguistic meaning that he cannot control and that holds the discouraging prospect of an infinity of similar future confusions, all of them potentially catastrophic in their consequences. Nor is this intervention really a part of the minitext constituted by the figure, which holds our attention only as long as it remains suspended and unresolved. . . . Rhetoric radically suspends logic and opens up vertiginous possibilities of referential aberration.[15]

The problem with de Man's conclusion is this: if what we are considering is an illocutionary act, a speech act – as de Man seems to assume – then it is not the case that the speaker's intention is 'extratextual' or that the 'intervention' of this 'extratextual intention' is not 'really a part of the minitext constituted by the figure'. For the very notion of a speech act necessarily involves reference to the speaker's intentions; otherwise it is not an act, but simply an event. Hence the 'vertiginous possibilities of referential

---

[14]Paul de Man, 'Semiology and Rhetoric', in Harari, ed., *Textual Strategies*, p. 139.
[15]De Man, 'Semiology and Rhetoric', p. 129.

aberration' turn out to be simply the usual, uninteresting possibilities of misunderstanding what someone is saying.

Furthermore, if de Man is right about the irrelevance of intention, then it is hard to see why it would make a difference whether Archie Bunker uttered the sentence or somebody else: 'But if a *de*-Bunker rather than a Bunker, a de-bunker of the *archè* (origin), an ''Archie Debunker'' such as Nietzsche or Jacques Derrida, asks the question ''What is the Difference?'' we cannot even tell from his grammar whether he ''really'' wants to know ''what'' difference is or is merely telling us that we should not even try to find out . . . grammar allows us to ask the question, but the sentence by means of which we ask it may deny the very possibility of asking'.[16] And in a self-conscious display of deconstruction at work, de Man continues: 'For what is the use of asking, I ask, when we cannot even authoritatively decide whether a question asks or doesn't ask?'[17]

But if we cannot tell here whether the question really asks or doesn't ask, the reason is certainly not that the grammar doesn't tell us. After all, who ever thought that grammar *could* tell us whether a question really asks (i.e. is used to ask) or doesn't ask?

Nor is it true that 'the grammatical model of the question becomes rhetorical, not when we have, on the one hand, a literal meaning and, on the other hand, a figural meaning, but when it is impossible to decide by grammatical or other linguistic devices which of the two meanings (that can be entirely contradictory) prevails'.[18] Instead it would seem that a question becomes rhetorical when we have decided that it is used to make a statement, rather than to ask a genuine question.

One might wonder who, in the Archie Bunker example, 'asserts and denies the authority of [the] rhetorical mode'[19] of the text. Since asserting and denying are speech acts, they can be performed only by people. But it is not Archie Bunker who is both asserting and denying the authority of the rhetorical mode of his text. If, as de Man assumes, he means 'I don't give a damn what the difference is',[20] then he is clearly not asking a question.

So who then is asserting and denying the authority of the rhetorical mode of the text? Obviously nobody. Hence it cannot be claimed that the text 'asserts and denies the authority of its own rhetorical mode'.[21]

Of course, if Nietzsche or Derrida were to ask the question 'What is the Difference?', then it might indeed 'assert and deny the authority of its own rhetorical mode'. However, the reason is not that the sentence somehow independently of the speaker does both of these things, but that now it would be plausible to suppose that the speaker is both asking what difference is and suggesting that it doesn't much matter. And this is

[16]*Ibid.*
[17]*Ibid.*
[18]*Ibid.*
[19]De Man, 'Semiology and Rhetoric', p. 139.
[20]De Man, 'Semiology and Rhetoric', p. 128.
[21]De Man, 'Semiology and Rhetoric', p. 139.

indeed confirmed by the fact that even de Man supposes that it makes a difference whether Archie Bunker or 'an Archie Debunker' asked the question.

IV De Man on Proust: Deconstructive Rhetoric and Speech Acts

If this example is too prosaic, consider de Man's analysis of the following passage from Proust's *A la recherche du temps perdu*:

> I had stretched out on my bed, with a book, in my room which shel-tered, tremblingly, its transparent and fragile coolness from the after-noon sun, behind the almost closed blinds through which a glimmer of daylight had nevertheless managed to push its yellow wings, remaining motionless between the wood and the glass, in a corner, poised like a butterfly. It was hardly light enough to read, and the sensation of the light's splendor was given me only by the noise of Camus . . . hammer-ing dusty crates; resounding in the sonorous atmosphere that is peculiar to hot weather, they seemed to spark off scarlet stars; and also by the flies executing their little concert, the chamber music of summer: evo-cative not in the manner of a human tune that, heard perchance during the summer, afterwards reminds you of it but connected to summer by a more necessary link: born from beautiful days, resurrecting only when they return, containing some of their essence, it does not only awaken their image in our memory; it guarantees their return, their actual, per-sistent, unmediated presence.
>
> The dark coolness of my room related to the full sunlight of the street as the shadow relates to the ray of light, that is to say, it was just as luminous and it gave my imagination the total spectacle of the sum-mer, whereas my senses, if I had been on a walk, could only have enjoyed it by fragments; it matched my repose which (thanks to the adventures told by my book and stirring my tranquility) supported, like the quiet of a motionless hand in the middle of a running brook, the shock and the motion of a torrent of activity.[22]

De Man claims that 'the passage acts out and asserts the priority of meta-phor over metonymy in terms of the categories of metaphysics and with reference to the act of reading'.[23] Thus, 'in a beautifully seductive effect of chiaroscuro, mediated by the metaphor of light as a poised butterfly, the inner room is convincingly said to acquire the amount of light necessary to reading. In the wake of this light, warmth can also enter the room, incarnate in the auditive synaesthesia of the various sounds. According to the narrator, these metaphorical substitutions and reversals render the presence of summer in the room more completely than the actual experi-ence of summer in the outside world could have done'.[24]

[22]De Man, 'Semiology and Rhetoric', p. 133.
[23]De Man, 'Semiology and Rhetoric', p. 134.
[24]*Ibid*.

And a little further: 'As opposed to the random contingency of metonymy (*"par hasard"*), the metaphor is linked to its proper meaning by, says Proust, the "necessary link" that leads to perfect synthesis. In the wake of this synthesis, the entire conceptual vocabulary of metaphysics enters the text: a terminology of generation, of transcendental necessity, of totality, of essence, of permanence, and of unmediated presence'.[25]

However, de Man also claims that this assertion of the 'superiority of metaphor over metonymy'[26] is undermined, deconstructed by the fact that the text 'proceeds to constitute itself by means of the epistemologically incompatible figure of metonymy'.[27] This is evident notably in the last sentence:

> . . . it [the dark coolness of my room] matched my repose which (thanks to the adventures told by my book and stirring my tranquility) supported, like the quiet of a motionless hand in the middle of a running brook, the shock and the motion of a torrent of activity.

And de Man comments:

> The proximate, contiguous image of the brook awakens, as it were, the sleeping beauty of the dozing metaphor which, in its common use, had become the metonymic association of two words united by sheer habit and no longer by the inner necessity, the 'necessary link', of a transcendental signification. 'Torrent' functions in a double semantic register: in its reawakened literal meaning it relays the attribute of coolness that is actually part of the running water, whereas in its figural nonmeaning it designates the quantity of activity connotative of the contrary property of warmth. The rhetorical structure of this sentence is therefore not simply metaphorical. It is at least doubly metonymic, first because the coupling of words in a cliché is governed not by the necessary link that reveals their potential identity but by the contingent habit of proximity; second, because the reawakening of the metaphorical term 'torrent' is carried out by a statement that happens to be in the vicinity, but without there being any necessity for this proximity on the level of the referential meaning. The most striking thing is that this doubly metonymic structure is found in a text that also contains highly seductive and successful metaphors (as in the chiaroscuro effect of the beginning, or in the condensation of light in the butterfly image) and that explicitly asserts the superiority of metaphor over metonymy in terms of metaphysical categories.[28]

De Man claims then that the text both asserts and denies the 'superiority of metaphor over metonymy'.[29] Now the question is what entitles us to take the instances of metonymy that de Man mentions as *denying* such

---

[25]*Ibid.*
[26]De Man, 'Semiology and Rhetoric', p. 137.
[27]De Man, 'Semiology and Rhetoric', p. 140.
[28]De Man, 'Semiology and Rhetoric', pp. 135–6.
[29]De Man, 'Semiology and Rhetoric', p. 137.

superiority? What entitles us to take them as meaning anything?

If a man waves his arm at me, I may take that as a friendly gesture. But if it turns out that I was mistaken and what I thought to be a man was in fact a scarecrow whose 'arm' was moved by the wind, then the movement of the 'arm' no longer means anything. Similarly here: unless I take the instances of metonymy as something the author has 'done' or is using for some purpose, i.e. unless I take the instances of metonymy as having a function in terms of the author's speech act, they mean nothing at all. And if they have such a function, what is asserted or denied logically depends on the speaker's and/or author's intention.

Of course, the text might be said to 'show' that we can't do without metonymy, irrespective of the author's intention. But (a) that is a far cry from showing that metonymy is superior to metaphor and (b) even if it did show the superiority of metonymy over metaphor, it would not warrant the claim that such superiority is *asserted* or, to put it differently, that it is part of the *meaning* of the text that metonymy is superior, or metaphysically prior, to metaphor.

De Man rightly notes that the narrator is a metaphor: 'The narrator who tells us about the impossibility of metaphor is himself, or itself, a metaphor, the metaphor of a grammatical syntagm whose meaning is the denial of metaphor stated, by antiphrasis, as its priority. And this subject metaphor is, in its turn, open to the kind of deconstruction to the second degree, the rhetorical deconstruction of psycholinguistics, in which the more advanced investigations of literature are presently engaged, against considerable resistance'.[30]

I am not quite sure what the deconstruction to the second degree would look like, but what we have here is already a good bit. I don't know how de Man arrives at the claim that the narrator 'tells us about the *impossibility* of metaphor' (my italics),[31] since, so far at least, the narrator has, according to de Man, been talking about the superiority or priority of metaphor over metonymy and vice versa.

In any case, de Man clearly thinks that the fact that the narrator is a metaphor means something: in particular, that this again reasserts the priority of metaphor over metonymy. But again, unless you assume that the fact that the narrator is a metaphor functions in a speech act, here the speech act or acts Proust is performing in writing the passage, that fact means nothing at all; no more than the 'wave' of the scarecrow's 'arm'. If, for example, Proust were not aware of such subtleties as the fact that a narrator in a fictional text can be said to be a metaphor and regarded the narrator simply as a fictional construct, then it would be difficult to construe the sentences in which the narrator 'tells us about the impossibility of metaphor'[32] as asserting the priority of metaphor simply on the basis of the fact that the narrator can be said to be a metaphor.

[30]De Man, 'Semiology and Rhetoric', p. 140.
[31]De Man, 'Semiology and Rhetoric', p. 140.
[32]*Ibid.*

The upshot of this is as follows: we cannot account for the kinds of things de Man wants to say about the meaning of a literary text without assuming that it is a speech act of its author. And if it is a speech act of its author, then there is no reason to suppose that 'a literary text simultaneously asserts and denies the authority of its own rhetorical mode'.[33] It may, of course. But whether it does will depend on what the author meant, not on the nature of 'poetic writing'.[34]

V Assertion and Truth

What I have been saying can be stated in another way. De Man claims that 'Figures are assumed to be inventions, the products of a highly particularized individual talent, whereas no one can claim credit for the programmed pattern of grammar. Yet our reading of the Proust passage shows that precisely when the highest claims are being made for the unifying power of metaphor, these very images rely in fact on the deceptive use of semi-automatic grammatical patterns. . . . After the deconstructive reading of the Proust passage we can no longer believe the assertion made in this passage about the intrinsic, metaphysical superiority of metaphor over metonymy'.[35] But does the passage now *mean* that metonymy is superior to metaphor? Do the 'semi-automatic grammatical patterns' alter the meaning of the passage such that it now means that metaphor is not really superior to metonymy? Is that what the narrator 'tells us'?[36] Surely, the answer to these questions is not obvious. Surely, the instances of metonymy which de Man mentions are not *necessarily* significant, in the sense that they necessarily bear on what the passage means, on what the narrator is saying.

What I am suggesting is that we need to make a distinction between the *assertion* of certain views in the text and their *truth*. What the instances of metonymy in the text (perhaps) show is that the assertion about the superiority of metaphor over metonymy is false. But those instances of metonymy do not necessarily show that the assertion about the superiority of metaphor over metonymy is in effect being retracted and the opposite asserted, and hence that it is now part of the *meaning* of the text that metaphor is not superior to metonymy, that rather metonymy is superior to metaphor. If 'after the deconstructive reading of the Proust passage we can no longer believe the assertion made in this passage about the intrinsic, metaphysical superiority of metaphor over metonymy',[37] it is because we no longer believe that assertion to be true, but not necessarily because we now believe that the narrator is denying what we took him earlier to be asserting.

In other words, what the 'deconstructive reading' deconstructs is the

[33]De Man, 'Semiology and Rhetoric', pp. 138–9.
[34]De Man, 'Semiology and Rhetoric', p. 139.
[35]De Man, 'Semiology and Rhetoric', p. 137.
[36]De Man, 'Semiology and Rhetoric', p. 140.
[37]De Man, 'Semiology and Rhetoric', p. 137.

truth of certain views asserted in the text, but not necessarily the *assertion* of these views. Once we make this distinction, it becomes obvious that though the rhetoric of a text may, of course, deconstruct *both* the *assertion* of certain views and their *truth*, it need not. And if it need not, then there is no longer any reason for supposing that what is 'shown', what is 'revealed' by the rhetoric, is necessarily part of the meaning of a text. It will be if and only if the author is using the rhetorical features in question to deny what he, or the speaker is explicitly asserting.

VI Nietzsche and 'The Birth of Tragedy'

To see that in actual practice even de Man operates with a notion of the meaning of a text which his explicit metacritical claims repudiate, let us look at his deconstruction of Nietzsche's *The Birth of Tragedy*.

De Man argues that the rhetoric of the work undermines, deconstructs what Nietzsche is explicitly asserting in the work. 'The system of valorization that privileges Dionysos as the truth of the Appolonian appearance, music as the truth of painting, as the actual meaning of the metaphorical appearance, reaches us through the medium of a strongly dramatized and individualized voice'.[38]

What de Man does is undermine the credibility of this voice by showing that it is not Nietzsche's. Thus he calls this 'voice' the 'orator' who 'has our best interests at heart' and who guarantees us

> intellectual safety as long as we remain within the sheltering reach of his voice. The same seductive tone safeguards the genetic continuity throughout the text, easing the listener over difficult transitions by means of helpful summaries, marking out the truly important points by attention-catching signals. The more delirious passages are clearly marked off as digressions, after which 'we glide back into the mood befitting contemplation' (3:139; 21), thus gaining at once our confidence with the reassuring thought that someone who allowed himself such verbal excesses in his digressions must be very cool and contemplative indeed in his argumentations. The voice is not beyond crediting us, the readers, with praise that it lavishes upon itself, as when we are endowed with Dionysian insight in being told that 'we penetrate' with piercing clarity, into an inner world of motives.[39]

Thus, according to de Man, Nietzsche has his 'orator' speak in a 'seductive tone', lets him indulge in 'delirious' 'verbal excesses', and has this 'voice crediting us, the readers, with praise that it lavishes upon itself', in order to undermine that voice's 'shaky system of valorization'.[40] That this is indeed what de Man is showing here is made quite clear when he quotes 'Nietzsche's resolution'[41] in the *Philosophenbuch* – of which de Man had

[38]Paul de Man, *Allegories of Reading* (New Haven and London, Yale U.P., 1979), p. 93.
[39]De Man, *Allegories*, p. 94.
[40]*Ibid.*
[41]*Ibid.*

noted earlier that it is 'near-contemporary'[42] with *The Birth of Tragedy* –
namely, ' "to write, in general, in an impersonal and cold manner. Avoid
all mention of 'us' and 'we' and 'I'. Also limit the number of sentences
with relative clauses" '.[43] And de Man comments: 'The opposite happens,
of course, in *The Birth of Tragedy*. The complicity between the "I" of the
narrator and the collective "we" of his acquiescing audience functions
relentlessly, underscored by the repeated address of the audience as "my
friends" '.[44] In other words, de Man is suggesting that Nietzsche is quite
clearly and consistently, if implicitly, casting doubt on the assertions of the
narrator by dramatizing 'emphatically the stance of the convinced man'.[45]

A little further, de Man quotes a passage in which the narrator speaks of
the intolerability of nonrepresentational music:

> I must address myself only to those who have a direct filiation with
> music, for whom music is like a maternal womb, and whose relation-
> ship with things is determined almost exclusively by unconscious musi-
> cal ties. To these authentic musicians, I put the question if they could
> imagine a human being able to hear the third act of *Tristan and Isolde*
> without the assistance of word and image, as if it were a single, over-
> whelming symphonic movement? Such a listener would expire, carried
> away on the overexpanded wings of his soul. Could a man whose ear
> had perceived the world's very heart chamber, who has heard the
> roaring desire for existence as if it were a thundering river or the gentlest
> of brooks pouring out into the veins of the world, fail suddenly to break
> down? How could he endure to hear the echo of innumerable shouts of
> joy and pain, coming from 'the wide spaces of the world's night' and
> reaching him within the miserable glass vessel of the human individ-
> ual? Would not this metaphysical bacchanal compel him to flee back to
> his primordial home?[46]

And de Man comments:

> Who would dare admit, after such a passage, to not being one of the
> happy few among the 'authentic musicians'? The page could only have
> been written with conviction if Nietzsche's personal identification
> would make him into the King Mark of a triangular relationship. It has
> all the trappings of the statement made in bad faith: parallel rhetorical
> questions, an abundance of clichés, obvious catering to its audience.[47]

Again, de Man's deconstructive reading consists in showing that Nietzsche
did not, indeed *could not*, really mean what he seems to mean, that
Nietzsche is not saying what his narrator is saying.

Furthermore, de Man mentions (and quotes from) 'the unpublished

[42]De Man, *Allegories*, p. 83.
[43]De Man, *Allegories*, p. 94.
[44]*Ibid.*
[45]*Ibid.*
[46]De Man, *Allegories*, p. 97.
[47]*Ibid.*

fragments, contemporaneous with the main text [of *The Birth of Tragedy*]' which 'deny [the] very possibility [of bridging the distinction between essence and appearance] and thus reduce the entire *Birth of Tragedy* to being an extended rhetorical fiction devoid of authority'.[48] And de Man finds it 'hermeneutically satisfying . . . that the statement forced upon us by the deconstruction of the main text would reach us, formulated by the same author who also produced this text'.[49]

If de Man is right that 'a literary text simultaneously asserts and denies the authority of its own rhetorical mode' and hence that 'the existence of [the deconstructive] moment' is 'constitutive of all literary language',[50] then it is difficult to explain why de Man should be so concerned to show that the 'voice' in the text is not really Nietzsche's, that Nietzsche, at least as de Man presents the matter, intentionally undercuts what the narrator is saying by the rhetorical mode in which he has him speak.

If indeed a literary text necessarily deconstructs its own assertions, then it is altogether unclear why it should matter in the slightest whether or not the narrator's voice is Nietzsche's, whether or not Nietzsche really believes what the narrator is saying.

For if de Man is right, the rhetorical mode of the text should deconstruct the assertions in the texts regardless of whether they are Nietzsche's, regardless of the way Nietzsche would have made those assertions had he really believed them.

Moreover, if it were irrelevant what Nietzsche meant, then it is difficult to see why, in his attempt to show that the rhetoric undermines the assertions in the text, de Man should feel a need to remind us of Nietzsche's resolution, formulated in the contemporaneous *Philosophenbuch*, and why de Man should want to claim that given what we know about Nietzsche, he 'could' not have written the passage about the intolerability of nonrepresentational music 'with conviction'.[51]

And finally, it is hard to see why de Man should feel a need to point out that in the unpublished fragments Nietzsche formulates explicitly 'the statement forced upon us by the deconstruction of the main text'.[52] For if the rhetoric of a text necessarily deconstructs its own assertions, then this could not have the faintest bearing on de Man's reading one way or the other and hence could hardly be called 'hermeneutically satisfying'.[53]

What all this shows is that the implicit notion of the meaning of a literary text underlying de Man's interpretive practice is that appropriate to speech acts and hence necessarily involves reference to, or assumptions about, the author's intention. Consequently, even de Man's own practice shows that deconstructionist theory of literary interpretation is untenable.

---

[48]De Man, *Allegories*, p. 101.
[49]*Ibid.*
[50]De Man, *Allegories*, p. 17.
[51]De Man, *Allegories*, p. 97.
[52]De Man, *Allegories*, p. 101.
[53]*Ibid.*

VII Playing with Texts?

Deconstruction can be regarded as, in certain important respects, an extension of developments which began with New Criticism. The New Critics loosened (or thought they loosened) the connection between the meaning of a work and the author's intention as a result of a greater interest in formal and aesthetic aspects of a text. There was greater emphasis on the aesthetic pleasure which a text provides. Thus instead of relying mainly on biographical documents to show what the work means, the New Critics tended to concentrate on textual evidence in an attempt to show that and how meaning and form constitute a harmonious whole.

Since then, the connection between meaning and intention, at least as far as *theories* of interpretation are concerned, has become increasingly looser; the evidence has become more subtle, more diffuse. And it has now become evidence for something else; in fact, the opposite of what the New Critics sought: namely, to put it very roughly, the antithesis of meaning and form. In consequence, the notion of meaning, at least in theory, has changed as well, since we now have at least two 'meanings', neither one nor both of which can be said to be 'the meaning' of a text.

Hand in hand with the increasing loosening of the connection between meaning and intention has gone again a greater emphasis on aesthetic pleasure. But whereas in New Criticism this aesthetic pleasure was provided by the work, in the latest theory it includes in equal measure the aesthetic pleasure provided by the activity of criticism. In fact, criticism has become a genuinely creative activity in its own right. Its task is no longer the discovery, but rather the creation of 'the meaning' of a text. Thus it has come to rival, in its creativity and in the aesthetic pleasure it affords, the object it originally set out to serve.

And yet when one looks at the actual practice, as opposed to the theory of criticism – even the practice of some of the most radical defenders of deconstruction – the hold which the 'old' notion of meaning has on us is undeniable. Moreover, I see very little evidence that critical practice is in a process of transition in which the 'old' notion of the meaning of a work is gradually changing such that interpreting a 'text', in Barthes' sense, is – or will soon become – a fundamentally creative activity, a playing with texts.

Note

Life

Virginia Woolf was born Adeline Virginia Stephen on 25 January 1882 in London. She was the daughter of Julia and Leslie Stephen, the latter a recognized scholar and editor. Educated at home, Virginia began to contribute to the *Times Literary Supplement* while still in her early twenties. With her sister Vanessa and brother Adrian, she lived in the Bloomsbury section of London and there gathered about her numerous artists and writers who became known as the Bloomsbury Group. She married journalist Leonard Woolf in 1912, and together they founded the Hogarth Press. Known mostly for her innovative novels, Virginia Woolf was also an essayist and literary critic. Threatened by another episode of the periodic mental crises she had suffered most of her life, Virginia Woolf drowned herself in 1941.

Writings of Virginia Woolf

Novels: *The Voyage Out* (1915); *Night and Day* (1919); *Jacob's Room* (1922); *Mrs Dalloway* (1925); *To the Lighthouse* (1927); *Orlando* (1928); *The Waves* (1931); *Flush* (1933); *The Years* (1937); *Between the Acts* (1941).

Essays: *The Common Reader: First Series* (1925); *A Room of One's Own* (1929); *Letter to a Young Poet* (1932); *The Second Common Reader* (1932); *Three Guineas* (1938); *The Death of the Moth and Other Essays* (1942); *The Moment and Other Essays* (1947); *The Captain's Death Bed and Other Essays* (1950); *Granite and Rainbow* (1958); *Contemporary Writers*, 1965; *Collected Essays* (4 vols., 1967); *Moments of Being* (1976).

Feminist criticism:

Collected Essays (New York, Harcourt, Brace and World, 1967); *The Death of the Moth and Other Essays* (New York, Harcourt Brace, 1942); *The Moment and Other Essays* (New York, Harcourt Brace, 1947); *A Room of One's Own* (New York, Harcourt Brace Jovanovich, 1980); *Three Guineas* (New York, Harcourt Brace, 1938); *Virginia Woolf: Women and Writing*, ed. Michele Barrett (New York: Harcourt Brace Jovanovich, 1980); *A Writer's Diary*, ed. Leonard Woolf (New York, Harcourt Brace Jovanovich, 1973).

Criticism

Simone de Beauvoir, *The Second Sex* (tr. H.M. Parshley; New York, Knopf, 1953); Wayne C. Booth, 'Freedom of Interpretation: Bakhtin and the Challenge of Feminist Criticism', *Critical Inquiry* IX, i (autumn, 1982), pp. 45–76; Mary Daly, *Beyond God the Father: Toward a Philosophy of Women's Liberation* (Boston, Beacon Press, 1973); Josephine Donovan, ed., *Feminist Literary Criticism: Exploration in Theory* (Lexington, Univ. of Kentucky Press, 1975); Andrea Dworkin, *Woman-Hating* (New York, Norton, 1979); Mary Ellmann, *Thinking About Women* (New York, Harcourt Brace & World, 1968); Sandra M. Gilbert and Susan Gubar, *The Madwoman in the Attic: The Woman Writer and the Nineteenth-Century Literary Imagination* (New Haven, Yale U.P., 1979); Carolyn G. Heilbrun, 'A Response to "Writing and Sexual Difference" ', *Critical Inquiry* VIII, iv (summer, 1982), pp. 804–10; Mary Jacobus, ed., *Women Writing and Writing About Women* (London, Croom Helm, 1979); Alice Jardine, 'Gynesis', *Diacritics* XII (summer, 1982), pp. 54–65; Peggy Kanuf, 'Replacing Feminist Criticism', *Diacritics* XII (summer, 1982), pp. 42–7; Annette Kolodny, 'A Map for Rereading; or, Gender and the Interpretation of Literary Texts', *New Literary History* IX (1980), pp. 45–55; Kolodny, 'Some Notes on Defining a Feminist Literary Criticism', *Critical Inquiry* II, i (autumn, 1975), pp. 75–92; Herbert Marder, *Feminism and Art: A Study of Virginia Woolf* (Chicago: Univ. of Chicago Press, 1968); Sally McConnell-Ginet, Ruth Borker and Nelly Furman, *Women and Language in Literature and Society* (New York, Praeger, 1980); Nancy K. Miller, 'The Text's Heroine: A Feminist Critic and Her Fictions', *Diacritics* XII (summer, 1982), pp. 48–53; Kate Millett, *Sexual Politics* (New York, Doubleday, 1970); Tillie Olsen, *Silences* (New York, Dell, 1978); Annis Pratt, *Archetypal Patterns in Women's Fiction* (Bloomington, Indiana U.P., 1981); Pratt, 'The New Feminist Criticism', *College English*

6

'A Wreath Upon the Grave': The Influence of Virginia Woolf on Feminist Critical Theory

Barbara Hill Rigney

Although Virginia Woolf was decidedly intolerant of academic treatises on 'The Influence of Somebody on Something',[1] one can scarcely avoid the topic in reference to Woolf herself, for her influence on feminist critical theory of the past two decades is profound indeed. She was the first woman writer who is also readily identifiable as a feminist critic, and her methods as well as the ideology which informed those methods, her questions and self-contradictions, still constitute the methods, the questions and the contradictions which are the central concerns of feminist theorists today. Woolf's numerous critical essays, and *A Room of One's Own* (1928) in particular, are yet a kind of touchstone, a departure point, even a prototype for subsequent attempt at self definition in an area which continues to challenge and therefore to revitalize mainstream literary criticism.

Writing on the stated subject of 'women and fiction' in *A Room of One's Own*, Woolf maintained an argument which yet today is considered revolutionary: that literature, particularly literature by women, cannot be evaluated apart from the historical, economic, political, psychological and sociological conditions which produce it. Women have always been prevented from writing and constrained from thinking, Woolf argued, by social circumstances which deprived them of adequate education and denied them equal opportunities to publish. She concluded that such conditions have profound effects upon the psychology of women and therefore on the quantity and the

---

[1] In *To the Lighthouse*, Charles Tansley, who maintains that 'women can't paint; women can't write', is satirized for his pedantic dissertation on 'The Influence of Somebody on Something'.

XXXII (May 1971), pp. 872–8; Adrienne Rich, *On Lies, Secrets and Silences* (New York, Norton, 1979); Elaine Showalter, 'Feminist Criticism in the Wilderness', *Critical Inquiry* VIII, ii (winter 1981), pp. 179–205; Showalter, *A Literature of Their Own: British Women Novelists from Brontë to Lessing* (Princeton, Princeton U.P., 1977); Patricia Meyer Spacks, *The Female Imagination* (New York, Avon, 1972); Catherine R. Stimpson, 'On Feminist Criticism', in Paul Hernadi, ed., *What is Criticism?* (Bloomington, Indiana U.P., 1981), pp. 230–41.

quality of literature they produce. Woolf's imaginary sister for Shakespeare, for example, lives and dies as a victim of social injustice, controlled and finally silenced by universal forces which Woolf recognized as patriarchal; Judith Shakespeare is Woolf's symbol for the woman as artist, for 'who shall measure the heat and violence of the poet's heart when caught and tangled in a woman's body?'[2]

Woolf's most fundamental contribution to modern feminist theory, then, is her insistence that literary critical analysis must take social and political factors into consideration, must recognize that women's peculiar relationship to that social order in which they remain outsiders determines their experience as well as their perceptions. The very essence of modern feminist theory, and that factor which unifies modern feminist critics despite other disagreements as to the proper scope and function of their craft, is the insistence that art must be viewed contextually and therefore politically.

A great deal of feminist literary criticism in the 1960s and 1970s almost exclusively reflected Woolf's emphases on materialist concerns, on the restoration of lost women writers to the canon, and on the exposing of misogynistic stereotyping in non-feminist literature. Simone de Beauvoir's earlier book, *The Second Sex*, Kate Millett's *Sexual Politics*, and Tillie Olsen's *Silences* are among the best examples of such overtly polemical critical writing, their concern, like Woolf's, being to delineate the grievances of the woman writer, to analyse her cultural deprivation, and, ultimately, to transform institutions which perpetrate that deprivation. Once established as existing problems, however, such factors as domestic conflicts, economic and educational disadvantage, lack of privacy and adequate leisure, proved to become limiting rather than creative topics for feminist critics of this period, who, at their least effective, indulged personal anger and frustration under the aegis of 'engaged criticism'. Similarly, outrage over sexist bias and stereotyped portrayals of female characters codified in literary texts led to a raised consciousness, but also too often to a stylistically reductive confusion of emotion and ideology.

Woolf, too, faced this dilemma in her work, whether a writer can maintain a stand that is exploratory as well as expository, heuristic as well as polemical, speculative as well as analytical, artistic as well as adversarial. Certainly, Woolf found fault with women writers of the past who wrote 'in a rage'; Charlotte Brontë, for one, therefore, 'will never get her genius expressed whole and entire. Her books will be deformed and twisted. . . . She is at war with her lot. How could she help but die young, cramped and thwarted?' (pp. 69–70). Yet Woolf herself derived great energy from anger and was never successful in divorcing art from didacticism even in her novels, which, as Herbert Marder remarks in *Feminism and Art*, themselves constitute 'a kind of

[2]Virginia Woolf, *A Room of One's Own* (New York, Harcourt Brace Jovanovich, 1981), p. 48. All subsequent references are to this edition.

latent propaganda'.[3] When one is denied entrance to a library because of one's sex, as is the case in *A Room of One's Own*, the temptation is to refuse the very validity of that library. Woolf wrote:

> That a famous library has been cursed by a woman is a matter of complete indifference to a famous library. Venerable and calm, with all its treasures safe locked within its breast, it sleeps complacently and will, so far as I am concerned, so sleep forever. Never will I wake those echoes, never will I ask for that hospitality again, I vowed as I descended the steps in anger. (p. 8)

The price of rage, however justified, is sometimes, as Woolf recognized, a kind of impotence. Carolyn Heilbrun, too, extends a gentle warning: 'if women forfeit the culture men have dubbed "male" when it is, in fact, human, they will have deprived themselves of too much.'[4]

Woolf's conflict is, of course, also the conflict of all feminists who write critical theory. Women have a right to their anger, any feminist would argue, and it would have been impossible for feminist theory to have evolved to its present more complex and analytical state were it not for the salutary and purgative effects of that rage vented upon male authors from John Milton to John Barth, upon tradition and institutions. Without a recognition and a castigation of what Mary Ellmann in *Thinking About Women* terms 'phallic criticism', the manifestation of that school of thought perpetrated by leading academicians for whom 'femaleness is a congenital fault, rather like eczema or Original Sin',[5] a feminist criticism would never have developed. Woolf's archetypal 'professor', who controls everything in London except the fog, has thus provided an object for feminist satire and a focus for female anger since his introduction in *A Room of One's Own*.

Recognizing the limitations of accusatory polemics as a subject for literary evaluation and anger for psychological sustenance, however, Woolf also anticipated the direction of more recent feminist critical theory which moves toward more affirmative evaluations of the works of women writers. A majority of contemporary feminist critics now see themselves as celebrating a newly-found heritage and exploring its ramifications, creating new traditions rather than merely blaming the old. As Carolyn Heilbrun has written,

> I worry about the effects of a feminist criticism or history that necessarily focuses on the constraints of female life, constraints that, however overcome or subverted or subtly recognized in novels and in life, remain nevertheless crippling and are, of course, neither necessary

[3]Herbert Marder, *Feminism and Art: A Study of Virginia Woolf* (Chicago, Univ. of Chicago Press, 1968), p. 2.

[4]Carolyn G. Heilbrun, 'A Response to "Writing and Sexual Difference" ', Critical Inquiry VIII, iv (summer, 1982), p. 808.

[5]Mary Ellmann, *Thinking About Women* (New York, Harcourt, Brace and World, 1968), p. 34.

nor desirable. . . . Women must discover their difference and their own culture. . . .[6]

Woolf also recognized that women writers needed to establish their own literary identities in relation to women writers of the past, that a 'woman writing thinks back through her mothers' (p. 97). This amounts to a great deal more than the compensatory activity of merely discovering who those mothers were and ensuring the publication of their long-hidden works; it means judging and analysing those works for their relationship to a female literary tradition, a tradition which exists, at least in part, because Virginia Woolf said it did and labelled it as such. 'For masterpieces are not single and solitary births', Woolf wrote in *A Room of One's Own*; 'they are the outcome of many years of thinking in common, of thinking by the body of the people, so that the experience of the mass is behind the single voice. Jane Austen should have laid a wreath upon the grave of Fanny Burney' (p. 65).

Like all sacred books, *A Room of One's Own* is not free of self-contradiction. Woolf's attempts to analyse those factors which led to the establishment of a female literary tradition which was distinct and separate from a male tradition are, on occasion, problematic. While she sought to identify and understand a female aesthetic, a problem which also occupies many feminist theoriticians today as we will see, Woolf also proposed the idea that the androgynous mind alone was capable of creating art:

> And I went on amateurishly to sketch a plan of the soul so that in each of us two powers preside, one male, one female; and in the man's brain, the man predominates over the woman, and in the woman's brain, the woman predominates over the man. The normal and comfortable state of being is that when the two live in harmony together, spiritually co-operating. If one is a man, still the woman part of the brain must have effect; and a woman also must have intercourse with the man in her. Coleridge perhaps meant this when he said that a great mind is androgynous. It is when this fusion takes place that the mind is fully fertilised and uses all its faculties. Perhaps a mind that is purely masculine cannot create, any more than a mind that is purely feminine. . . .' (p. 98)

Carolyn Heilbrun's book *Toward a Recognition of Androgyny* was one of several important and valuable studies which supported Woolf's concept, but it is a concept by which we now feel betrayed and misled. Elaine Showalter in *A Literature of Their Own* is severely critical of Woolf's non-fiction, largely because of the androgyny theory which Showalter describes as the 'psychological equivalent of lobotomy'.[7] In spite of the fact that her own title is derivative of Woolf's, Showalter

[6]Heilbrun, p. 805.
[7]Elaine Showalter, *A Literature of Their Own: British Women Novelists from Brontë to Lessing* (Princeton, Princeton U.P., 1979), p. 287.

calls *A Room of One's Own* a death book: 'If one can see *A Room of One's Own* as a document in the literary history of female aestheticism, and remain detached from its narrative strategies, the concepts of androgyny and the private room are neither as liberating nor as obvious as they first appear. They have a darker side that is the sphere of the exile and the eunuch.'[8] Showalter continues, 'Woolf's view of womanhood is as deadly as it is disembodied. The ultimate room of one's own is the grave.'[9]

Perhaps, however, feminist critics might begin to view Woolf's androgyny theory less literally; perhaps Woolf intended it as a metaphor for unity or wholeness, a resolution of opposites rather than as itself an example of polar thinking. Certainly Woolf frequently described herself as a divided woman, split between 'the angel in the house'[10] and the artist at work, the 'butterfly' as creator and the 'gadfly' as politician, the image of womanhood and herself as woman. Recognizing these divisions as symptomatic of the female condition in general, Woolf strove for harmony, the combination of male and female in the androgynous soul perhaps representing little more than a symbolic image of what she recognized as an unattainable unity. Although the metaphor of androgyny has now been almost universally and unequivocally rejected, feminist critics today are still wrestling with the problem of opposites, that very dilemma of duality which has occupied Western philosophers and theologians for so long. Feminist theoreticians, as did Woolf, reject what they see as a characteristically masculine emphasis on polar thinking, a perception of the world as divided between good and evil, black and white; instead, they seek alternative perceptions of both art and reality, perceptions that reflect resolution and wholeness rather than division.

Many feminist theorists now contend that women writers in fact manifest profound differences from male writers, not only in matters of polar thinking, but in all modes of perceiving reality. Questions as to the validity and viability of a female aesthetic centre on discussions of imagery and language and their relevance to a female perspective, even a female consciousness. Woolf, for one, declared the existence of such an entity. Despite the fact that Woolf claimed that 'it is fatal for any one who writes to think of their sex' (p. 104), she also repeatedly remarked the profound differences which she saw between the perceptive abilities and the sensibilities of men and women. Both Jane Austen and Emily Brontë, Woolf declared, were superior artists mainly because 'they wrote as women write, not as men write' (pp. 74–5); perceptions of the world differ as to gender, Woolf went so far as to say, because 'the nerves that feed the brain would seem to differ in men and women' (p. 78). So, she exhorts her imaginary Mary Carmichael to record her

[8]Showalter, p. 285.
[9]Showalter, p. 297.
[10]Woolf, 'Professions for Women', *The Death of the Moth and Other Essays* (New York, Harcourt Brace Jovanovich, 1974), p. 237.

female impressions, which are, after all, very distinct and, in Woolf's terms, superior to those of male authors:

> All that you will have to explore, I said to Mary Carmichael, holding your torch firm in your hand. Above all you must illumine your own soul with its profundities and its shallows, and its vanities and its generosities, and say what your beauty means to you or your plainness, and what is your relation to the everchanging and turning world of gloves and shoes and stuffs swaying up and down among the faint scents that come through chemists' bottles down arcades of dress material over a floor of pseudo-marble . . . for it is a sight that would lend itself to the pen as fittingly as any snowy peak or rocky gorge in the Andes. And there is the girl behind the counter too – I would as soon have her true history as the hundred and fiftieth life of Napoleon or seventieth study of Keats and his use of Miltonic inversion which old Professor Z and his like are now inditing.(p. 90)

Woolf, then, points the way to entire new areas of enquiry for the feminist critic: the discovery and restoration of a female perspective to literature, the search for a female aesthetic which yet does not exclude women writers and critics from humanist endeavours, the examination of imagery and language itself as reflective of a female experience or even a female consciousness. Among the contemporary feminist theorists who have followed Woolf's direction is Patricia Meyer Spacks who, in *The Female Imagination*, declares: 'Surely mind has sex, minds learn their sex – and it is no derogation of the female variety to say so.'[11] The implications of this for the feminist critic, Spacks indicates, are clear: 'So what is a woman to do, setting out to write about women? She can imitate men in her writing, or strive for an impersonality, beyond sex, but finally she must write as a woman: what other way is there?'[12]

Sandra Gilbert and Susan Gubar in *The Madwoman in the Attic* also see female experience and female biology as sources of symbolism and imagery in the works of women writers. Using Harold Bloom's theory of the 'anxiety of influence' which contends that literary works embody their authors' struggles against the intrusive influence of their predecessors, Gilbert and Gubar maintain that the autonomy of the woman writer is even more tenuous and must depend on the inversion and subversion of imagery inherited from patriarchal tradition. Traditional linguistic associations of the penis and the pen as metaphor for literary achievement are viewed by Gilbert and Gubar as indicative of male cultural supremacy, and thus women writers must and often do assert their own perspectives, patterns of imagery, thematic concerns and even stylistic devices. According to Gilbert and Gubar, readily

[11]Patricia Meyer Spacks, *The Female Imagination* (New York, Avon, 1976), p. 6.
[12]Spacks, p. 41.

identifiable patterns of images recur in the works of women writers throughout history, transcending genre and culture. Gilbert and Gubar thus argue for a distinct female literary tradition based on images of 'enclosure and escape, fantasies in which maddened doubles functioned as asocial surrogates for docile selves, metaphors of physical discomfort manifested in frozen landscapes and fiery interiors', images which but reflect a social reality, that women were 'enclosed in the architecture of an overwhelmingly male-dominated society'.[13]

While the revelation of a female experience through an examination of imagery in the works of women writers is a most valuable contribution to feminist theory, discussions of the phallic versus the ovarian theory of art, the paternity versus the maternity of creative production are perhaps, however, aspects of that biological criticism which Elaine Showalter, for one, sees as 'cruelly prescriptive'.[14] Undoubtedly, there exist cultural determinants of expression; there are differences in allusion, choice of images, even style, based on women's experience and sensibility. Female biology, however, while it may provide a source of imagery for women writers, can never be proven to determine style and aesthetic.

Similarly, when we claim a female aesthetic which is somehow superior or the existence in women of some super-natural and tropismic level of awareness of the inner workings of consciousness, we risk validity as human beings and credibility as thinking scholars. Women, whether as writers or as characters in fiction, become like the goddesses and witches perceived by Jungian feminist critics, reduced rather than elevated to archetypes, somehow not human and therefore not relevant. It seems counterproductive for women to conform to any ideal of femininity, whether as defined by male culture or by feminist critics, after Woolf herself struggled so valiantly against 'the angel in the house',[15] that prescribed role which she found so destructive to her individuality and to her creative abilities.

Ultimately, we are led by some contemporary feminist critics to a re-evaluation of the function of language itself: does language have a gender; have women been even more culturally disadvantaged than we knew by the existence of a hitherto unrecognized 'oppressor's language',[16] as poet and critic Adrienne Rich maintains; ought we to find or devise some new language or, perhaps, even communicate in 'ultra-sonic sound', as Mary Daly suggests?[17] Andrea Dworkin writes in *Woman-Hating*: 'I write . . . with a broken tool, a language which is sexist and discriminatory to its core. I try to make the distinctions,

[13]Sandra M. Gilbert and Susan Gubar, *The Madwoman in the Attic: The Woman Writer and the Nineteenth-Century Literary Imagination* (New Haven, Yale U.P., 1979), p. xi.
[14]Showalter, 'Feminist Criticism in the Wilderness', *Critical Inquiry* VIII, ii (winter, 1981), p. 189.
[15]Woolf, 'Professions for Women', pp. 236–8.
[16]Adrienne Rich, *On Lies, Secrets and Silence* (New York, Norton, 1979.)
[17]Mary Daly, *Beyond God the Father: Toward a Philosophy of Women's Liberation* (Boston, Beacon Press, 1973).

not "history" as the whole human story, not "man" as the generic term for the species, not "manhood" as the synonym for courage, dignity, and strength. But I have not been successful in re-inventing the language.'[18]

These are radical arguments, surely, but Woolf, while she would never have considered abandoning her language, might also be seen as advocating a theory of woman's separate relationship to language. In *A Room of One's Own*, she imagines Jane Austen's reaction to the work of a male author: 'That is a man's sentence; behind it one can see Johnson, Gibbon, and the rest. It was a sentence that was unsuited to a woman's use . . . Jane Austen looked at it and laughed at it and devised a perfectly natural, shapely sentence proper for her own use and never departed from it' (pp. 76–77). Similarly, in a review of Dorothy Richardson's work, Woolf wrote: 'She has invented, or if she has not invented, developed and applied to her own uses, a sentence which we might call the psychological sentence of the feminine gender. It is of a more elastic fibre than the old, capable of stretching to the extreme, of suspending the frailest particles, of enveloping the vaguest shapes.'[19]

Yet Woolf does not convince even herself that 'sentences of the feminine gender' resulted from any factor other than female experience. Woolf's argument is social and psychological, not biological. Earlier women writers more often chose the novel form rather than poetry or drama, Woolf remarks in *A Room of One's Own*, not because the novel was somehow more sympathetic to female nature, but simply because 'all the older forms of literature were hardened and set by the time she became a writer. The novel alone was young enough to be soft in her hands' (p. 77).

Although Woolf was at times severely critical in her assessments of the works of women writers of the past and often, as we know from her diaries, highly competitive in her relationships with her contemporaries (for example, her guilty jealousy of Katherine Mansfield), she none the less manifested a great deal of empathy and respect for the woman as artist. One example occurs in Woolf's diary as she records the death of writer Stella Benson in 1933:

> I was walking through Leicester Square . . . just now when I read 'Death of Noted Novelist' on the posters . . . it is Stella Benson. . . . A very fine steady mind: much suffering; suppressed; – there seems to be some sort of reproach to me in her death, as in K.M.'s [Katherine Mansfield's]. I go on; and they cease. Why? Why not my name on the posters? . . . A curious feeling, when a writer like S.B. dies, that one's response is diminished . . . My effusion – what I send out – less porous and radiant – as if the

[18] Andrea Dworkin, *Woman-Hating* (New York, Dutton, 1974), p. 26.
[19] Woolf, *Women and Writing*, ed. Michele Barrett (New York, Harcourt Brace Jovanovich, 1980), p. 191.

thinking stuff were a web that were fertilized only by other people's (her that is) thinking it too: now lacks life.[20]

Novelist Mary Gordon, too, sees this sympathetic aspect of Woolf in an introduction to the recent edition of *A Room of One's Own*: 'She looks friendly; she may be approachable. It is November 6, 1929. She is writing to her friend G. Lowes Dickinson, explaining the reasons for *A Room of One's Own*: "I wanted to encourage the young women – they seem to get fearfully depressed" ' (p. xiv). Woolf's compassion for women of the past, her recognition of their influence on her own life and work, her hope for women artists of the future are elements of her critical works which serve as models for today's feminist critics to reiterate and reaffirm their stated commitment to tolerance and sisterhood.

When we ask ourselves questions, as we often do in print and in classrooms, about the proper function of feminist criticism, whether we should write only about women and their work or whether we should concern ourselves also with corrective and prescriptive analyses of the classics, whether feminist theory should be 'mainstreamed' or kept a separately identifiable entity, we might recall Woolf's advice that women should 'write all kinds of books, hesitating at no subject however trivial or however vast' (p. 109). Feminist critics would perhaps benefit from Woolf's direction to 'escape a little from the common sitting-room and see human beings not always in their relation to each other but in relation to reality; and the sky, too, and the trees or whatever it may be in themselves'. Women writers in all genres, Woolf continues, must 'face the fact, for it is a fact, that there is no arm to cling to, but that we go alone and that our relation is to the world of reality and not only to the world of men and women' (pp. 113–14). Thus Woolf directs us toward a feminist perspective that is, at the same time, humanistic and interdisciplinary, unlimited in scope and universal in application.

Woolf herself maintained that 'no human being should shut out the view' (p. 114), and that the primary function of writers and critics is to question authority and to explore the territories beyond tradition. As feminist critics, we are by definition revisionists. Our evaluation of Woolf's own work and contributions should, of course, retain a critical and a questioning stand. Yet, we owe her a truly significant debt, both in theory and method. If, as Woolf wrote, 'Jane Austen should have laid a wreath upon the grave of Fanny Burney' (p. 65), then we, too, should gratefully bestow on Virginia Woolf a similar honour.

---

[20]Woolf, *A Writer's Diary*, ed. Leonard Woolf (New York, Harcourt Brace Jovanovich, 1973), pp. 206–7.

Note

Examples of Roland Barthes' ideas about literature and history can be found in his polemic with Raymond Picard and traditional French literary historians (see 'What is criticism?' and other essays in his *Critical Essays* (Evanston, Northwestern U.P., 1972; first published Paris, Seuil, 1964), 'History or literature?' in *On Racine* (New York, Hill & Wang, 1964; first published Paris, Seuil, 1963), Picard's *New Criticism or New Fraud?* (Pullman, Washington State U.P., 1969; first published Paris, Pauvert, 1965), and Barthes' response in *Critique et vérité* (Paris, Seuil, 1966)); in *Sade/Fourier/Loyola* (London, Cape, 1977; first published Paris, Seuil, 1971); and in his 'Inaugural Lecture', in Susan Sontag, ed., *A Barthes Reader* (London, Cape, 1982; the lecture first published Paris, Seuil, 1978). Relevant texts by Jacques Derrida include *Writing and Difference* (London, Routledge & Kegan Paul, 1978; first published Paris, Seuil, 1967), especially the essay 'Structure, Sign, and Play'; the early chapters of *Of Grammatology* (Baltimore, Johns Hopkins U.P., 1977; first published Paris, Minuit, 1967); and *Margins of Philosophy* (Brighton, Harvester, 1982; first published Paris, Minuit, 1972).

For a critique of anti-historical elements in literary structuralism, see Fredric Jameson, *The Prison-House of Language* (Princeton, Princeton U.P., 1972). For a critique of such elements in poststructuralism, see Frank Lentricchia, *After the New Criticism* (London, Athlone Press, 1980); Edward Said, 'Abecedarium Culturae', in his *Beginnings* (Baltimore, Johns Hopkins U.P., 1975) and 'The Problem of Textuality: Two Exemplary Positions', in *Critical Inquiry* IV (1978); and M.H. Abrams, 'How To Do Things With Texts', in *Partisan Review* XLIV (1978) and 'The Deconstructive Angel', in *Critical Inquiry* III (1977).

Hans-Georg Gadamer's *magnum opus* is *Truth and Method* (London, Sheed & Ward, 2nd edition 1979; first published Tübingen, Mohr, 1972). His collected essays have been published as *Kleine Schriften* (Tübingen, Mohr, 1967–77), and a selection of these is available in English as *Philosophical Hermeneutics* (Berkeley, Univ. of California Press, 1976). See also his 'The Problem of Historical Consciousness', in Paul Rabinow and William Sullivan, eds., *Interpretive Social Science: A Reader* (Berkeley, Univ. of California Press, 1979). For practical applications of Gadamer's ideas to literary studies, see the work of his pupil Hans Robert Jauss, especially *Towards an Aesthetic of Literary Reception* (Brighton, Harvester Press, 1983). For examples of more critical responses to his ideas, see the work of the major interpretation-theorist writing in English, E.D. Hirsch, Jr, especially *Validity in Interpretation* (New Haven, Yale U.P., 1967) (Hirsch's 'The Politics of Theories of Interpretation' in the special issue of *Critical Inquiry* (IX, 1982) devoted to that subject and his 'Derrida's Axioms' in the *London Review of Books*, 21 July to 3 August 1983, are also relevant); and Jürgen Habermas's long dispute with Gadamer. This can be traced in Habermas's *Knowledge and Human Interests* (London, Heinemann Educational, 1972; first published Frankfurt, Suhrkamp, 1968), in Gadamer's response in 'Rhetorik, Hermeneutik und Ideologiekritik' (in *Kleine Schriften*), and in essays in the anthology *Hermeneutik und Ideologiekritik* (Frankfurt, Suhrkamp, 1971). See also Martin Jay, 'Should Intellectual History Take a Linguistic Turn? Reflections on the Habermas – Gadamer Debate', in Dominick La Capra, ed., *Modern European Intellectual History: Reappraisals and New Perspectives* (Ithaca, Cornell U.P., 1982); Anthony Giddens, 'Habermas's Critique of Hermeneutics', in his *Studies in Social and Political Theory* (London, Hutchinson, 1977); and Paul Connerton, 'Gadamer's Hermeneutics', in E.S. Shaffer, ed., *Comparative Criticism* v (Cambridge, Cambridge U.P., 1983), a volume devoted to hermeneutic criticism, with bibliography.

Gadamer's ideas should be understood within the long tradition of German hermeneutical philosophy, as represented most notably by the work of Schleiermacher (e.g. 'The Hermeneutics: Outline of the 1819 Lectures', in *New Literary History*'s symposium on 'Literary Hermeneutics' (X, 1978)), Dilthey (see his *Selected Writings* (Cambridge, Cambridge U.P., 1976)), and Heidegger (in *Being and Time* (Oxford, Basil Blackwell, 1978; first published Tübingen, Max Niemeyer, 1927)). For contrasting reworkings of that tradition, see the work of Paul Ricoeur (e.g. *The Conflict of Interpretations* (Evanston, Northwestern U.P., 1974; first published Paris, Seuil, 1969)) and Emilio Betti, *Teoria generale della interpretazione* (Milan, A. Giuffrè, 1955).

7

History, Hermeneutics, Deconstruction

Iain Wright

A few years ago Robert Weimann wrote hopefully of the emergence of 'a new consciousness of the need for historical theory, historiography, and hermeneutics' in Anglo-American literary studies.[1] His optimism has turned out to be premature. Attempts to formulate a new conception of literary history – of literature in history – have been checked, not so much by an a-temporal structuralism, whose influence on the actual practice of British and American criticism was never very great, but by the unlooked-for flowering of a neo-Nietzschean 'poststructuralism'. Structuralism was evidently anti-historical. Its very point of origin, after all, was Saussure's displacement of diachronic explanations by synchronic ones, his attempt to picture language-systems as inhabiting an eternal present without memory of their own past and origins. But it was indeed *evidently*, blatantly, so, and therefore repeatedly drew attention to that term – history – which it attempted to exclude. How in fact can one even begin to grasp the notion of synchrony without constantly holding in one's mind its contrary? The repressed continually returned, and the great debate – between 'genetic' and 'structural' accounts of human culture – was kept very much alive both within the ranks of mainstream structuralism (see Lévi-Strauss's 'History and Dialectic', for instance[2]) and in the rapid appearance of an antagonistic fifth-column in the form of so-called 'genetic structuralism' (see the work of Lucien Goldman). At the beginning of the seventies it even looked as though the long-term effects might turn out to be beneficial: diachronists had had to sharpen their wits and defend their gut-sympathies more energetically and rigorously when faced with the challenge of ultra-synchrony.

---

[1]Robert Weimann, *Structure and Society in Literary History* (London, Lawrence & Wishart, 1977), p. 19; first published in 1969.
[2]In Claude Lévi-Strauss, *La Pensée sauvage* (Paris, Plon, 1962); translated as *The Savage Mind* (London, Weidenfeld & Nicolson, 1966).

Surveys of the hermeneutical tradition are to be found in R.G. Palmer, *Hermeneutics* (Evanston, Northwestern U.P., 1969) and (more specifically relevant to the present essay) in D.C. Hoy, *The Critical Circle: Literature, History, and Philosophical Hermeneutics* (Berkeley, Univ. of California Press, 1978).

To say, in short, that synchronic systems cannot deal in any adequate conceptual way with temporal phenomena is not to say that we do not emerge from them with a heightened sense of the mystery of diachrony itself. We have tended to take temporality for granted; where everything is historical, the idea of history itself has seemed to empty of content. Perhaps that is, indeed, the ultimate propaedeutic value of the [Saussurean] linguistic model: to renew our fascination with the seeds of time.[3]

Perhaps. But when Fredric Jameson closed his preface to *The Prison-House of Language* with this stirring rallying-call in 1972, the American Derrida-cult was still a fairly small cloud on his horizon. Very shortly afterwards 'radical relativism'[4] was in full swing and, paradoxically, it turned out to be a far more insidious and effective enemy of the historical approach than its predecessor. I say 'paradoxically' because poststructuralism is seldom as explicitly anti-historical as structuralism. Indeed, its Anglo-Saxon advocates, anxious to render it acceptable to a liberal academy where an antagonism to history might be regarded as a threat to civilization as we know it and to senior staff members' scholarly reputations, have gone out of their way to assure their colleagues that deconstruction is potentially *highly* historical. 'Deconstruction', Jonathan Culler tells us, 'couples a philosophical critique of history and historical understanding with the specification that discourse is historical and meaning historically determined, both in principle and in practice.'[5] But the fact is that even if deconstructive philosophy 'in principle' has the potential to advance historical knowledge – as Derrida himself would certainly claim – that potential has shown little sign of being released 'in practice'. The work simply hasn't been done, either within deconstructive philosophy itself (where, as Edward Said has pointed out, Derrida's method has proved 'finally unable to get hold of the local material density and power of ideas as historical actuality'[6]) or in the various attempts to apply it to literary studies. The most striking feature of the last 10 years has been a movement in precisely the opposite direction, a movement exemplified, vividly and influentially, by the 'poststructuralist turn' in the work of Roland Barthes.

Let us look at some representative moments of that 'turn'. Barthes's earlier writings proclaimed his strong attachment to a hermeneutical model which was strikingly similar to the one which I shall be cautiously recommending as an alternative or antidote to deconstructionist relativism, the 'philosophical hermeneutics' of the German tradition. It was

---

[3]Fredric Jameson, *The Prison-House of Language: A Critical Account of Structuralism and Russian Formalism* (Princeton, Princeton U.P., 1972), p. xi.
[4]Paul de Man's name for the new critical method he advocated in the first chapter of *Blindness and Insight: Essays in the Rhetoric of Contemporary Criticism* (New York, Oxford U.P., 1971), p. 10.
[5]Jonathan Culler, *On Deconstruction: Theory and Criticism after Structuralism* (London, Routledge, 1983), p. 129.
[6]Edward Said, 'The Problem of Textuality: Two Exemplary Positions', *Critical Inquiry* IV (1978), p. 701. A revised version has been published in his *The World, the Text, and the Critic* (London, Faber, 1984).

above all a dialectical – perhaps it would be better to say 'dialogical' – model, one which envisaged and celebrated the continual tension between the claims of history and the present, old text and new reader. You could only put on a modern production of the *Oresteia* which made any sense, Barthes wrote in 1955, if you were prepared clearly to answer two separate questions: what exactly did the work mean for Aeschylus's contemporaries? and what use are we, a twentieth-century audience, to make of the work's ancient meanings? We must understand the trilogy simultaneously as 'progressive in relation to its own past, but barbarous in relation to our present'. We should be moved by it as an account of the Greeks' struggle to overcome obscurantism and dispel the darkness of the old gods, but it tells us at the same time that 'for us, these efforts are ana-chronistic, and that the new gods which they wished to enthrone are the gods which we in our turn have vanquished.' Only by taking the full weight of the work's otherness, its *altérité flagrante*, can we make it modern: 'To grasp the historical specificity of the *Oresteia*, its *originalité exacte*, is the only way for us to make a dynamic and responsible use of it.'[7]

Eight years later, in an essay on La Bruyère, Barthes still seemed to hold to the same model and put its claims with equal emotional force when he recommended a reading of La Bruyère's works which would pay special attention to 'everything which separates his world from ours and every-thing which that distance teaches us about ourselves . . . let us discuss everything in him which little concerns us: then perhaps we shall at last grasp the modern meaning of his work.'[8] Again, an image of paradoxical reciprocity: understand the past's otherness and it will speak most directly to us.

But in the same year, writing in the *Times Literary Supplement*, Barthes very deliberately unbalanced his own model. Certainly, criticism is a kind of dialogue between two historical situations, he said, but he now wished to present it as a dialogue which 'shows a complete egotistical bias' (*'est égoïstement tout entier déporté'*) towards the present; criticism is nei-ther a 'tribute' (*'hommage'*) to the truth of the past nor to the truth of the 'other'; it is the 'ordering of that which is intelligible in our own time' (*'construction de l'intelligible de notre temps'*).[9] In *Sur Racine*, also pub-lished in 1963, one partner in the dialogue seems to have fallen silent altogether: we are to 'try out all the languages our century suggests to us' on Racine 'in virtue of his very silence', and his plays are 'an empty site [*un place vide*], eternally open to signification'.[10] Eight years later, in *Sade/ Fourier/Loyola*, it sounds as if old empty textual sites are not to be treated even with an archaeologist's reverence, and the tomb-robbers have been

[7]Roland Barthes, 'Comment représenter l'antique', in his *Essais critiques* (Paris, Éditions du Seuil, 1964), pp. 77–8; first published 1955. An English translation is available (Evanston, Northwestern U.P., 1972).
[8]Barthes, 'La Bruyère', in his *Essais critiques*, p. 223; first published 1963.
[9]Barthes, 'Criticism as Language', *The Times Literary Supplement*, 27 September 1963, p. 740; and 'Qu'est-ce que la critique?', in his *Essais critiques*, p. 257.
[10]Barthes, *Sur Racine* (Paris, Éditions du Seuil, 1963), p. 12. An English translation is available (New York, Hill and Wang, 1964).

licensed to loot: Barthes speaks of aiming 'to fragment the old text of culture, knowledge, literature, and disseminate its features in unrecognizable formulations, in the same way that one disguises stolen goods.'[11] Eventually, metaphors are dropped altogether, and the modern *théorie du texte* is defined as that theory which 'removes all limits from the freedom of reading (authorizing the reading of a past work from an entirely modern standpoint)'.[12] Clearly then, Barthes' later writings can be made to yield many snappy *anti-passéiste*, reader's-liberationist slogans, and, in practice, they have certainly played a key role in encouraging or legitimizing the kind of anti-historical trend which this essay sets out to describe and resist. But they did not actually establish an anti-historical orthodoxy. Barthes was, in the first place, uninterested in constructing a general hermeneutical theory for himself, and in the second, simply too inconsistent to provide the basis for anyone else's. As Jonathan Culler has pointed out, his description of the new criticism as authorizing 'entirely modern' readings of old texts is at once followed by the remark that 'it also insists greatly on the productive equivalence of reading and writing' – that is, of the present and past.[13] The dialogue-model persists. Barthes the historian – even the antiquarian – is never entirely displaced by Barthes the iconoclastic champion of the *modernes*, and Culler is right to end his recent essay by quoting the passage from the 1977 *Leçon inaugurale* in which he speaks movingly of the pleasure of returning to gaze upon the 'old and lovely things' of the past once one has been liberated to do so by the desacralization of that past.[14] Desacralization is what Barthes stands for. His enemy is not the past itself, but the past as dead hand. He says 'Shed your guilt and your passivity and feel free, on occasion, to read the past's texts anachronistically, for the present's purposes', not 'It is always wrong to grant the past semantic authority'.

But deconstruction, especially in its North American forms, often seems to go much further than that. The historical approach *per se* is equated with that worship of origins which in turn is the distinguishing feature of the infantile 'metaphysics of presence' whose reign is now ended. How else are we to read the much-quoted passage in Derrida's 'Structure, Sign, and Play' essay in which he contrasts 'the two interpretations of interpretation', the 'Rousseauist' version –'sad, *negative*, nostalgic, guilty'– which is always turned towards the presence, lost or impossible, of the absent origin, and the 'Nietzschean' one, 'the joyous affirmation of the freeplay of the world, and without truth, without origin'?[15] Jonathan

[11]Barthes, *Sade/Fourier/Loyola* (Paris, Éditions du Seuil, 1971), p. 15. An English translation is available (London, Jonathan Cape, 1977).
[12]Barthes, 'Texte, théorie du', *Encyclopaedia universalis* (Paris, 1968–75) XV, pp. 1013–17.
[13]Culler, *Barthes* (London, Fontana, 1983), p. 118.
[14]Barthes, *Leçon inaugurale de la chaire de sémiologie littéraire du Collège de France* (Paris, Éditions du Seuil, 1978), pp. 40–1. An English translation is available in Susan Sontag, ed., *A Barthes Reader* (London, Jonathan Cape, 1982).
[15]Jacques Derrida, 'Structure, Sign, and Play in the Discourse of the Human Sciences', in Richard Macksey and Eugenio Donato, eds., *The Structuralist Controversy* (Baltimore and

Culler can try as hard as he likes to convince us that Derrida is not trying to say that one of these kinds of interpretation is better than the other one, nor 'affirming a free play of meaning', but it won't do.[16] It is quite clear what the intention of this emotion-laden rhetoric is, and what in practice its effects have been: to stigmatize origin-oriented hermeneutics as fuddy-duddy, immature and destructive of individual freedom and creativity. Culler himself, fired by the appeal of 'joyous affirmation', actually *defines* the 'historical approach' in the second chapter of his book as that which 'appeals to historical narratives . . . in order to control the meaning of rich and complex works by ruling out possible meanings as historically inappropriate', and is so pleased with the formulation that he repeats it a hundred pages later.[17] That one of the most influential of contemporary American commentators can not simply make such a statement but can make it in the apparent confidence that he can get away with it is a telling indicator of the tendency which I have been attempting to describe: the tendency which *has* 'affirmed free play of meaning' and indeterminacy, and which has reduced 'the historical approach' to that which opposes 'richness and complexity'; the tendency which devotes itself to promoting a series of highly selective re-runs of Nietzsche's 'Use and Abuse of History' essay – the hidden *ur*-text of the whole movement – with its scorn for the 'laborious beetle-hunters climbing up the great pyramids of Antiquity' and all those who would 'let the past become the grave-digger of the present', its praise of the man of action who 'forgets most things to do one', its continual stress on how our ability to live fully in the present and for the future can be undermined by too great an interest in the past.[18]

It is clear to me that this tendency must be resisted. I say this not because I suppose historical approaches to literature to be somehow more truthful or more 'correct' than unhistorical ones, but because I think they are likely to be more productive at the present time. We are all pragmatists now, philosophically speaking, and my concern is with what the *effects* of the anti-historical tendencies within (or hiding behind) poststructuralism are likely to be, both in academic literary studies and (in the unlikely event of their ever being noticed there) in the wider culture. As Richard Rorty has observed, the serious objections to this style of criticism are 'not epistemological but moral'.[19] And at this point in the late twentieth century I have serious doubts about the heuristic value of a pedagogy which flees from history.

How then is resistance to be organized? Three main strategies seem to offer themselves. The first, which is the one most favoured on this side of

London, Johns Hopkins U.P., 1970), p. 264. French version in *L'écriture et la différence* (Paris, Éditions du Seuil, 1967).

[16]Culler, *Deconstruction*, p. 132.

[17]Culler, *Deconstruction*, pp. 129, 215.

[18]Friedrich Nietzsche, 'The Use and Abuse of History', in Geoffrey Clive, ed., *The Philosophy of Nietzsche* (New York, Mentor Books, 1965), pp. 218–38.

[19]Richard Rorty, 'Nineteenth-Century Idealism and Twentieth-Century Textualism', in his *Consequences of Pragmatism* (Brighton, Harvester, 1982), p. 156.

the Atlantic, is to pull one's blankets over one's head and hope that the poststructuralist intruder will go away. (This strategy is also to be found in a marginally more combative version, characterized by Frank Kermode as 'manning the walls with dusty banners'.[20]) This approach seems to me unhelpful. Deconstructive criticism probably will go away: it is in the nature of sudden reflex-movements of absurdist cognitive scepticism to be short-lived. In any case, the readings which it produces are simply too repetitive and uninteresting, too 'entirely absorbed in demonstrating their own validity',[21] to keep it going for long, and five-year subscriptions to *Glyph* and *Diacritics* may turn out to have been bad investments. But what will it leave in its wake? Traditional versions of literary history have not survived the theoretical challenges of the last 20 years, and their practitioners will not be able simply to clamber out of their deep shelters and mouldering keeps when the present critical war is over and put up 'business as usual' signs. Whatever we think of the sillinesses and excesses of American deconstruction, a genuine anti-positivist and anti-empiricist revolution has taken place in philosophical and social scientific thought – a revolution represented at least as potently by Gadamerian hermeneutics, or Habermas's version of Critical Theory, by Kuhn or by Feyerabend, as by Derrida – and any attempt simply to deny this and stop the clock will bring English and other literary studies even further into intellectual disrepute than they are at the moment. What is needed, as Weimann suggests, is a new start, and a theoretically self-conscious one.

That is why Strategy Two, although necessary, will also be insufficient on its own. Strategy Two would attempt an immanent critique of the anti-historical tendencies in poststructuralism. That is, it would seek to demonstrate that even if one accepts the value of the main tenets of deconstructive philosophy, one is not thereby committed to nor drawn ineluctably into the kind of 'cultural Kantianism' (E.D. Hirsch's phrase) or 'silly relativism' (Richard Rorty's) which is being carried on in its name in American literary academies. Richard Rorty's work in fact provides us with a useful point of reference here. It is often cited by defenders of literary deconstruction in support of their cause, and it is true that Rorty has expressed considerable admiration for Derrida. But examine his *Philosophy and the Mirror of Nature*. It provides a clear demonstration of how a critique of the idea that there can be 'foundations of knowledge' which is every bit as wide-ranging as (and a good deal more readable than) the deconstructionist version can lead to a rediscovery of history rather than its loss. Rorty's purpose is, precisely, to expose 'traditional philosophy as an attempt to escape from history' and to provide an alternative.[22] The moral of his book, he says, is 'historicist' in this sense, and his heroes are the thinkers who 'take history seriously'.[23] And surely this is what one

---

[20]Frank Kermode, *Essays on Fiction 1971–82* (London, Routledge, 1983), p. 7.
[21]Kermode, *Essays*, p. 6.
[22]Rorty, *Philosophy and the Mirror of Nature* (Oxford, Basil Blackwell, 1980), p. 9.
[23]Rorty, 'Overcoming the Tradition: Heidegger and Dewey', in Michael Murray, ed.,

would expect from any of the heirs of Heidegger, the whole thrust of whose work was to insist on the primacy of human historicity – that is, to persuade us to think of our being as constituted by our situatedness in particular historical moments rather than by transcendental essences. How is it then that the literary-deconstructionist extrapolation of Heidegger seems to lure its practitioners in the very opposite direction, into an a-temporal *aporia*, a 'textualism' in which history itself has become only one ungrounded and unprivileged text among the myriad that endlessly subvert and 'differ/defer' one another? Rorty again – this time in a direct critique of poststructuralist criticism and in a neatly-turned aphorism – seems to me to make the important point when he remarks that 'Epistemology still looks classy to weak textualists.' A weak textualist, in Rorty's account, is a literary critic who thinks that the claim that there are nothing but texts has vast and far-reaching consequences and has at last revealed the only true method of analysing literary works because it reveals the fundamental problematic (their own textuality, rather than, say, their relation to 'history' or 'reality') with which these works deal.

> As usual with pithy little formulae, the Derridean claim that 'There is nothing outside the text' is right about what it implicitly denies and wrong about what it explicitly asserts. The *only* force of saying that texts do not refer to nontexts is just the old pragmatist chestnut that any specification of a referent is going to be in some vocabulary. Thus one is really comparing two descriptions of a thing rather than a description with the thing-in-itself.

It is merely one of several celebrated but misleading ways of 'saying that we shall not see reality plain, unmasked, naked to our gaze'. There is no harm in this kind to thing as long as it is done jokily. 'The claim that the world is nothing but texts is simply the same sort of light-hearted extravagance as the claim that it is nothing but matter in motion'. The trouble is that many people, including Derrida himself, now seem to be taking this rather seriously:

> There are, alas, people nowadays who owlishly inform us 'philosophy has *proved* that language does not refer to anything nonlinguistic, and thus that everything one can talk about is a text. This claim is on a par with the claim that Kant proved that we cannot know about things-in-themselves. Both claims rest on a phony contrast between some sort of nondiscursive unmediated vision of the real and the way we actually talk and think. Both falsely infer from 'We can't think without concepts, or talk without words' to 'We can't think or talk except about what has been created by our thought and talk'.

There is in fact a further inference which is commonly made in American 'textualism' which is even more misleading: not only that texts (and

Heidegger and Modern Philosophy: Critical Essays (New Haven and London, Yale U.P., 1978), pp. 241–2; reprinted in *Consequences of Pragmatism*.

therefore textual critics) cannot talk about 'reality', but that *all* they can talk about is their inability to do so. Rorty quotes Gerald Graff's remark that 'from the thesis that language cannot correspond to reality, it is a short step to the current revisionist mode of interpretation that specializes in reading all literary works as commentaries on their own epistemological problematics', and comments:

> It is in fact a rather long step, and a step backward. The tendency Graff speaks of is real enough, but it is a tendency to think that literature can take the place of philosophy [something which Rorty would not be entirely averse to] by *mimicking* philosophy – by being, of all things, *epistemological*. Epistemology still looks classy to weak textualists. They think that by viewing a poet as having an epistemology they are paying him a compliment. They even think that in criticizing his theory of knowledge they are being something more than a mere critic – being, in fact, a philosopher. Thus conquering warriors might mistakenly think to impress the populace by wrapping themselves in shabby togas stripped from the local senators. Graff and others who have pointed to the weirdly solemn pretentiousness of much recent textualist criticism are right, I think, in claiming that such critics want to have the supposed prestige of philosophy without the necessity of offering arguments.[24]

This is surely right. The sillier elements in poststructuralism emerge, and it becomes ultra-relativist, at the point at which it begins to offer itself as *ersatz*-philosophy, and loses sight of some essential distinctions between philosophical deconstruction and literary analysis (something which is of course encouraged by Derrida's notion of *le texte général* and his scorning of the traditional discipline-boundaries). It really isn't so easy to transfer the Derridean method to literary analysis. As Jonathan Culler has the grace to admit, 'the implications of deconstruction for the study of literature are far from clear',[25] and it is notable that Derrida himself has shown little interest in spelling them out. His concern, after all, despite his dazzling range of reference, is primarily with philosophy – or, more precisely, with metaphysics. And literature simply isn't often or centrally metaphysical in ways which would make it an appropriate subject for his investigations. His main aim (in the words of the title of Rorty's essay on him) is to expose 'Philosophy as a Kind of Writing'[26] – that is, as radically metaphorical, as self-deluding when it claims to use language as a transparent or neutral medium. But we always knew that *writing* was a kind of writing, didn't we?

What does all this have to do with my subject here – the scepticism of the possibility of historical knowledge which deconstruction fosters? I can answer most succinctly by pointing to the somewhat slippery and various ways in which the notion of 'origin' is used in such criticism. It plays a central role in Derrida's own writings, as my quotation from 'Structure, Sign, and Play' has already shown. If his great adversary is metaphysics, it is metaphysics defined as 'the enterprise of returning "strategically", in idealization, to an origin or to a "priority" seen as simple, intact, normal, pure, standard, self-identical'.[27] Fine. For *philosophical* discourse. But what does this have to do with *literary* texts? Nothing, except in so far as it can be used to undermine those approaches which propose that one should always value 'the pure before the impure, the simple before the complicated' and so on. And it is very difficult to name a single considerable literary critic who argues *that*. Here is the point at which the rhetorical trickery or the category confusion begins: the only way of transferring deconstructive vocabularies to literary studies is to set up literary critical equivalents of Derrida's 'metaphysics', and the only available candidates are all Aunt Sallies. Hillis Miller can only make deconstruction's 'centerless repetition . . . without origin or end' sound attractive and liberating by defining it in contradistinction to a caricatured opponent (M.H. Abrams) whose notion of literary history is said to rest on the improbable belief that a literary text has 'a single and unequivocal meaning' defined by its historical origin.[28] Jonathan Culler ('owlishly'?) informs us that deconstruction's great contribution to interpretation is that 'it demonstrates the difficulties of any theory which would define meaning in a univocal way'.[29] But even the most committed advocates of the importance of 'originary meaning' – E.D. Hirsch, say, in his earlier work – hardly argue *that*, nor that the purpose of excavating origins is to *hypostatize* textual meaning. Deconstruction, according to Culler, effects a significant displacement in the way we think, such that 'origin is no longer originary; it loses its metaphysical privilege.'[30] But readers and critics of literature are not on the whole interested in salvaging or reconstructing what they can of a text's history and origins because they think them *metaphysically* privileged, but because, in ways which have very little to do with epistemology, they think that historical knowledge is on the whole a good thing and are inclined to agree with Santayana that progress depends on retentiveness (rather than Nietzsche's 'forgetting') and that those who cannot remember the past are condemned to fulfil it.

Let me summarize Strategy Two then. Centring on deconstructionists' frequent failure to make the necessary distinctions between what an historian means by an origin and what an epistemologist means by the same word, it would seek to demonstrate how fatally easy it then becomes to slide unresistingly from the statement 'No text has an ultimate, "univocal", metaphysically guaranteed meaning' to the statement that 'Any meaning is "as good as" – epistemologically on a level with – any

[27]Derrida, *Limited Inc*, Supplement to *Glyph* II (Baltimore, Johns Hopkins U.P., 1977), p. 66. An English version was published in *Glyph* II.
[28]J. Hillis Miller, 'Tradition and Difference', *Diacritics* II, 4 (1972), p. 11.
[29]Culler, *Deconstruction*, p. 131.
[30]Culler, *Deconstruction*, p. 88.

other' to the assertion that 'Certainly, the *past*'s meanings can claim no special status and are indeed not even "as good as" mine, the modern reader's, since they distract me from living fully in the "richness and complexity" of my own present'; and thence out into the abyss of pure relativism and subjectivism. Such an investigation might then help to explain the extraordinary degree to which this kind of criticism has taken in writers who do not appear to be the least anti-historical in their interests. It might look at Tony Bennett's influential attack on the 'metaphysics of the text' in his *Formalism and Marxism*, for instance, and unravel an assertion such as the following: 'Ultimately, there is no such thing as "the text". There is no pure text, no fixed and final form of the text which conceals a hidden truth which has but to be penetrated for criticism to retire, its task completed.'[31] It might point out how Bennett's rhetoric attempts to make us suppose that these two sentences are equivalent. Clearly they are not: Bennett's eagerness to oppose the idea of the originary meaning of a text as tyrranical and univocal has led him, in a characteristic *glissade*, to sacrifice *all* notion of a text-in-itself. Rather than yielding to the lure of 'radical relativism' in this way, it would seem to me more useful to think through a much more difficult set of ideas, a hermeneutical model which would retain a notion of the text-in-itself, with its own right to assert its meanings against the reader's, while at the same time being thoroughly sceptical of the unexamined but highly problematic ideas of 'objectivity' on which traditional literary–historical approaches have depended.

That is precisely the project of Hans-Georg Gadamer's hermeneutical theory, and here I come to my third strategy for defending or refounding literary history. Suppose we argue for a moment (following deconstruction's own favoured tactic of reversing apparent cause–effect relations) that the flight from history in contemporary literary studies is not a *by-product* of Derridean scepticism, but rather that Derrida's ideas have been seized on because they seem to provide an impressively 'philosophical' new guise or stalking-horse or legitimation for that formalism and fear of history which is so deep-rooted in literary academies, especially in North America? If that is so, then the best way of countering poststructuralism in its anti-historical forms would neither be to reassert an unexamined traditional literary history nor (although that would be valuable and necessary) to point out the internal inconsistencies and *non sequiturs* of the new theories, but directly to confront the hard question which deconstruction continually circles and continually evades: what bases can there be for historical understanding? – the central question of Gadamer's major work, *Truth and Method*.

Truth and Method does not make easy reading and it is not by any means the ideal basic handbook around which to rally a diachronic resistance movement. It is immensely long-winded and prolix. Its central propositions are reached only after a long haul through such matters as

[31]Tony Bennett, *Formalism and Marxism* (London, Methuen, 1979), p. 148.

late-eighteenth-century Pietism and its reinterpretation of the *sensus communis*, anticipations of Husserl's phenomenology in the manuscript fragments of Graf Yorck, and 'the ontological value of the occasional and the decorative'. It is remarkably Germanocentric. It stakes a great deal on a very shakey concept of 'the tradition' (a point I shall return to later). And all these difficulties are exacerbated for English readers by the fact that the only available translation is woefully inadequate. But *Truth and Method* has one great virtue which, for my present purposes, outweighs all its flaws. In it, Gadamer is able to locate historically, and then to find a way around, the falsely polarized alternatives which have blocked and bedevilled hermeneutics from Schleiermacher to the Yale poststructuralists – doctrinaire objectivism versus doctrinaire subjectivism, pure intentionalism versus pure anti-intentionalism, slavish 'homage to the truth of the past' versus 'intelligibility for our time', ultra-Rousseauism versus ultra-Nietzscheanism, the rights of the text versus the rights of the reader. Like Derrida and the later Barthes (and like Rorty for that matter), Gadamer's chief purpose is fundamentally to challenge the dominance of pseudo-scientific or 'objectivist' models of understanding the human world. Unlike many of Derrida and Barthes' admirers, he has a very lively sense of how easy it has been historically and how easy it still is to swing violently from false objectivism into extreme subjectivism. If, as I suspect, the present vogue for deconstruction represents one of those pendulum-swings – specifically, a swing away from the 'scientific' pretensions of structuralism and some recent Marxist theory – then Gadamer provides a vocabulary which might both help us to understand that process and to damp down its wilder oscillations.

He charts a difficult middle course. He is emphatic that there is 'something absurd about the whole idea of a uniquely correct interpretation' of a text (which is, roughly speaking, the goal of 'objectivism'), but in the same section of *Truth and Method* he pours scorn on the notion that art (for instance) can be understood as 'the variety of changing experiences whose object is each time filled subjectively with meaning like an empty mould' (or Barthes' 'empty site'?).[32] His response to the venerable *querelle des anciens et des modernes* is not yet another attempt to enforce the final victory of one side over the other, but, like Barthes in that early essay on the *Oresteia*, to *celebrate* their conflict as creative and to toast its continuance. Historical consciousness, in Gadamer's account, is a consciousness of collision and incompatibility. It 'involves the experience of the *tension* between the text and the present. The hermeneutic task consists in not covering up this tension by attempting a naïve assimilation but consciously bringing it out' (p. 273).

In the process of true historical understanding there occurs a *Horizontverschmelzung*, a fusing of horizons, in which the value-systems and

---

[32] Hans-Georg Gadamer, *Truth and Method* (London, Sheed and Ward, 1979), pp. 107, 104. Further references are given in the text. (Translation of *Wahrheit and Methode* (Tübingen, J.C.B. Mohr, 1960).)

presuppositions of past and present collide. The real problem with the attempt to apply a scientific model of understanding to the human sciences is that it refuses the challenge of such collisions. It tries to banish the (historically-situated) observer and his or her predispositions –'the scientific nature of modern science consists precisely in the fact that it . . . methodically eliminates any influence of the interpreter on understanding' (p. 297) – and thus aims to view the object as in itself it really is, through a neutral, historically *un*situated camera-like eye. This, says Gadamer, is an illusion. 'There can be no such thing as a direct approach to the historical object that would objectively reveal its historical value. The historian has to undertake the same task of reflection as the jurist' (p. 292) – that is, simultaneously to exercise what the old rhetoricians called the *subtilitas intelligendi* and the *subtilitas applicandi*, both the understanding of a text's original meaning and reflection on how it is to be applied in a new and changed context. To hold otherwise is to posit an impossible ideal of the self-extinction of the observer and what makes him or her a man or woman of the present. 'We might say that historical consciousness is not so much self-extinction as the intensified possession of itself' (p. 207) – intensified not by self-absorption but by its increased sense of the other.

> To think historically means, in fact, to perform the transposition that the concepts of the past undergo when we try to think in them. To think historically always involves establishing a connection between those ideas and one's own thinking. To try to eliminate one's own concepts is not only impossible, but manifestly absurd. To interpret means precisely *to use one's own preconceptions* so that the meaning of the text can really be made to speak for us. (p. 358)

Here is the heart of Gadamer's case: a defence of preconceptions, or *Vorverständnis* (foreunderstanding – a term he takes from Heidegger), or, bluntly, of *prejudice*. Some of his liveliest pages are those in which he attacks the 'prejudice against prejudice' which he sees as one of the Enlightenment's most dubious legacies.

> This is the point at which the attempt to arrive at an historical hermeneutics has to start its critique. The overcoming of all prejudices, the global demand of the Enlightenment, will prove to be itself a prejudice . . . the idea of an absolute reason is impossible for historical humanity. Reason exists for us only in concrete, historical terms . . . [pp. 244–5]. . . . Does understanding in the human sciences understand itself correctly when it relegates the whole of its own historicality to the position of prejudices from which we must free ourselves? (p. 251)

Once we have overcome our 'prejudice against prejudice' (and begun the much more difficult task – about which Gadamer is irritatingly vague – of distinguishing 'legitimate' prejudices from illegitimate ones), then we shall be in a position to abandon the arrogant attitude which pictures the past's texts as inert laboratory specimens upon which the cool neutral modern subject performs his or her empirical 'value-free' research. But that will not involve an equally arrogant subjectivism. Gadamer's balancing-act would attempt to treat the subject and the object of inter-pretation as *equivalent* in status. 'There is one thing common to all con-temporary criticism of historical objectivism or positivism, namely the insight that the so-called subject of knowledge has the same mode of being as the object' (p. 479). Thus it becomes possible to conceive of our rela-tionship to a text of the past as a *dialogue*, and it is to an analysis of the nature of this dialogue that the most stimulating sections of *Truth and Method* are devoted. A false dialogue is one-sided. A true one (and Gadamer's ideal touchstone is the Platonic dialogue) involves a mutual learning-process, in which each interlocutor retains his or her identity but is prepared to learn from the other. The present allows the past to inter-rogate it: 'For an historical text to be made the object of interpretation means that it asks a question of the interpreter' (p. 333). (And at this point in the argument, rather to our surprise, the otherwise invisible British intellectual tradition makes a brief appearance: this key concept of *Die Logik von Frage und Antwort*, the logic of question and answer, turns out to derive from the 'Question and Answer' chapter in Collingwood's *Autobiography*, where he argues that to understand a proposition (or a text?) one must 'find out what question it was meant to answer': and since that is itself an historical question it 'cannot be settled except by historical methods.'[33]) When the interpreter allows himself or herself to be ques-tioned, the prejudices that inhere in his or her own historical situation are not denied. On the contrary, they are brought into full self-consciousness and, if necessary, modified during the course of the 'dialogue':

> a person trying to understand a text is prepared for it to tell him something. That is why a hermeneutically trained mind must be, from the start, sensitive to the text's quality of newness. But this kind of sensitivity involves neither 'neutrality' in the matter of the object nor the extinction of one's self, but the conscious assimilation of·one's own fore-meanings and prejudices. The important thing is to be aware of one's own bias, so that the text may present itself in all its newness and thus be able to assert its own truth against one's own fore-meanings. (p. 238)

All this seems admirable. But I must conclude with a caveat. Although Gadamer's model of historical understanding as a dialogue of equals is attractive, *Truth and Method* itself is in fact weighted heavily towards one partner in the dialogue: the past, conceived of as 'tradition'. Gadamer quite openly admits that one of his aims is to demonstrate 'how little the traditions in which we stand are weakened by modern historical conscious-ness' (p. xiii) and, in the closing words of his preface, to counter the excesses of the 'utopian or eschatological consciousness with something

[33]R.G. Collingwood, *An Autobiography* (Oxford, Clarendon Press, 1939), p. 39.

from the truth of remembrance: with what is still and ever again real'
(p. xxvi). In other words, this is a strongly political work as well as a
philosophical one, and of a strikingly conservative character, and its
tendentious purpose gets mixed up with its attempt to develop a hermeneutical model of general validity in ways which are often confusing. I
would wish to stress that, in the final analysis, the latter – the general
model – retains its value despite the former, and that they can be kept
conceptually separate. I would wish to resist the caricaturing of Gadamer's
notion of tradition which Frank Lentricchia and Terry Eagleton have gone
in for.[34] But I have to concede the justice of his critics' main point (most
fully developed by Jürgen Habermas) that Gadamer seems to allow little
possibility in practice of challenging the authority of tradition and that as a
result his implicit picture of historical process and of our relationship to it
is too bland and quietistic. If we are to employ his writings in the cam-
paign to reinvent literary history, it will need to be in the service of a history far more fragmentary, alien and discordant than the one which he
himself envisages.

I can summarize as follows. Gadamer's dialogue-model, based on his
fundamental conviction that 'understanding begins when something
addresses us' (p. 266) and addresses us from its *alterity*, its otherness, but
without the listener sacrificing his or her (historical) identity, seems to me
greatly to be preferred to pictures of the past's texts either as inert specimens beneath the scientist–historian's microscope, or as empty sites for
deconstructive revelry. But the way in which he actually describes that
dialogue makes it sound much too genteel and professorial for my taste.
Why should we not allow it develop into a slanging-match at times? Why
should not the old *querelle* flare up fiercely on occasion? To understand a
text, for Gadamer, is 'like understanding another person' (p. 158). That
seems acceptable. But he then goes on to *define* understanding as 'primarily agreement with another person'. Not so. Understanding, both
personal and textual, can just as well and as productively be an understanding or clarification of irreconcilable dissension and discord. Agreement can be agreement to differ. If it cannot admit *that*, a
'hermeneutical' literary discourse will soon become as monotonous and as
unproductive of genuine historical knowledge as a deconstructionist one.

---

[34]Gadamer does *not* counsel 'wise Heideggerian passivity' towards the past (Eagleton). Nor
does he hold that tradition has an authority 'outside reason'. Eagleton follows Lentricchia in
quoting Gadamer to that effect, but neither of them has noticed that Gadamer is here
characterizing the *Romantic* notion of tradition, to which he is fundamentally opposed.
Frank Lentricchia, *After the New Criticism* (London, Athlone Press, 1980), p. 154. Terry
Eagleton, *Literary Theory: An Introduction* (Oxford, Basil Blackwell, 1983), pp. 71–3.
Truth and Method, pp. 249–50.

Note

Rather than duplicate material here and in the footnotes, I have tried to give very full information in the latter. My essay refers to a number of different (if related) areas of work which have produced very extensive bodies of secondary material; I do not refer to all the relevant writing in the pages that follow, but some of the most important sources are mentioned there.

8

Blanche

Maud Ellmann

What you depart from is not the way
and olive tree blown white in the wind
washed in the Kiang and Han
what whiteness will you add to this whiteness,

what candour?

Ezra Pound, Canto LXXIV

A Lover's Discourse

This essay speaks of love.

Love, according to Lacan, is the only thing that analytic discourse ever really speaks about. 'Speaking of love, in analytic discourse, basically one does nothing else.'[1] Lacan, here, may be remembering Freud who, in his essay on 'A Special Type of Choice of Object Made by Men', hinted that analysis and literature were rivals for the same elusive object: the power to address oneself to love.[2] Literature, however, has concealed the truth of love in the embroidery of the imagination. It is left to science to unwind the veil of fiction clinging round the stuff of love, as subtly as the Emperor's new clothes.[3] But this exposure is a ruse to conceal the darker truth that psychoanalysis is in love with literature.

Psychoanalysis drew its most famous theory from *Oedipus*, and many of its other principles betray a literary genealogy.[4] As if it were impossible,

[1]Jacques Lacan, 'God and the *Jouissance* of The Woman. A Love Letter', in Juliet Mitchell and Jacqueline Rose, eds., *Feminine Sexuality: Jacques Lacan and the Ecole Freudienne* (London, Macmillan, 1982), p. 154.

[2]Sigmund Freud, *On Sexuality*, The Pelican Freud Library V (London, Penguin, 1977), p. 231. I have used the Pelican Freud Library where possible because it is easily available and includes references to the Standard Edition of *The Complete Psychological Works of Sigmund Freud*, trans. James Strachey (London, Hogarth Press, 1953–74).

[3]See Jacques Derrida's discussion of Freud's analyses of dreams of being naked in 'The Purveyor of Truth', *Yale French Studies* LII (1975), pp. 33–9; and Freud, *The Interpretation of Dreams*, The Pelican Freud Library IV (1976), pp. 341–3.

[4]See Cynthia Chase, 'Oedipal Textuality: Reading Freud's Reading of *Oedipus*', *Diacritics* IX, i (1979), pp. 54–68.

however, to gaze on Oedipus's crime without succumbing to Oedipus's blindness, psychoanalytic discourse blinds itself to the letter of the text; to the insistence of the literary in its own procedures; to the uncanny reappearance, in the purest moments of its theory, of a scene of writing or a scene of reading.[5] Even analytic practice is a stage. Together, analyst and patient must play 'another scene', a scene which can be laid to rest only through the vicissitudes of phantasmatic, re-enacted love. This essay will explore love's other scene, as Chaucer presents it in *The Book of the Duchess*: a scene of dialogue forever vexed by the absent object of desire.[6]

'To make love, as the term indicates, is poetry', writes Lacan.[7] Love *is* its discourse and its declarations. Such is the story of love: from the troubadours who competed for prowess in the language, rather than the act, of love, to Prufrock's *scriptus interruptus*.[8] Deprived of the performance, desire resorts to the performative. 'What analytic discourse brings to bear – which may after all be why it emerged at a certain stage of scientific discourse – is that speaking of love is in itself a *jouissance*.'[9] So speaks Lacan, in 'A Love Letter': a letter addressed to woman, 'The Woman', the silent interlocutress of all apostrophes, the illegible address from which all love letters return to sender. Woman's place is to be out of place, perpetually displaced by a discourse that depends on her effacement. A lover's discourse can only really flourish in the absence of the woman, whatever name one calls that absence, be it 'death', as in Chaucer, truth or beauty, silence, mystery, pride, indifference, or virginity. Discourse is the process by which woman is erased, blanched out. It is this blanche in every lover's discourse that I, a woman, also speak about.

Blanche is the name that Chaucer chose to speak of 'woman', or rather of the vagrant gap where woman does not appear, does not *take place*. Blanche is dead. And *The Book of the Duchess* is the tomb in which she lies encrypted. 'The Deeth of Blaunche the Duchesse' was the title Chaucer gave his dream-poem – but it seems that the Duchess, true to her name – 'She loved so wel hir owne name' (1018) – has blanched herself out of the title.[10] The change from 'Deeth' to 'Book' in the title also hints that the *Book* is an accomplice to the death of Blanche, her death in discourse, a death on which the life of discourse and the book depends. This is no ordinary death, but a death that seeps into the very fabric of the text, where every letter frames a blank, entombs a silence.

[5]See Derrida, 'Freud and the Scene of Writing', *Writing and Difference*, trans. Alan Bass (London, Routledge, 1978), pp. 196–231.

[6]All references to *The Book of the Duchess* are to F.N. Robinson, ed., *The Works of Geoffrey Chaucer* (2nd ed., London, Oxford U.P., 1966), pp. 267–79.

[7]Lacan, 'God and the *Jouissance* of The Woman', p. 143.

[8]I discuss the connection between loving and writing in Eliot's 'The Love Song of J. Alfred Prufrock' in my forthcoming book, *Modernist Writing and the Problem of the Subject* (Brighton, Harvester, 1984).

[9]Lacan, 'God and the *Jouissance* of The Woman', pp. 154, 144.

[10]Alceste lists 'the Deeth of Blaunche the Duchesse' among the author's works in *The Legend of Good Women*, 418, 406 (Robinson, p. 492); the Man of Law also mentions an early 'Ceys and Alcione', *Canterbury Tales*, 11, 57 (Robinson, p. 62).

Many centuries divide *The Book of the Duchess* from psychoanalysis. But Lacan suggests that they belong to the same history, because psychoanalysis issued out of courtly love. He defines courtly love as an 'altogether refined way of making up for the absence of sexual relation by pretending that it is we who put an obstacle to it.'[11] *The Book of The Duchess* certainly invites a psychoanalytic reading. A dream-poem, it challenges the dream-interpreter: 'Y trowe no man had the wyt/To konne wel my sweven rede' (278–9). A work of mourning, it anticipates the talking cure. 'And telleth me of your sorwes smerte', the Dreamer coaxes the Black Knight, 'Paraunter hyt may ese youre herte' (555–6). The Black Knight's 'compleynt' unveils the secret sorrows of his interlocuter, and it is the Dreamer, too, whose heart is eased. The text hints that they double one another.[12] Who is the analysed and who the analyst? Chaucer's dialogue unfixes these positions, by showing that the analyst confesses in the discourse of the other.

Lacan also argues that the analyst is implicated in the tales that he elicits from his patients. 'There is no meta-language.'[13] That is, there is no discourse which can understand another discourse without participating in its dreams and its delusions. Lacan reads Freud as Freud would read a dream, uncovering the way that psychoanalytic theory blinds itself to its own desire through the delusion of its objectivity. Not that interpretation is 'subjective', for that would be to privilege the subject, and it is the very notion of a stable subject or a stable object that Lacan appeals to us to doubt. But the analyst defends himself against the anguish of his own complicity when he pretends to be objective and detached. The same applies to psychoanalytic criticism, which is never more deceived than when it claims to undeceive. The reader is embroiled in the fictions he pretends to penetrate. The text redoubles back upon the critic, interpreting its own interpreter.

This essay, then, does not propose to find 'the truth' of *The Book of the Duchess*. For Chaucer's text interprets Freud as well as Freud's interprets Chaucer. Freud's work on mourning and melancholia, on transference and countertransference, on trauma, deferred action, death, and dreams, and most importantly, on sexuality and gender difference: all these may enlarge one's meditation on *The Book of the Duchess*.[14] But Chaucer's

[11]Lacan, 'God and the Jouissance of The Woman', pp. 141, 158.

[12]Freud, in 'The Disposition to Obsessional Neurosis', Standard Edition XII, p. 320, wrote that 'everyone possesses in his own unconscious an intrument with which he can interpret the utterances of the unconscious in other people'.

[13]Lacan, 'Of Structure as an Inmixing of an Otherness Prerequisite to Any Subject Whatever', in Richard Macksey and Eugenio Donato, eds., *The Structuralist Controversy: The Languages of Criticism and the Sciences of Man* (Baltimore, Johns Hopkins U.P., 1970), p. 188. See also Lacan, *Ecrits: A Selection*, trans. Alan Sheridan (London, Tavistock, 1977), pp. 310–11.

[14]My description of Chaucer's narrative strategy is particularly influenced by Nicolas Abraham and Marie Torok's essay on '*Deuil ou mélancolie, introjecter - incorporer*', ch. 4, section 3 of *L'Écorce et le noyau* (Paris, Aubier Flammarion, 1978). See Derrida, 'Fors', pref. to Abraham and Torok, *Cryptonomie: Le verbier de l'homme aux loups* (Paris, Aubier Flammarion, 1978), pp. 1–73; trans. by Barbara Johnson as 'Fors: The Anglish Words of Nicolas Abraham and Maria Torok', *The Georgia Review* XXXI, i (1977), pp. 64–116; see also

text will show how Freud's in turn is secretly compelled to blanche out femininity.

'To rede, and drive the night away'

No one really knows when *The Book of the Duchess* was written. Still, most critics have agreed that Chaucer's poem pays posthumous tribute to Blanche of Lancaster, whose bereaved husband, John of Gaunt, figures in the text as the Black Knight.[15] Yet the death of the Duchess is equally undateable. The text anticipates its historians' confusions in the complexities of its internal temporality. The narrative moves unpredictably, through sudden leaps and long digressions. Its narrator is too fullsome and too reticent by turns.

The narrator begins by bemoaning his insomnia and the mysterious sickness he has 'suffered this eight year' (36–7). Requesting a book to 'drive the night away' (49), he chooses a romance from Ovid, and forgets his own tale for the while in the retelling of the tragedy of Ceyx and Alcyone. This story soon sends him to sleep, and the song of little birds 'awakens' him into the antechamber of his dream, a chamber 'Ful wel depeynted' with the texts the dream incorporates: 'holly al the story of Troye' (326), together with 'both text and glose/Of al the Romaunce of the Rose' (333–4). Just as the dream is framed within the Dreamer's reading, so the Dreamer, here, is literally framed with texts.[16] A hue and cry breaks in upon his intertextual reverie, and the Dreamer leaps to his horse to join the Emperor Octovyen in his hunt. But the hart they are pursuing 'staal away/Fro alle the houndes a privy way', leading the Dreamer into a forest (381–2). Here he is greeted by a 'whelp', who guides him deeper into the intricacies of the wood. And thus, by its own privy way, the narrative conducts the reader to the kernel episode of the Black Knight.

Derrida, 'Me – Psychoanalysis: An Introduction to the Translation of *The Shell and the Kernel* by Nicolas Abraham', in *Diacritics* IX, i (1979), pp. 4–12.

[15]Robinson, p. 266, states that the 'duchess died in September, 1369, and the *Book* was probably composed within the next few months'. However, J.J.N. Palmer, in 'The Historical Context of *The Book of the Duchess*: A Revision', *Chaucer Review* VIII (1973–4), pp. 253–61, argues that Blanche died on 12 September 1368 as opposed to 12 September 1369, as argued by chroniclers: see N.B. Lewis, 'The Anniversary Service for Blanche, Duchess of Lancaster, 12th September, 1374', *Bulletin of the John Rylands Library* XXI (1937), pp. 3–19. Edward I. Condren, in 'The Historical Context of *The Book of the Duchess:* A New Hypothesis', *Chaucer Review* V (1970–1), pp. 195–212, argues that the poem was completed in 1377. See also D.W. Robertson, Jr, 'The Historical Setting of Chaucer's *Book of the Duchess'*, in John Mahoney and John Esten Keller, eds., *Medieval Studies in Honor of Urban Tigner Holmes, Jr*, Univ. of North Carolina Studies in Romance Languages and Literatures, LVI (Chapel Hill, Univ. of North Carolina Press, 1965), pp. 195–212; Condren, 'Of Deaths and Duchesses and Scholars Coughing in Ink', *Chaucer Review* X (1975–6), pp. 87–95.

[16]For sources, see James Wimsatt, *Chaucer and the French Love Poets: The Literary Background of the Book of the Duchess*, Univ. of North Carolina Studies in Comparative Literature CLIII (Chapel Hill Univ. of North Carolina Press, 1968); B.A. Windeatt, *Chaucer's*

The Dreamer gradually becomes aware of a 'man in blak', all alone, who sings, or rather says, 'Withoute noote, withoute song' (472), a mournful lay to his dead lady. He is so caught up in his misery, so lost in 'his owne thogt', that he cannot see the Dreamer standing in front of him. Taking pity on his plight, the Dreamer urges the Black Knight to speak his woes. The Knight, at first, speaks indirectly. The message of his words is simple: Blanche is dead. But his prolixity suggests there is no end to the discourse that death inspires and sustains. He begins with an elaborate conceit about a chess-game, in which he lost his '*fers*', or Queen, to Fortune. The Dreamer takes him literally, forcing him to change his rhetoric: their whole dialogue revolves around this ambiguity between the literal and figural meaning of words. He now recounts the whole story of his courtship, his 'firste speche' (1131), his first refusal: the only word, indeed, he ever quotes from Blanche is 'nay' (243). After great trials, Blanche at last accepted him in her 'governaunce'. 'Where is she now?' the Dreamer asks the Knight (1298). 'Therwith he wax as ded as stoon' (1300), and he is forced to cry 'She ys ded!' With these words scarcely uttered, their speaker vanishes. A castle rises in his place, built out of both these lovers' names: 'A long castel with walles white, / Be seynt Johan! on a ryche hil' (1318–19).

Now, as if the dream itself could not sustain the name of death, the Dreamer suddenly awakens. He finds himself, like the reader, with a closed book in his hand.

'In youthe he made of Ceys and Alcione'

Blanche is dead. Or there would be no book. Her book was built upon her death, in order to commemorate her life, but also to ascertain her death, and to ensepulchre her troubling spirit. It is not known whether Chaucer's *Book* was written just after her death, or for any of her death-day anniversaries. In either case, the poem discursively performs the act of burial: an act which demanded repetition every year. The *Book* encrypts itself, walling up its narrators in narratives, its dreamers in their dreams. The Dreamer, for example, reads the dream of Alcyone, a dream within a reading; but the content of the dream is less important than the way the dreaming gods of dreaming made the dream. Juno instructs her messenger to fly to Morpheus, the 'god of slep' (137), who must 'crepe into the body' of the drowned king (144), and tell the story of his death to dreaming Alcyone. This story prefigures Blanche's death, her lover's mourning; but it does much more. It is concerned with death's enunciation, the transmission of its message, a message lying at the heart of every dream and every story, at the centre of narrativity itself. Death is known by its effects alone: effects of doubling, relay, re-inscription, whereby books of dreams inspire dreams of books, till Chaucer's dream-book brings death's message to the

Dream Poetry: Sources and Analogues (Cambridge, D.S. Brewer, 1982); Karl Young, 'Chaucer and Peter Riga', *Speculum* XII, iii (1937), pp. 299–303.

reader, bound in a mummy-cloth of dreams and readings. Perhaps, as Freud speculates, 'life' *is* death's own circuitous enunciation of itself.[17]

Encryptment is the only word for such a narrative. For books within books, dreams within dreams, are all depicted as rooms within rooms: and each of these interiorities beckons further inwards to a safe more secret, a crypt more cryptic, enclosing what remains of Blanche. The movement from narrative to narrative is always figured as a change of *topos* and a change of architecture. This structure suggests that *The Book of the Duchess* is itself the 'long castel' where Blanche is entombed in the white walls of the family vault – her name.

'Long castel' is Chaucer's famous pun on Lancaster, the name of Blanche's family. The 'walles white' of this castle bear Blanche's signature. The castle stands upon the 'rych hil' of Rich-mond – her widower, more often known as John of Gaunt – just as her *Book* is perched upon his riches and his patronage. These puns have played a crucial role in criticism because they surreptitiously refer the text to the circumstances of its composition. Edward Condren, for example, argues that the puns in the text 'suggest an historical context which seems to explain thoroughly how the poem came into existence, and why it took the form that it did.' Even so, the dating of the *Book*, and the dating of the death the *Book* commemorates, has never ceased to vex the pages of *The Chaucer Review*. Since *The Book of the Duchess* is the 'only major Chaucerian poem offering any hope of being precisely dated', the chronology of his entire *oeuvre* rests upon these puns, the moments of his greatest impudence, equivocality.[18]

The text suggests another form of temporality, subversive of chronology and dates. No 'event' occurs in *The Book of the Duchess*: the whole text tells the story of the mournful reconstruction of 'another scene'. This scene cannot take place within the text, and yet the whole text suffers the effects of that which, in its very whiteness, never appears. The death of the Duchess may be compared to Freud's notion of the primal scene: the blanche at the node of the neurosis; the primal scene which can only be imputed and may never have occurred, yet lurched the psyche into all its future phantasmatics. History is produced to fill the gap in which the primal scene should be.

Blanche stands for this non-event whose violence her history is built upon. The Black Knight is not alone in mourning her. Chaucer's poem intimates that mourning is native to narrative itself, which arises in and through the loss of origin. It mourns the loss of any cause of which it be seen as the effect, a loss called Blanche because it has no name. In 'Mourning and Melancholia', Freud argues that the complaints of melancholics do not just refer to loss, but depend on the repression of that loss – the loss of loss – a double cancellation.[19] Only the death of that which is already blanche can bring this woeful and interminable discourse into being.

[17]See Freud, *Beyond the Pleasure Principle*, Standard Edition XVIII, pp. 7–64, also published as a separate volume (London, Hogarth Press, 1974); see also Derrida, 'Speculations – on Freud', *Oxford Literary Review* III, ii (1978), pp. 78–97.
[18]Condren, 'The Historical Context', pp. 195, 197.
[19]Standard Edition XIV, pp. 248, 245.

'She loved so wel hir owne name'

It is such a loss which spurs the Black Knight into speech. Mournfully, indefatigably, he inventories Blanche's virtues. From the purity of her soul to her vital statistics, it is as if his black words, like a mantle draped around a phantom, might lend shape to the whiteness and the emptiness within. One could say that Blanche's body is a map on which the Black Knight plots his grief, the outer image of the inner 'topography' of melancholia:

> Ryght faire shuldres and body long
> She had, and armes, every lyth
> Fattyssh, flesshy, not gret therwith;
> Ryght white handes, and nayles rede,
> Rounde brestes; and of good brede
> Hyr hippes were, a streight flat bak. (952–7)

With these words the Black Knight draws to the end of a description a good deal fatter and fleshier than its subject, itemizing not only the graces Blanche possessed but the faults that she mercifully escaped. 'No countrefeted thyng' nor 'wikked sygne' could stain the blancheur of her countenance (869; 917). Blanche is no less blanche when these hyperboles subside than she was before her lover's discourse had begun. It is as if the Knight's 'black' words were struggling against the deathly pallour of the page, to create White out of white, Blanche out of nothing.

'She loved so wel hir owne name' (1018), concludes the Knight. He means she is 'so fair, so fresh, so fre' as 'White' implies (484). But he also hints that she stands for the propriety of discourse: the name's love of its referent, and the referent's chastity to its name.[20] 'She hadde not hir name wrong' (951), the text reiterates. The puns on Lancaster and Richmond have already shown how closely proper names ally themselves to place and property. Blanche's name is built into the very walls that define the limits of her family's property. Her love of her own name is a different and related form of regulating property. Blanche comes to represent the proper meaning of words, the identity between the name and what it names.

In loving her own name, Blanche logically must love her namelessness, her own blancheur: it is as if the name must be erased in the perfection of its own propriety. But is it not through whiting out the name of woman that patrilineal proprieties must always institute themselves? Namelessness enables women to circulate between the names and properties of men. Blanche herself, as her name implies, has no intrinsic properties: she represents the currency through which names, places and proprieties are realigned.[21] Another way in which she loves her name is through the

---

[20]For the complex of terms related to the 'proper', see, *inter alia, Of Grammatology*, pp. 26, 107–12, 244, and Derrida's long footnote on Marx's critique of the linguistic association of 'proper' and 'property' in *The German Ideology*, in 'White Mythology: Metaphor in the Text of Philosophy', trans. F.C.T. Moore, *New Literary History* VI, i (1974), p. 15.

[21]See May McKisack, *The Fourteenth Century* (Oxford, Clarendon, 1959), pp. 267–8, for John of Gaunt's marriages.

whiteness of her chastity. Woman's chastity protects the proper name, for if her honesty cannot be trusted, the father's name no longer guarantees his fatherhood, and name and person break asunder. The 'walles white' of Blanche's chastity defend the castle of propriety against the threat of woman's *jouissance*. It is as if male discourse and its dream of meaning could commence only through her bloodless body and her whitened signature.

But her whiteness also haunts this discourse as the stigma of its founding violence. Blanche signifies that which discourse must exclude, but which also leaves a mark or signature behind, even though that signature no longer names, identifies, appropriates, but only traces a primordial obliteration. Woman is indeed displaced, erased. But *The Book of the Duchess* also seems to show that the remaining blanche is all that discourse has to talk about. Tortured by her spirit, the discourse that entombs her compulsively repeats the trauma of her loss.

Most ghosts – and Blanche is no exception – are trespassers: their menace is directly related to property. It is the home they haunt, the hub of all that one can call one's own. In German, the very word for the 'uncanny' is haunted by the sense of impropriety: *Unheimlich* literally means unhomely. Freud, however, shows that what is now regarded as uncanny was once familiar, 'homely' to the home it haunts, estranged.[22] The home, in other words, returns to haunt itself as its own outcast. The proper has become improper to itself, its own white shade. The ghost stands for an outside that was once an inside, and returns from the outerness of death, an outerness encrypted in the innermost recesses of the house and the proprieties for which is stands. The 'walles white' which should divide the living from the dead are porous membranes relentlessly traversed by phantoms.

Fers

One reason why *The Book of the Duchess* only refers to Blanche as 'White' is to align her with the whiteness that inhabits writing as its ghost – the unconquerable whiteness of the page. '*Le vide papier que le blancheur défend*' – in the words of Mallarmé.[23] The 'work of Thanatos', as Jean-Michel Rabaté has written, is 'inscribed in the production of writing':[24] while striving to subdue this blancheur, writing only endlessly displaces it. Blanche is the unnaming of death or woman or exteriority – all that the order of the proper name excludes to institute itself. Like the blank page, she both enables discourse to commence and vexes the proprieties of speech with the silence of the grave that they are built upon.

If Blanche stands for the whiteness of the page, the Black Knight repre-

[22]See Freud, 'The "Uncanny" ', Standard Edition XVII, pp. 219–26.
[23]Stephane Mallarmé, 'Brise Marine', in Henri Mondor and G. Jean-Aubry, eds., *Oeuvres complètes* (Paris, Gallimard, 1945).
[24]See Jean-Michel Rabaté, 'Silence in *Dubliners*', in *James Joyce: New Perspectives* (Brighton, Harvester, 1982), p. 46.

sents the ink with which it is deflowered. Yet it is the Knight who presents *himself* as a 'whit wal' (780), prefiguring the 'walles white' of the 'long castel' of Lancaster:

> Paraunter I was thereto most able,
> As a whit wal or a table,
> For hit ys redy to cacche and take
> Al that men will theryn make,
> Whethir so men wil portreye or peynte,
> Be the werkes never so queynte. (779–84)

Once Blanche has left her mark upon this 'whit wal', it is never to be white again. Now it is *her* whiteness which the Knight's black discourse must articulate. Whiteness, in Derrida's words, is an 'elytron' that Chaucer leaves 'to float between the masculine and the feminine'.[25] The Knight, at different moments, represents both the white wall and the craft that marks it: that craft being the craft of love – 'I ches love to my firste crafte' (791). In his own rhetoric, the craft of love is implicated in the craft of discourse. Similarly, Blanche stands for the immaculacy of the page and for the marking which has always already deflowered it, opening its white and gaping chasm.

The signifiers 'black' and 'white' shuffle back and forth between the genders in the same way that black and white change places in a game of chess. It was in such a game that the Black Knight lost his white '*fers*' to Fortune. The derivation of the fers confirms the suspicion that gender is not so black and white a matter as it first appears to be. Its sex has changed three times in the course of its chequered history. Male at first, then female, the *fers* has now reverted into a masculine noun.[26] Curiously, this etymology recapitulates *The Book of the Duchess*, in which the male figure splits into two, while the female is vanquished and erased. Perhaps all three persons should be perceived as moments in a single structure, rather than as fixed, opposing entities. Chess is a game of places and displacements, in which the identity of any of the pieces depends on its position and its movements. On the chessboard black *is* only in its difference to white. The *fers* became a Queen in Chaucer's time because it hovered defensively around the King, and in spite of its own masculine origin. Topography determines gender.

If love is a game of chess, then writing is a game of love.[27] The flickering of black and white brings writing, love, and chess together, and suggests that all three consist of games of difference. The chess conceit betrays the mutability of gender, together with the mutability of love. In writing, likewise, the gender of the page remains to be determined, and so too does the pen that cleaves its virgin surface.

[25]See Derrida, *Spurs: Nietzsche's Styles*, trans. Barbara Harlow (Chicago and London, Univ. of Chicago Press, 1979), p. 39.
[26]See H.J.R. Murray, *A History of Chess* (Oxford, Clarendon, 1913), pp. 386, 285, 423.
[27]Murray shows that the comparison of the course of love to a game of chess was a favourite with the troubadours and Minnesingers: see p. 753.

'And Ecquo died, for Narcisus / Nolde nat love hir'

Chaucer's chess game compares to a divertissement of Freud's in which he, too, suggests that gender 'ys nothyng stable' (645). This is his analysis of dirty jokes. Mary Jacobus has brilliantly explored the way in which 'male bonding' is achieved at the expense of woman in Freud's analysis of 'smut'.[28] The dirty joke arises from the wish to overwhelm the woman sexually. This wish, however, is denied. Like Blanche, the only word the woman speaks in Freud's scenario is 'nay'. In the face of her resistance, the man 'postpones' the satisfaction of his own desire and diverts it into smut's ingenious detour. Left to herself, however, the woman would soon abandon her rigidity. She would give in to the man's desire, and the joke would die. Another man, therefore, must supplement her own resistance, for 'in that case an immediate surrender by the woman is more or less out of the question.' Freud calls this other man 'the third person'. It is the third person who provides the conditions whereby sexual desire turns from deeds to words. In effect, he institutes language as the obverse of repression. It is he, the diversion, who is now to be diverted: he is the 'third in whom the joke's aim of producing pleasure is fulfilled'.

As smut evolves, the woman withers away. Freud contrasts the cheery, common hoard, where the presence of the woman encourages a smutty gaiety, to high society, where men tell dirty jokes only when the woman is not there. What was once a colloquy of three has turned into a dialogue of two, in which the woman is erased. Afterwards, however, she is 'retained as of she were still present, or in her absence her influence has an intimidating effect on the men.'[29]

Woman, therefore, is never truly absent nor truly present. Pale shade, she slips out of either of these categories. When she is present, she functions merely as an inhibition, a facilitating negativity, her *jouissance* forsworn to a third person. When she is absent, her presence is retained, her power exercised. Smut is a dialogue which blanches woman out, but also reinscribes her in a structure that demands her fading, aphanasis.

Both *The Book of the Duchess* and the art of smut demand three persons, though one of these must always be effaced. The Knight takes the place of the joker, the Dreamer takes the place of third person, and Blanche corresponds to the woman whom the dialogue displaces. Originally the object of desire, woman is evicted from the dialogue that takes desire's place. But it is the woman who now becomes third, and supplements the supplement. Dialogue is always haunted by a third person. 1 + 1 = 3: such is the logic of smut, a logic to dismantle opposition. Even the opposition of the sexes is to be undone.

Freud argues that the exposure of sexual difference is one of the many aims of smut. But he argues that the other aim is the exposure of sexual

---

[28]Mary Jacobus, 'Is There a Woman in this Text?', lecture delivered at the University Teachers of English Conference, Leicester, 1982.
[29]Freud, *Jokes and Their Relation to the Unconscious*, The Pelican Freud Library VI (1976), pp. 140–5.

similitude.[30] This double, contradictory aim may be perceived at work in the shifting persons of this trinity. The third person introduces an excess, a remainder which can never be reduced to two. The apparent opposition of the sexes stands for a defence against the mobile, relative domain of difference. One reason why woman, in the text, is White is so that her gender may remain as undecideable as an x-factor in algebra. Because its sex is not determinate, the third person puts both sexes in their places, and renders both these places treacherous, unstable.

Like the woman in the joke, Blanche stands for the undead third that dialogue must bury, only so that she may continue to 'intimidate' the men who speak from the silence of the crypt their speech has built. What Chaucer calls 'White', Freud calls darkness, as in the phrase 'dark continent' of femininity. Both signify erasure, a whiting or a blacking out. Throughout Freud's work, the figure of woman is marked by some form of obliteration. The theory of castration implies that the woman's body is perceived as marked by an omission, a perception too terrible to bear. A blind spot in vision commemorates the erasure of her erasure.[31]

It would not suffice to lift the erasure which has blanched out femininity. The 'true identity of woman' does not lie hidden underneath the mask of her blancheur, for identity itself belongs to a structure which is always haunted by an absent third. Blanche does not stand for 'woman' as such, but for 'the opaque place of the *jouissance* of the Other', as Lacan writes, 'that Other which, if she existed, the woman might be.'[32]

Blanche is dead, because woman is not. Woman is the evasion of 'is', laughing at being and nothingness. Neither absent nor present, neither dead nor alive, woman 'is' the laughter of such oppositions at themselves, at their own labour to reduce 3 into 2, and 2 into 1. The law of gender is the law of the third person, the law of one too many. It means that there is somewhere, always elsewhere, 'a supplementary *jouissance*'.[33] Does woman – if she existed – have the last laugh after all, because she supplements the third who supplements the smut? Could Blanche be laughing, somewhere, orgiastically, at her own joke? Is there somewhere – always elsewhere – another Blanche, consuming the white walls of propriety in the flames of woman's *jouissance*?

'Alway deynge and be not ded'

Chaucer may have meant his 'White' to refer to an historical personage named Blanche of Lancaster. None the less, her name re-marks a lack within the narrative, the lack which drives the text to its impossible fulfilment. Lacan suggests that something must be lost or absent in any narrative for it to unfold: if everything stayed in place there would be no story to

[30]Freud, *Jokes*, p. 141.
[31]See Freud, 'Fetishism', *On Sexuality*, p. 353.
[32]Lacan, 'God and the *Jouissance* of The Woman', p. 153.
[33]Lacan, 'God and the *Jouissance* of The Woman', p. 144.

tell. Blanche signifies the gap that teases lovers' discourse into being; the gap, also, that lovers' words can never fill. The white sheets of her wedding-bed return as the white sheets of her book, that book itself at last her winding-sheet. Indefectibly, as Mallarmé would say, 'the blank space returns.'[34]

She dies in discourse. The Black Knight entombs her in his words, but he can never talk away her silence. Her crypt was 'built by violence', as Derrida has written in another context: 'it is erected in its very ruin, held up by what never stops eating away at its foundation.'[35] Blanche does not allow male discourse to forget what it has buried, for she returns in every blank or silence woven into speech.

Chaucer's text offers a paradigm for the predicament of woman, 'excluded by the nature of things which is the nature of words'.[36] Woman is blanched out in the very word that brings her into being. Her namelessness is the condition of the proper name, her death the womb of male proprieties. In a dialogue only heard and understood by men, woman figures as the blanche which marks the absence of a third. Yet the third person, in Chaucer as in Freud, also circumvents the fixities of gender. Blanche's name, no longer limited to woman, now intimates a moving cancellation. The very birth of man and woman depends upon the death of a third person, whose ghost will always trouble their duality. One too many, the third person means that blanching is a movement in a structure, rather than the stamp of the eternal feminine. Blanche's whiteness is the stain of difference itself.

The absence at the centre of this narrative should not be considered a *carte blanche* to all interpretations. Death, whiteness, continence, virginity all signify the text's resistance to the very readings it solicits. Blanche designates the limits as well as the possibilities of reading. She stands for that which calls for mastery yet cannot be appropriated. Her name does not anticipate the *Book*'s apocalypse, the moment when its truth will be revealed, but rather marks the moment when the whiteness of the text will close like snow over all the Black Knights who have fought for its possession. The *Book* – for all its lovers – remains immaculately Blanche.

[34]Quoted by Derrida in 'The Double Session', *Dissemination*, trans. Barbara Johnson (Chicago, Univ. of Chicago Press, 1981), p. 257.
[35]Derrida, 'Fors', p. 80.
[36]Lacan, 'God and the *Jouissance* of The Woman', p. 144.

Note

The editions of John Fowles' works referred to in the text are: *The French Lieutenant's Woman* (St Albans, Triad Granada, 1977); *The Aristos* (St Albans, Triad Granada, 1981).

John Fowles' critical reputation was established with the publication of his first novel, *The Collector* (London, Cape, 1963), and has been consolidated with each subsequent novel: *The Magus* (London, Cape, 1966), *The French Lieutenant's Woman* (London, Cape, 1969), a revised edition of *The Magus* (London, Cape, 1977), *Daniel Martin* (London, Cape, 1977), and most recently, *Mantissa* (London, Cape, 1982). He has also written poetry, and short stories, and has articulated some of the ideas which inform his novels in *The Aristos* (London, Cape, 1966), a collection of philosophical *pensées*. Unusually, this critical reputation is combined with tremendous popular success.

Harold Pinter, who wrote the screenplay of *The French Lieutenant's Woman* (London, Cape, 1981), is known primarily of course as a playwright. His most celebrated plays include *The Birthday Party, The Homecoming, No Man's Land, Betrayal*, and *Family Voices*. But he also has established a reputation for his literary adaptations for the screen. Other screenplays include *The Servant* (from Robin Maugham's novel), *The Pumpkin Eater* (from Penelope Mortimer), *The Go-Between* (L.P. Hartley) and *The Last Tycoon* (F. Scott Fitzgerald).

Karel Reisz, who directed the film, was one of the film-makers associated with the Free Cinema movement of the fifties. His adaptation of Alan Sillitoe's *Saturday Night and Sunday Morning* placed him, with Lindsay Anderson, as one of the leading directors of the British New Wave.

9

Feminism and Form in the Literary Adaptation: *The French Lieutenant's Woman*

Terry Lovell

Novel and film of *The French Lieutenant's Woman* are separated by some 10 years and by the contemporary Women's Movement, and in his foreword to the screenplay John Fowles recalls the writer who turned down the project 'on the grounds that he could not help propagate a story so biased to the female side'.[1] Another critic declares that Fowles was a feminist 'before it was fashionable to be one'.[2] And it is true that the novel broaches questions central to feminism: sexuality, prostitution, economic and sexual exploitation of women.

Fowles' novel has been widely acclaimed from a number of different critical perspectives. His structuralist interpreters argue that *The French Lieutenant's Woman*'s modernism forces the reader into an active relationship with the text, disrupting its narrative flow, and foregrounding its constructed, fictional status.[3] The film of *The French Lieutenant's Woman*, while hardly modernist, interrupts the Victorian tale with its parallel modern story. Feminist theorists, influenced by structuralism, have also claimed that modernist disruption of 'classic narrative' is a necessary if not sufficient condition for a feminist challenge to 'patriarchal ideology'.

The French Lieutenant's Woman is of course open to other readings. If it really is 'biased to the female side', in what terms are these 'sides' drawn up? Does it follow that feminist readers might be expected to respond more favourably? Should they?

I will begin by considering the novel's construction of sex and gender identities and relationships, and go on to look at the ways in which these were reproduced or changed in the particular kind of film which *The French Lieutenant's Woman* became, a literary adaptation.

If films and novels were absolutely different, comparison would be impossible, and adaptations a mistake. Some critics come close to this

[1] John Fowles, 'Foreword' in Harold Pinter, *The Screenplay of The French Lieutenant's Woman* (London, Janathan Cape, 1981), p. viii.
[2] Barry N. Olsen, *John Fowles* (New York, Frederick Ungar, 1978), p. 14.
[3] David H. Walker, 'Subversion of Narrative in the Work of John Fowles and Andre Gide', *Comparative Criticism: a Yearbook* II (1980).

view, taking 'pleasure in scrutinising this practice while ultimately condemning it to the realm of the impossible'.[4] Others minimize the differences.[5] The structuralist intervention in film theory offers examples of both tendencies. Where interest lies in specifically cinematic production of meaning, difference is emphasized. Where narrative strategies are the focus, it is underplayed. Colin MacCabe's influential concept of classic realism implies that 'classic realist' film and prose fiction have more in common with each other than they have with 'modernist' texts in the same medium. Ulrich Wicks' suggestion that different levels of narrative fiction are differentially transposable across media offers a perhaps more tenable intermediary position so I will compare film and novel along these lines.[6]

John Fowles has achieved a considerable literary reputation on the basis of some half a dozen published novels, which have stimulated a growing body of critical study. But before his novels were recognized in Britain as 'literature' one, *The French Lieutenant's Woman*, had become a bestseller, 'At first sight . . . indistinguishable from the rest of the pulp fiction on the station bookstall'.[7] Although many have noted this unusual combination of literary reputation and popular appeal, few link the two. He is, typically, praised in terms of such things as the existentialist philosophy which informs his novels;[8] for his mannerist style;[9] for his relationship to 'great' novelists who have influenced him – Hardy, Gide, Eliot, Camus, Sartre, Fournier, even Shakespeare; for his modernist subversion of narrative. His name has been linked in flattering terms with other contemporary writers of repute, including Murdoch, Barth, and Lessing. But his popular success places him in different company. It has been estimated that in 1970 the sales of *The French Lieutenant's Woman* were exceeded only by Erich Segal's *Love Story*. Significantly, this piece of information is divulged by one of Fowles' detractors. Brantlinger treats Fowles' popular success as *prima facie* evidence against him. 'Probably all best-sellers flatter us in some way'. 'The identification of his (Charles's) abandonment of Ernestina for Sarah with sanity and with modern superiority to "Victorianism" is . . . one source of the popularity of Fowles' story, because it is always pleasing to have our weaknesses presented to us as strengths'.[10] While this need not be taken too seriously, Brantlinger's

[4]Dudley Andrew, 'The Well-worn Muse: Adaptation in Film History and Theory', in Syndy M. Conger and Janice R. Welsch, eds., *Narrative Strategies* (Western Illinois U.P., 1980), p. 12.
[5]Keith Cohen, *Film and Fiction: the Dynamics of Exchange* (New Haven and London, Yale U.P., 1979). Morris Beja, *Film and Literature* (New York and London, Longman, 1979). Geoffrey Wagner, *The Novel and the Cinema* (Rutherford, Fairleigh Dickinson U.P., 1975).
[6]Ulrich Wicks, 'Borges, Bertolucci and Metafiction' in Conger and Welsch, *Narrative Strategies*.
[7]Ronald Binns, 'John Fowles: Radical Romancer', *Critical Quarterly* XV (1973).
[8]Robert Scholes, 'The Illiberal Imagination', *New Literary History* IV (1972-3). Peter Conradi, *John Fowles* (London and New York, Methuen, 1982).
[9]Prescott Everts, 'Fowles' French Lieutenant's Woman as Tragedy', *Critique* XIII (1972). Conradi, *John Fowles*.
[10]Patrick Brantlinger, Ian Adams and Sheldon Rothblatt, 'The French Lieutenant's Woman: a Discussion', *Victorian Studies* XV (1971-2).

hostility brings into focus the inability of Fowles' more admiring critics to confront his popular appeal. The effect of their sophisticated interpretations is merely to make the novel's popularity more puzzling. Novels which 'hint at the falsification of existential experience inherent in narrative patterns'[11] are not often best-sellers and never on that account.

The opposition between classic realism and modernism has tended to conflate popular non-realist genres with realism, especially where it has been applied to film. The term is often used interchangeably with 'classic narrative', defined in terms of Todorov's theory of narrative process.[12] Yet Todorov's theory was developed out of the analysis of popular, non-realist forms, such as the fantastic. He sees narrative as progression through order–disturbance–reordering. It is the introduction of something out of place into the expected order on to which the fictional world opens which initiates the narrative process for Todorov. Some feminist theorists have drawn attention to the frequency with which women serve this narrative function.[13] It may be the sexual desire she provokes which constitutes the 'problem' which the narrative must resolve, or the anomalous position she occupies. Women may also function within the narrative as catalyst, stumbling block or test of some kind, for the male protagonist. This type of plot is usually told from the hero's point of view, but where it is not, as for instance in *Diana of the Crossways*, the result can be interesting from a feminist perspective.

Fowles' *The French Lieutenant's Woman* is poised between nineteenth-century realism, popular romance/melodrama, and modernism. MacCabe takes *Middlemarch* as his paradigm of classic realism, noting Eliot's use of the god-like narrator whose 'discourse' bears the Truth which measures the events of the story, and characters' behaviour and speech. In fact nineteenth-century realism yields a rich variety of narrative strategies. If we take MacCabe's definition for the moment, then *The French Lieutenant's Woman* shares *Middlemarch*'s form of narration, but with a difference. *Middlemarch*'s narrator is separated from the events narrated by about 30 years – distance enough to establish the position of narrative superiority, close enough for its 'lessons' to have contemporary relevance. Fowles' 100-year gap places narrator and story in different epochs.

An impersonal god-like narrator is not of course necessary to realism, which may be carried through the development of 'well-rounded characters', and descriptive accuracy. These slow down the pace of narration, and are typically minimized in popular plot-laden forms such as melodrama, romance, mystery, etc. *The French Lieutenant's Woman* shares the strong narrative drive typical of popular forms, and uses the language of melodrama/romance. Finally its claim to modernism is based on the nature and extent of direct authorial intervention, on its unusually large narrative distance, and on its absence of closure.

[11]Walker, p. 203.
[12]Tzvetan Todorov, *The Fantastic* (New York, Cornell U.P., 1973).
[13]Annette Kuhn, *Women's Pictures* (London, Routledge, 1982).

Fowles draws widely from the Victorian novel. The game of 'spot-the-source' is undoubtedly a major pleasure it affords. Charles has an obvious predecessor in Lydgate, the idealistic young doctor-scientist of *Middle-march*, while Ernestina is another Rosamund, the agent of Lydgate's reduction to stultifying social conformity. Charles side-steps his Rosamund, and in choosing Sarah, also chooses social ostracism, but reaches beyond historico-social determination towards his species' evolutionary destiny. (Fowles, like Eliot who was deeply influenced by the ideas of Comte and Spencer, uses the metaphor of social evolution.)

Sarah is a composite figure, reminiscent of a good many Victorian heroines. She acts the tragic 'fallen woman' role of Hardy's Tess but the plot reveals to Charles and to us that this is a persona which she chooses to assume. More surprisingly perhaps she bears a striking resemblance, in situation and character, to Jane Eyre. She shares Jane's bitter resentment at her low status, as well as her displaced fear of madness, associated with female sexuality. She is threatened with the fate of Jane's *alter ego*, Bertha Mason: incarceration in a private asylum. If her dissembling and her sexuality threaten Charles, he has at his command a more terrible reprisal.

Fowles' modernism permits him to lift these figures out of the narrative and subject them to critical scrutiny alongside the literary conventions which produced them and their predecessors, and the historical contexts, Victorian and contemporary, which they reference. They are used to trigger the discursive and documentary interruptions to the narrative flow, in which comparisons are drawn between nineteenth- and twentieth-century attitudes and practices, sexual, social and literary. This strategy certainly occasions the broaching of questions central to feminism, and therefore might seem to offer support to the view which links narrative disruption with progressive politics and aesthetics.

The narrative functions and ideological effects of Fowles' various narrative strategems become clearer however when we compare the film, in which they are absent or different.

Novel into Film

Story

The film's Victorian story is close to but not identical with that of the novel. It might appear to be a fictional story of the love affair between Anna and Mike which developed during the making of a film of *The French Lieutenant's Woman*, interlarded with the film that was made. But it merely gestures in this direction, and is in effect two parallel love stories, with the Anna–Mike sequences functioning like a subplot. Many minor characters disappear of necessity in any adaptation of a full-length novel, and the plot is simplified. The Sam–Mary subplot disappears and Charles's lost inheritance is omitted. The film's Sarah becomes an artist. Despite these changes, which are not without their effects, the two stories are substantially the same.

Narrative Organization

Here the most obvious differences are visible. For it was here that the film-makers confronted the notoriously 'unfilmable' aspects of the novel. Narrative organization and control are more problematic in film than in prose fiction. But many of the devices used by Fowles would have been perfectly feasible on celluloid. The changes introduced go beyond the dictates of the change of medium. Walker, who wishes to claim the novel for modernism, notes Fowles' strategy of leaving characters suspended, as it were, for several chapters while the situation of other characters, likewise suspended at an earlier point, is resumed and brought up to date. Walker argues that this amounts to ironic disruption of narrative by narrative itself, in the style of *Tristram Shandy*. This device, he claims, foregrounds the telling at the expense of the tale, and reduces the whole enterprise of 'realistic' narration to absurdity. 'To tell the full story, the story has to interrupt itself: it is defeated by its own logic'.[14] He might have pointed to the novel's use of the cinematic device of flashback which also has the effect of returning us to an earlier point in narrative time. The film does neither of these things. It tells the Sarah–Charles–Ernestina story in chronological order, possibly because the interlarded modern sequences already make for a high degree of narrative complexity; possibly also because the novel's flashback is anchored to the narrator, not to a character. In cinematic convention, flashback is almost always from a character's point of view. Without this anchorage point, it would cease to *be* flashback. It would simply become a story told out of sequence.

Paradoxically the effect of the film's narrative reorganization into a more regular linear structure is to slow its pace. I believe that Walker misinterprets the 'Tristram Shandy' device. For it is commonly used, in popular fiction, for its cliffhanger effect. It produces not so much readerly distancing and forced reflection on the fictional, constructed nature of the work, as the 'I-could-not-put-it-down' effect, appropriate to a best-seller. Fowles uses it to provoke and tease the reader, in a way that is sexual as much as intellectual. What Walker fails to note is that the rhythm of movement back in narrative time intensifies as the novel approaches its and Charles's climax in the Endicott Family Hotel.

Authorial and documentary interventions which interrupt the narrative also serve to heighten it by delay. The novel has an inverse relationship to pornography. The classic pornographic text has a skeletal narrative which provides the occasion for as many and varied sexual encounters as possible. *The French Lieutenant's Woman* is organized around a single encounter whose effect is the more stunning because so swift when it comes, so long delayed and anticipated. It takes we are told by the narrator, just 90 seconds.

The novel's complex narrative organization then, as well as its mixture of genres, facilitates a high degree of manipulation of the reader. The film's reorganization of that narrative gives it a more even tenor and flow.

[14]Walker, p. 202.

The film depends on the modern sequences to create ironic distance from the Victorian story. I shall consider in a moment whether it is successful in this.

Narrative Voice

The novel of *The French Lieutenant's Woman* uses two narrational voices. It has a dramatized narrator, who appears in the railway carriage with Charles. He is unreliable, mischievous, tongue-in-cheek. The dominant narrational voice is however impersonal, objective and reliable. The double vision provided by the twentieth-century point of narration on a nineteenth-century story necessarily distances the author/narrator from the characters. Yet despite the ironic distance at which Charles is held – in the opening sequence we see him and Ernestina as though through the wrong end of a telescope – we are persuaded into sympathetic identification with Charles, as narrative voice merges with Charles's point of view. This movement of convergence across the gulf of a century and across ironic distance cannot be analysed in formal terms alone. For it is in part a function of the links which Fowles creates between Charles, the reader, the authorial persona and the ideas around which the novel is constructed.

Construction of Imputed Reader through Narration

We can trace these links as they are established in the sequence in which Charles wanders through London following his humiliating encounter with Ernestina's father.

> I hold no particular brief for the Gentleman in 1867. . . . But . . . we can trace the Victorian gentleman's best qualities back to the parfit knights of the Middle Ages: and trace them forward into the modern gentleman, that breed we call scientists . . . there is a link: they all rejected or reject the notion of *possession* as the purpose of life, whether it be of a woman's body, or of high profit at all costs, or of the right to dictate the speed of progress. . . .
>
> You have just turned down a tempting offer in commercial applied science in order to continue your academic teaching? Your last exhibition did not sell as well as the previous one, but you are determined to keep to your new style? You have just made some decision in which your personal benefit, your chance of possession, has not been allowed to interfere? Then do not dismiss Charles' state of mind as a mere condition of futile snobbery. See him for what he is: a man struggling to overcome history. . . .[15]

Fowles, too, is 'struggling to overcome history'. The 100-year gap he has opened up must be closed. The philosophy which informs this passage is most clearly articulated in *The Aristos*.[16] While Fowles likes to dismiss this

---

[15]John Fowles, *The French Lieutenant's Woman* (St Albans, Triad Granada, 1977), pp. 256–7.
[16]John Fowles, *The Aristos* (St Albans, Triad Granada, 1981).

work, he has revised it recently, indicating a degree of continuing commitment to it. *The Aristos* identifies the chief difference in society as that
which separates the élite, or 'aristos' from the many. Aristos share, across
historical time, their struggle to escape fossilization within their own time.
They seek rather to advance in their species' time through integrity and
the exercise of free choice.

The first section quoted above establishes ironic distance between
Charles and his author. The second reduces this by linking Charles to the
aristos of other epochs, including our own. The third directly addresses the
reader-as-aristo – as artist, scientist, teacher, 'man' of integrity. This
identity flatters not only the reader, but also the author, aristo by virtue of
his status as 'artist'. And it elevates Charles in turn, allowing us to move,
without noticing, to a position of identification with Charles's point of
view.

The novel uses narrative distance, then, to broach and acknowledge
differences (between nineteenth- and twentieth-century sexuality, men
and women then and now, class difference, etc.). These differences are
then reduced in favour of a broader, more universal distinction between
'few' and 'many'. Chapter 35 provides us with another instance. Here the
sexual double standard is broached, along with Victorian middle-class
hypocrisy.

> What are we faced with in the nineteenth century? An age where
> woman was sacred: and where you could buy a thirteen-year-old girl for
> a few pounds. . . . At first sight the answer seems clear – it is the
> business of sublimation. The Victorians poured their libido into those
> other fields. . . . I sometimes wonder if this does not lead us into the
> error of supposing that the Victorians were not in fact quite as highly
> sexed as our own century . . . I suspect we are in reality dealing with a
> human constant . . . I think too, there is another common error: of
> equating a high degree of sexual ignorance with a low degree of sexual
> pleasure. . . . a much more interesting ratio is between desire and the
> ability to fulfill it.[17]

What has been effectively submerged at the close of this passage is its
starting point, the gender- and class-based exploitation of Victorian
women. Differences of class and sex are covered as the passage progresses
in its rhetoric by the use of generalized terms which are not class or sex
specific – 'us', 'we', 'they', 'the Victorians', etc. But 'the Victorians'
whose libido may have been channelled into 'other fields' are of course
male. Fowles himself documents the lack of outlets for pent up female
sexuality, outside the lunatic asylum.

The 'you' in the first sentence is male and wealthy, the 13-year-old girl
working class. Differences based on exploitation and ignorance are
reduced in rhetoric to 'human constants', denying what the narrative has
dramatized – the encounter in the Endicott Family Hotel between a

[17]Fowles, *French Lieutenant's Woman*, pp. 231–3.

wealthy upper-class male, and a poor working-class woman. The 'ratio between desire and the ability to fulfill it' is not a generalized measure in any epoch, for it is not independent of class and sex. Charles and Sarah cannot be merged into a single identity as 'Victorians'.

The narrative voice of the novel then is complex, but in spite of a 'bias' of sympathy towards women, it is fundamentally élitist and male.

However the construction of the reader in *The French Lieutenant's Woman* in not achieved through direct narrational address alone, and the majority of actual readers who make up the sales which give it best-seller status are unlikely to identify themselves as aristos. These lengthy discursive and rhetorical passages are less easily assessed than analysed. How many readers simply skip past them in order to press on with the narrative? If we want to assess the possible ideological effect of the novel, rather than its rhetoric, we must give primacy to narrative dramatization. Here Charles's point of view predominates, consistently supporting this rhetoric.

Again, the ideology behind the narrative strategy is openly declared in *The Aristos*. While differences of class give way to the differences between the aristos and the many, differences of sex and gender by contrast are never less than fundamental in Fowles' world view. Fowles uses gender as *the* polarity which structures all aspects of human life. Art, for instance, is essentially feminine, but not on that account the special provenance of women. On the contrary; there are, he tells us, 'Adam-women and Eve-men; singularly few, among the world's great progressive artists and thinkers have not belonged to the latter category'.[18] Hence the central role of women in Fowles' novels, combined with the predominance of the male point of view. Sarah does not stand in her own right, like Charles, as an aristo struggling to achieve mankind's species being. She stands for 'woman' – timeless, unchanging, mysterious, and performing an enabling function for the world's feminine–male aristos. There is an equivalent division on the female side between the few who, like Sarah, rise to this task, and the many who, like Ernestina and Rosamund, trap potential aristos into social convention and fossilization in historical time. The Sarahs are however catalysts not aristos. 'Eve societies are those in which the woman, the mother, female gods, encourage innovation and experiment, and fresh definitions, aims, modes of feeling'.[19] This is precisely what we see the enigmatic Sarah stimulating in Charles, and why we only see *her* effect on *him*. We never see her, or him, or her story, from her point of view. Again this is directly related to Fowles' philosophy. For women achieve their evolutionary function through mystery and conflict. 'Women . . . initiate marital quarrels more frequently than men: they know more about human nature, more about mystery, and more about keeping passion alive . . . and the women who resist emancipation also know what they are about'.[20]

18Fowles, *Aristos*, p. 94.
19Fowles, *Aristos*, p. 93.
20Fowles, *Aristos*, p. 47.

Spelled out in this fashion it is easy to see how far Fowles' ideas are from feminism.

The novel's plot is the woman-as-catalyst/test type discussed earlier. Such plots are almost always told from the male point of view, and where they are, they leave all too much room for male fear and loathing of the mysterious powerful 'eternal feminine' to come flooding in, swamping Fowles' own admiration of, indeed 'bias' towards, Sarah.

The French Lieutenant's Woman as Literary Adaptation

The French Lieutenant's Woman was, then, an enormously popular best-seller. Its success must be sought in its sexually charged narrative control, and in its use of popular forms such as romance and melodrama. Best-sellers are coveted properties among film producers. But they are not usually made into the kind of film which *The French Lieutenant's Woman* became – the literary adaptation. The difference is signalled in the credits, in the difference between 'based on the novel by . . .' and 'adapted from . . .'. It is true that the film version of a best-seller will be referred to the original novel, but the question posed will be 'is it as good' rather than 'is it faithful?' The literary adaptation, then, is the form of adaptation which is usually reserved for 'great literature', as may be seen in critical studies of adaptations. The *locus classicus* is Bluestone's work, written before contemporary structuralism transformed film theory.[21] It consists of a lengthy theoretical essay followed by detailed analyses of six films. All are adaptations of novels with considerable critical reputations as 'literature' and three are of nineteenth-century classics. Post-structuralist works on adaptation, written from a very different perspective to Bluestone's, nevertheless share his privileging of 'great literature'. At first sight this is not surprising, but must be set against the equally prevalent conviction that 'brilliant adaptations are nearly all of second-rate fictions'.[22] Literary adaptations present special problems of analysis which may actually make them systematically misleading *vis à vis* the differences between novel and film. I want to consider them here as constituting a loosely circumscribed genre of film instead.

'Great literature' may be adapted for the screen in more than one way. Dudley Andrew identifies three types, which he terms 'borrowing', 'fidelity' and 'intersection'. Borrowed titles, subjects, themes, etc. may gain respectability by association. Fidelity to the letter or the spirit aims at 'the reproduction in cinematic terms of something essential about an original text'.[23] In the third type 'the cinema, as a separate mechanism, records its confrontation with an ultimately intransigent text'.[24] Andrew uses Bresson's *Diary of a Country Priest* as his example of this third type which he identifies with cinematic modernism. Most adaptations of nineteenth-

[21]George Bluestone, *Novels into Film* (Baltimore, Johns Hopkins U.P., 1957).
[22]Beja, p. 85.
[23]Andrew, p. 12.
[24]Andrew, p. 11.

century classics fit the second type, and it is this which I have termed 'the literary adaptation'. What is common to literary adaptations and what above all is transposed from novel to screen in this genre, is the 'aura' of the original: that which registers its claim to high cultural status as literature. In all three types described by Andrew, this recognition is assumed for the original, sought for the adaptation. 'Borrowing' usurps aura in the most superficial way, by association. The other two types share respect for an original of widely acclaimed literary value, but register and transpose that value in different ways. The mode of 'fidelity' tries to reproduce the literary qualities of the original through cinematic equivalents. The mode of 'intersection' respects the 'great novel' by making a 'great' film, saluting and acknowledging its peer across the divide of different media. The conventions which have been developed in this genre to produce the aura of literariness on the screen centre around the concept of 'authenticity'. The film-makers strive to be 'faithful' by retaining as much as possible of the original. Story, plot, characters obviously, but also language. Paul Kerr has pointed to the critical importance of language in reproducing the aura of high culture in television adaptations of classic serials.[25] Television serial dramatizations have the advantage of length. They can reproduce intact more of the original dialogue than the longest film. The recent television adaptation of *Brideshead Revisited* used large chunks of the novel's language through the device of the voice-over, while Fay Weldon's adaptation of *Pride and Prejudice* used much of Austen's dialogue unaltered. Fowles' dialogue in *The French Lieutenant's Woman* is based not on the speech patterns of 1867, but on the language of popular romance and melodrama. Pinter's innovations in the screenplay do not touch this style of dialogue, and much of Fowles' own dialogue is retained in the 'Victorian' sections of the film.

'Authenticity' is also produced through period accuracy in costume, furniture, setting, etc. in the literary adaptation. Literary 'greatness' being more readily granted posthumously, literary adaptations are usually costume dramas set in the historical past, even where they were written originally as contemporary or near-contemporary fictions. *The French Lieutenant's Woman* allows ample scope for this treatment. Lyme Regis was taken over and transformed into a replica of its 1867 self, and remained in this state as a tourist attraction in the season which followed the completion of filming.

Where the limits of 'authenticity' have been reached, literary aura can be signalled through the collaboration of other 'high' arts. On the soundtrack, classical or at least 'serious' music by a named composer adds the right touch to the 'words of beauty and power' of the dialogue,[26] while visually, a painterly style may be consciously sought. 'In the Victorian scenes', Reisz told an interviewer, 'we very consciously went for an academic kind of lighting, the sort of high definition that you see in Victorian

[25]Paul Kerr, 'Classic Serials – to be Continued', *Screen* XXIII, i (1982).
[26]Kerr, p. 11.

paintings . . . a pre-Impressionist kind of light. . . . We had our own shorthand motto for this: "Constable, not Monet" '.[27] The choice of a prestigious screenwriter like Harold Pinter, man of literature in his own right, adds its own contribution in this mobilization of high culture in the service of literary aura.

The success of a literary adaptation will be judged as much by its critical reception as by box office receipts. But the latter, needless to say, are never irrelevant. British literary adaptations are important money-spinners in the USA, and John Fowles' reputation there would be an additional incentive to turn his novel into a literary adaptation.

Because the literary adaptation is signalled as and reproduces 'high culture', the favourable critical response is sought more broadly than the usual circles of specialized film criticism. Typically, the literary adaptation will appeal beyond the habitual cinema-goer, to consumers of other high cultural forms. And it will be discussed and publicized in appropriate forums, to attract this audience. There will be a good deal of publicity prior to its release and during its making, in the form of interviews and articles in Sunday supplements and daily press. *The French Lieutenant's Woman* received its full share of this type of publicity.

Apart from the evidence of the film itself and the way it was made and launched, *The French Lieutenant's Woman*'s status as literary adaptation is confirmed by the manner of its reception. I have been unable to find a single review which does not discuss the film almost entirely in its relation to the novel. Why was *The French Lieutenant's Woman* seen as a suitable case for literary adaptation? In principle it might have been made within the constraints of very different art movie conventions. We have seen that best-sellers do not usually become literary adaptations. But then neither do they usually become literature. *The French Lieutenant's Woman*'s double reputation as best-seller and literary success made it a unique property. Because of its commercial and critical success Fowles was in a position to retain an unusual degree of control over its filming. The critical success of the novel, enhanced in the 10-year gap between novel and film by Fowles' subsequent work, increased the likelihood that it would be treated as 'literature' rather than 'best-seller'. But finally the nature of the novel itself was, I believe, decisive. For *The French Lieutenant's Woman* is a pastiche of precisely that kind of Victorian novel which provides the chief source of literary adaptations. Its story and setting provide the opportunity for applying the conventions of the genre of the literary adaptation in a manner in which *Daniel Martin* or *The Collector* do not. And the fact that it is, finally, not a 'Victorian' novel accounts for the difficulties confronted by the attempt to turn it into a literary adaptation.

---

[27]Harlan Kennedy, 'The Czech Director's Woman', *Film Comment* (Sept.–Oct. 1981), p. 30.

Narrative Voice in the Film

The position of ironic superiority adopted by the novel's narrator places him in a position in which he knows, and reveals to us, more than the character from whose point of view the story is told. But it is necessary to Fowles' success in constructing his fiction around his gender-polarized view of the world, that Sarah should remain unknown and unknowable, enigmatic for her imputed author/narrator, as well as for the reader and for Charles. David Lodge points out that in neither of the novel's alternative endings do we discover what it is that Sarah wants, and comments that Fowles doesn't know either.[28] Narrative voice is more difficult to analyse on the screen. MacCabe argues that it is the camera which occupies the position of narrative dominance providing the 'dominant discourse' against which the 'discourse' of characters can be measured. This view, widely held, implies primacy of visual image over soundtrack and draws upon the belief that the camera cannot lie. What the camera shows us cannot conventionally be disputed, any more than can the voice of the impersonal, objective narrator in the novel. First person narrations are more problematic, especially where the narrator is also an interested party to the events. The reader is obliged to determine his/her reliability. While the cinema has a range of substitutes for the subjective 'I', in point of view shooting, voice-over and flashback, in all of these it is difficult to sustain a consistent subjective view. Point-of-view shots show us what the camera, placed in the position of the character, would reveal, which is not necessarily the same thing as what the character sees, or wants us to believe she/he sees. Where voice-over, often in combination with flashback, is used, the voice is unreliable, because it is always the voice of an interested party, an 'I' which has to be assessed. But again there is a possibility of dislocation between what the camera shows us and what the character tells.

Christine Gledhill suggests that this gap between what is seen and what is said opens up a space in cinema for struggle over narrational dominance, in which the 'woman's voice' may be heard.[29] But in her analysis of *Klute* she argues that where the woman's voice is only *heard*, and is contradicted by what is seen, it is contained. On the other hand, where the male voice is contradicted by what we see, the 'dominant discourse' is disrupted, if only momentarily.

Leaving aside the questions whether women necessarily speak 'women's discourse', and indeed whether there is such a thing, another problem immediately arises. It is true that what the camera shows us is privileged in cinematic convention, except in those films which license doubt by showing us more than one *visual* version of the same event (e.g. *Rashomon*). But there is a difference between seeing and knowing how to interpret what has been seen. The vast majority of films offer no room for doubt that

---

[28]David Lodge, 'Ambiguously Ever After', in *Working with Structuralism* (London, Routledge and Kegan Paul, 1981).
[29]Christine Gledhill, 'Klute', in E. Ann Kaplan, *ed.*, *Women in Film Noir* (London, British Film Institute, 1978).

what the camera shows really occurred in the fiction. In this respect, the camera is equivalent to the impersonal reliable narrator. But the impersonal narrator has relatively greater power to guide the reader's interpretation of what the narrative shows. At best, the narrative voice of film as it is established through the eye of the camera, is less readily decipherable. A second, related point is that what we see may be an act of dissembling. In the *Klute* example, we have to assess the authenticity and the power to last of what we see in the domestic idyll which develops between Klute and Bree, in the light of the knowledge we have gained about her. We already know, through voice and vision, that Bree herself is unsure and ambivalent, and therefore have as much reason to distrust what we see as she sits at Klute's feet as we have to doubt what she tells her analyst voice-over on the soundtrack.

This difficulty in assessing what we see, particularly when we know that the character may be dissembling, can again be illustrated in *The French Lieutenant's Woman*, in the filming of the love-making scene. The novel's narrator cuts brutally into the language of romantic melodrama in which the dialogue between Charles and Sarah is couched, to tell us that the encounter took 90 seconds. This cannot be doubted in terms of the novel's conventions. The information given therefore has to be accommodated within our reaction to the events shown. It may lead to an uneasy awareness of complicity through narrative involvement; to recognition of the vicarious sexual tease. The camera *shows* us the encounter, and we necessarily see not only Charles but also Sarah's reaction. But while the film time for this sequence may indeed be 90 seconds, we have no way of assessing this fact, since conventionally, film time and diegetic time do not necessarily correspond. The camera may show us exactly what the narrator has told us, but the effect is lost. Even had the sequence been shot from Sarah's point of view, we would not necessarily have gained any distance on the encounter, particularly if the film, in keeping with the conventions of the literary adaptation, remained 'faithful' to the novel. For Sarah is entirely supportive of Charles, even self-accusing. At this crucial point in the film, it would have had to depart from the policy of 'fidelity' if it wished to create the same effect as the novel.

But while authoritative visual narration may be more difficult to control, and may yield multiple readings, the general point that there is a greater possibility for discordant 'voices' in films which are not fully sutured into the dominant patriarchal ideology, may be correct. I believe that the film of *The French Lieutenant's Woman* had very real possibilities in this direction, which were not exploited because the film was made as a literary adaptation. There are two other types of film which it might conceivably have become; its melodramatic plot might have been emphasized more strongly, bringing out and perhaps even heightening the novel's debt to this form. (Interestingly, the story has some of the elements of *film noir*, in particular the investigative structure in which the object of investigation is 'woman' and her sexuality.) Just precisely how this might have been done, and with what effects from a feminist point of view, is not easy to say. But the point I am making is that the novel's triple identity as best-seller, nineteenth-century realist fiction, and modernist text offered a complex range of possible choices to the film-makers.

Another possibility which the film gestures towards in its interlarded modern sequence, is a film in the genre of Andrew's third type, 'intersection'. It is only where 'literature' is regarded as sacrosanct that fidelity to a novel on the screen seems to be a virtue. Fowles' modernism indeed suggests precisely that the film of his novel should *not* attempt fidelity. Rather it positively invites, in view of its subject matter and its tone, a further level of interrogation on the screen from the vantage point afforded by 10 years and the intervening women's liberation movement. The interlarded modern sequences were a brilliant idea, and could have afforded the space to exploit this possibility. There is the hint of a suggestion of this at times. For instance in the scene in which Anna, choosing some dress material for Sarah's Windermere costume, holds it up against herself in front of a mirror and says 'Yes, I think I'm going to like her in this'. Anna could have provided a contemporary, post-feminist, woman's perspective on Sarah, and broken the domination of Charles's point of view. But these most Pinteresque sequences, in some ways the most distinctive of the film, are used instead to evoke a particular kind of trendy cosmopolitan milieu and atmosphere rather than to provide any distance on Fowles' Victorian story, or on its construction of sex and gender. These sequences reference other films (*Accident*, *The Servant*), and other concerns. They take off from *The French Lieutenant's Woman* but then move away from its obsessions and point towards others of its own. But in any case, they are too short and slight to offer any counterpoint to the main story.

Without the frame provided by those aspects of the novel which were unfilmable *within the conventions of the literary adaptation* the film of *The French Lieutenant's Woman* has transposed Fowles' pastiche of Victorian romantic melodrama into . . . a Victorian costume romantic melodrama. It is possible to become completely immersed in its atmosphere of lush romance overcast with the threat of tragedy. The film's parallel story allows that story to be given the 'correct' narrative closure denied it in the novel, by giving the alternative ending to the minor story.

To conclude: there is no medium-determined imperative which dictated the making of *The French Lieutenant's Woman* as a literary adaptation, nor is there any great virtue in 'fidelity'. The novel may not be as I have argued, in any sense 'feminist', but the complexity of generic interplay within which it is constructed and the resources of cinematic narrative create great opportunities for a screen version of 'the same' story which could have prised open and interrogated its sexual politics and aesthetics. A film which was less faithful to the novel might have been both a more interesting film, and one which in the last resort treated its original with greater respect.

Note

This essay is primarily concerned with the contrast between the standard mimetic account of literary pleasure and that appropriate to 'postmodern' writing given by Roland Barthes in *The Pleasure of the Text* (trs. Richard Miller, New York, Hill and Wang, 1975). This, with the *Fragments d'un discours amoureux* (Paris, Seuil, 1977), merits a more extended analysis than I have been able to give it here. For general philosophical accounts of pleasure, see the works cited in footnotes, and also D.L. Perry, *The Concept of Pleasure* (Hague, Mouton, 1967). For the coherence theory as applied to literature see I.A. Richards, *Principles of Literary Criticism* (1924; rpt London, Routledge, 1967); and for a starting point in Freudian theory, Norman H. Holland, *The Dynamics of Literary Response* (New York, Oxford U.P., 1968). This is developed in verious ways by Jack Spector, *The Aesthetics of Freud* (London, Allen Lane, 1972), in post-Lacanian fashion by Fredric Jameson in *The Political Unconscious* (London, Methuen, 1981), ch. 3, and in her own idiosyncratic manner by Julia Kristeva, *Desire in Language* (Oxford, Blackwell, 1982). Other treatments of pleasure and desire within literature are e.g. Lionel Trilling, 'The Fate of Pleasure', in his *Beyond Culture* (London, Penguin, 1967), Leo Bersani, *A Future for Astyanax* (London, Marion Boyars, 1978), Rene Girard, *Deceit, Desire and the Novel* (Baltimore, Johns Hopkins, 1965) and Stephen Heath, *The Sexual Fix* (London, Macmillan, 1982). A larger social perspective is provided by e.g., Herbert Marcuse, *Eros and Civilisation* (London, Allen Lane, 1969) and Norman O. Brown, *Life Against Death* (Connecticut, Wesleyan U.P., 1979). See also the journal *Formations: of Pleasure* (London, Routledge, 1983). Frank Lentricchia argues that Derridan deconstruction is essentially hedonistic in his *After the New Criticism* (London, Athlone Press, 1980), ch. 5; Derrida's own discussion of Freud on pleasure is in his *La carte postale* (Paris, Flammarion, 1980); '*Sur Freud*', pp. 275ff. Also of interest is Jean Baudrillard, *L'economie libidinale* (Paris, Minuit, 1974).

10

The Pleasures of the Experimental Text

Christopher Butler

When art is produced on realist assumptions, the pleasures of the literary text might be thought to be very much like those of life, save that they take place 'only in the head'.[1] As we read, we desire certain outcomes to action; we are pleased or disappointed that Dorothea does not marry Lydgate; that the description of a sexual act may become more explicit; that justice will be done to good Mr Micawber, and so on. This is not to say that such desires and their associated sympathies are simple. On one level we don't want Paul Dombey to die: on the other we want him to travel off to his sea-like heaven, in a manner which seems to have been satisfying to Victorian readers at least. (Such an example, incidentally, should not allow the critic to fall for a simple division of matter (displeasing) and manner (pleasing) because Dickens' sentimentally imagistic description isn't mere manner, or 'style': it displaces the main concern of the happening (Paul's pain) on to another subject matter, Dickens' notion of heaven.)

We also like certain things in the world: the landscape where 'everything pleases', the Lake District in Wordsworth, the texture or feel of things in Keats' poems or Stephen Dedalus on the sea shore. They too are, for mimetic theory, objects satisfyingly described in the text. And so on, for all those many things we may claim, with irrefutable subjective authority, to like, enjoy or get pleasure from.[2]

But of course, in the text these persons, objects or situations are only cunningly ordered descriptions, enactments in language. And language affects the head, at least in the first place, even if as in I.A. Richards'

---

[1]This may be true of pleasures generally, and there is a philosophical problem here: e.g., does pleasure have an 'intentional object' rather than a cause? Cf. R.A. Sharpe in Eva Schaper, ed., *Pleasure Preference and Value* (Cambridge, Cambridge U.P., 1983), p. 90; and on 'mental pleasures' of G.E. Moore, *Principia Ethica* (1903; rpt Cambridge, Cambridge U.P., 1962), pp. 188f., 201. Moore asserts their existence and value, but says very little about their nature. Analytical philosophers in general offer very little to the critical theorist: they tell us that pleasure is 'favourable' attention, that we don't like it to be interrupted, and so on. But cf. J.C.B. Gosling, *Pleasure and Desire* (Oxford, Clarendon, 1969).
[2]On the truth value of first person hedonic judgments, cf. G.H. Von Wright, *Varieties of Goodness* (London, Routledge, 1963), pp. 78ff.

theory of emotion, or in erotic arousal, they may prepare us for actions which we are not actually going to perform.[3] However this may be, some such picture as I have sketched above has allowed critics to elaborate reader-oriented theories of narrative form, from Kenneth Burke, who defined form as the arousal and fulfilment of desires, to Wolfgang Iser,[4] and Robert Scholes' notion of the modern romance (whose most recent self-conscious embodiment is perhaps John Fowles' *Mantissa* (1982)):

> In the sophisticated forms of fiction, as in the sophisticated practice of sex, much of the art consists of delaying climax within the framework of desire in order to prolong the pleasurable act itself. When we look at fiction with respect to its form alone, we see a pattern of events designed to move toward climax and resolution, balanced by a counter-pattern of events designed to delay this very climax and resolution. Fiction which attends mainly to this formal pattern we have learned to call 'romance'.[5]

I think we would say in such cases (which approximate to what can be done in 'realist' fiction or poetry) that what we enjoy or hope to enjoy here is not language (the text) itself, but what the text reminds us of or makes us think about. Language appeals to experience, and offers us enticing visions of what our experience in the world *might be like*. The 'pleasures of the imagination' are thus at least partly the pleasures of imaging a world more or less conforming to our own desires; though of course we may be equally more or less aware of the distinction between imagining something possible (seeing Skiddaw's lofty height in such a way as to approximate to Wordsworth's description of it) and having a fantasy (escaping like James Bond). Fantasies by definition go beyond that which is possible for us, at the moment, or even for ever (heaven, science fiction). Such reactions to language and painting and even 'abstract' music (as in Forster's silly description of part of Beethoven's Fifth Symphony as goblins trampling over the universe) are familiar features in theories of the arts. The notion of fantasy of course suggests psychoanalytic theory. We may be concerned, as is the Freudian Norman Holland, to break down the distinction I have suggested between thinking about *realia* and fantasy, and to suggest that even in the most austerely realistic of novels, say, there may be an underlying fantasy, so that all

> Literature transforms our primitive wishes and fears into significance and coherence, and this transformation gives us pleasure.[6]

Less realistic works may be similarly reassuring; for example, detective

[3]Cf. I.A. Richards, *Principles of Literary Criticism* (1924; rpt London, Routledge, 1967), p. 78.
[4]Kenneth Burke, *Counter-statement* (Los Altos, Calif., Hermes Publications, 2nd. ed. 1953), p. 147, and Wolfgang Iser, *The Act of Reading* (London, Routledge, 1978), esp. pp. 129ff., 180ff.
[5]R. Scholes, *Fabulation and Metafiction* (London, Univ. Illinois Press, 1979), p. 26.
[6]Norman H. Holland, *The Dynamics of Literary Response* (New York, Norton, 1968), p. 30.

stories which, as argued by Auden in his 'The Guilty Vicarage', respond to our desire to see justice done in the world, by feeding us with a fantasy that reasoning (that of the detective) can master the violent event (murder).[7] Or in an alternative version, more applicable to film, we may enjoy libidinous thoughts about violence, provided that the superego is normally reassured that in the end it won't be allowed to pay. However, in what follows I shall not be concerned with psychoanalytic theories of pleasurable fantasies, and confine myself to making some 'philosophical' remarks about pleasure which are independent of such theories, even if, as I hope, compatible with them.

I wish to argue that the pleasures of the contemporary experimental text, as produced by writers like Abish, Apple, Barth, Barthelme, Coover, Davenport, Kundera, Calvino and others need a different *kind* of explanation. This is because these writers contest the form of the conventional realist text which provides the model I have outlined. As I shall try to show, they contest coherence-conferring interpretation, and thus liberate the reader from attempts to control the text in terms of serious frameworks of belief and ideology, and draw us into the game of their own disruptive procedures. In doing this they break with the aesthetic typical of modernism, which allowed interpretation to function as a kind of rationalizing *explanation*, not simply of matters such as allusion, but also of the way in which the apparently incoherent could be given a thematic ordering. Thus Wilde asserts that modernism looks for

> an image of total order. Whether the image is frankly of another world (Yeats' Byzantium) or of some symbolically sufficient enclave in this one (Howards End; the greenwood in *Maurice* or even of an ideal still to be, or only temporarily realised (Lawrence's star-balance; Woolf's lighthouse; Forster's 'only connect . . .'), in all of these cases emphasis falls on a unity in which all discontinuity is comprehended and dissolved.[8]

Many postmodern texts on the other hand are baffling because they refuse the coherence-conferring strategies of the critic.[9] Confronted by Pynchon's entropy, Federman's freewheeling concrete poetry monologue, Davenport's multilayered intertextual structures, Coover's contradictory narrative in 'The Babysitter' and so on, we are unlikely to succeed in the search for a hidden allegorical or thematic key to the whole. Nor very often, will we be able to tie the text down to a given or single mimetic situation. In reading a story like Donald Barthelme's 'The Indian Uprising',[10] we cannot say 'who' the Indians are, what they 'symbolize', why

---

[7]W.H. Auden, *The Dyer's Hand* (London, Faber, 1963), pp. 146ff.
[8]Alan Wilde, *Horizons of Assent* (Baltimore and London, Johns Hopkins U.P., 1981), p. 178.
[9]Cf. Christopher Butler, *After the Wake* (Oxford, Oxford U.P., 1980), and Marjorie Perloff, *The Poetics of Indeterminacy* (Princeton, Princeton U.P., 1981).
[10]Donald Barthelme, *Unspeakable Practices, Unnatural Acts* (New York, Farrar, Straus and Giroux 1976), pp. 9ff.

the narrator makes tables out of hollow-cored doors while living with various women, why Jane is beaten up by a dwarf in a bar in Tenerife, as notified to the narrator by International Distress Coupon, and so on. And even if we could explain these elements separately in symbolic terms, there seems little chance that such explanations would be compatible with one another. The text may refuse what the structuralists have taught us to call recuperation or naturalization;

the vocabulary of disorder is both copious and insistent; the expectation of irresolution pervasive; the syntax of parataxis overwhelming. All [such writers] welcome or at any rate subscribe to an aesthetic of openness and an ethic of improvisation or adaptation.[11]

The text may contain dreck ('matter which presents itself as not wholly relevant'), narrative becomes 'more additive than progressive', so that 'if much of modernism appears historic, hypotactical and formalist, postmodernism strikes us by contrast as playful, paratactical and deconstructionist.'[12] Ronald Sukenick in his novel *98.6* is not unusual in proclaiming

Interrruption. Discontinuity. Imperfection. It can't be helped. This very instant as I write you read a hundred things. . . . This novel is based on the Mosaic Law the law of mosaics or how to deal with parts in the absence of wholes.[13]

New fiction of this kind thus contests a basic and traditional assumption concerning the pleasure of the text; that in I.A. Richards' words, it confers upon us a satisfaction derived from coherence:

When we say that anything is good we mean that it satisfies, and by a good experience we mean one in which the impulses that make it are fulfilled, and successful, adding as the necessary qualification that this exercise and satisfaction shall not interfere with more important impulses.[14]

And he points further to 'The feeling of freedom, of relief, of increased competence and security, that follows any reading in which more than usual order and coherence have been given to our responses'[15] Such assumptions underlie much of the New Critical approach to the text; and the concern for convergent and hence satisfying significance runs right through to Frye's *Anatomy of Criticism*, which I see as the last fine flowering of the modernist, pre-deconstructive, aesthetic; 'the profound master-

---

[11]Wilde, p. 135.
[12]I refer here to Donald Barthelme, *Snow White* (New York, Atheneum, 1978), p. 106, P. Stevick, 'Scheherezade', in Malcolm Bradbury, ed., *The Novel Today* (Manchester, Manchester U.P., 1977), p. 200, and Ihab Hassan, *The Dismemberment of Orpheus* (2nd ed., Oxford, Oxford U.P., 1982), p. 267.
[13]Ronald Sukenick, *98.6* (New York, Fiction Collective, 1975).
[14]Richards, p. 44.
[15]Richards, p. 185. He goes on to describe the disequilibrium produced by bad art, p. 186.

piece draws us to a point at which we seem to see an enormous number of converging patterns of significance.'[16] If the new fiction refuses to allow for this ordering or ordered impulse, what then happens to the mimetic theory of pleasure, relying as it does on the correspondence of world to work, and on the satisfying coherence of both?

Suppose then that we are in a disordered textual world in which one is sceptical because one sees so many frameworks of belief compete, and so many bizarre incongruities in experience, that fact and fiction are as fantastic as one another. And further, that in default of a unified culture, artistic or political or moral beliefs will be in conflict or prone to deconstruction. And yet everyone goes on 'behaving' beyond the ability of crumbling ideologies (as moralities or psychological theories), or the ability of realist techniques in literature, to explain them.[17] But writers still want to write: what do they do when the older types of commitment to order, philosophical, moral, or religious, even existential, are not possible, and there is no reliable framework in which one can investigate character and action in depth? I wish to suggest that one possible solution is to become shallow,[18] and to see conflicts of belief as ironic or comic. (This is after all one way of making it tolerable; think of Beckett's remarkable stoic humour.) In the process one's art may become a form of *play* – with language, with the conventions of literature, and so on. If philosophical depth and a totalizing aesthetic are not available, then the comic mode, and a self-reflective view of the text as a focus for play, which includes the play of its possible interpretations, may take over.

These aspects of postmodern culture were particularly clear to (or perhaps just dear to) Roland Barthes. We can, using his terms, argue that the modernist text of pleasure has given way to the postmodern text of bliss. He says:

Text of pleasure; the text that contents, fills, grants euphoria; the text that comes from the culture and does not break from it, is linked to a *comfortable* practice of reading. Text of bliss: the text that imposes a state of loss, the text that discomforts (perhaps to the point of a certain boredom), unsettles the reader's historical, cultural, psychological assumptions, the consistency of his tastes, values, memories, brings to a crisis his relation with language.[19]

Barthes points out that the reader who likes both types of text, 'participates in the hedonism of all culture . . . and in the destruction of that culture'.[20] He is also willing to embrace logical contradictions; a condition

---

[16]Northrop Frye, *Anatomy of Criticism* (Princeton, Princeton U.P., 1957), p. 17.

[17]These assumptions, which really only presuppose an acquaintance with some experimental fiction, and an acceptance of the sceptical force of deconstruction, are more explicitly defended in my 'Scepticism and Experimental Fiction', forthcoming in Ileana Marcolescu, ed., *La Postmodernité* (Paris, Presses Universitaires de France).

[18]Cf. Stevick, p. 212.

[19]Roland Barthes, *The Pleasure of the Text* (trs. Richard Miller, New York, Hill and Wang, 1975), p. 14.

[20]Barthes, p. 14.

that Barthes may well have indicated with the new novel in France in mind, but which applies to many other postmodern writers. The reading subject is thus unstable, split, even perverse, 'decentred', in a way which has become familiar to us from critical theory.

He or she also lives, according to Barthes and to many other theorists, in a period in which ideologies are seen to be fictions, (and prone to Derridan deconstruction). In a sceptical age, we lack moral unity:

> The pleasure of the text does not prefer one ideology to another. *However*: this impertinence does not proceed from liberalism but from perversion: the text, its reading, are split. What is overcome, split, is the moral unity that society demands of every human product.[21]

Barthes' theory deserves a detailed exegesis, but what I wish to suggest, here at least, is that he describes very well our relationship as readers to much new writing. I think of Abish's 'Minds Meet', of Federman's *Twofold Vibration*, Max Apple's *The Oranging of America*, Calvino's *The Castle of Crossed Destinies* and *If on a Winter's Night*, of Sorrentino's *Mulligan's Stew* and Guy Davenport's *Eclogues*, amongst others. But since I have not the space to exemplify Barthes' view in so general a way, I would like to restrict myself to a single exemplary short story by Donald Barthelme, 'The Rise of Capitalism'.[22]

Here, it seems, is a 'serious' subject, which should give rise to profoundly engaging ideological positions, on which we all have 'views', philosophical, political, and stereotyped. We may think for example of 'Religion and the Rise of Capitalism' or of its inevitable decline, fissured by its own self-contradictions, exposing as it goes the false consciousness of those who would accept or sustain it. The way seems open to a direct confrontation between frameworks of belief: ours and those of the text: a confirmatory pleasure *à la* Barthes, or a challenging contradiction, that is what we look for. In any case we might expect to know where we are, within a 'comfortable' practice of reading. And indeed Barthelme seems to make things very comfortable for us by allowing the 'right' or stereotypical political notions to get into the story, for example at the beginning of the second paragraph:

> Capitalism places every man in competition with his fellows for a share of the available wealth. A few people accumulate big piles, but most do not. The sense of community falls victim to this struggle. Increased abundance and prosperity are tied to growing 'productivity'. A hierarchy of functionaries imposes itself between the people and the leadership. The good of the private corporation is seen as prior to the public good. (p. 124)

However, the fact that this is in Barthelme's 'child's copy book' style ironizes the stereotypical, comfortable character of the ideas expressed. It

---

[21]Barthes, p. 31.
[22]Donald Barthelme, *Sadness* (New York, Pocket Books, 1972; rpt 1980), pp. 123ff. Following page references are given in the text.

uses the context of literariness (in which we expect complexity) to produce a bathetic critique of ideas which can be put in this way. On the other hand, since we all I suppose understood this passage without too much difficulty, it is a tribute also to these ideas' accessibility *without* any 'high theory'. It is after all a simple story or model of the kind which may underlie the philosophical and theoretical pretensions of all ideologies. Indeed its simplicity reminds us of our perversity or bad faith in not accepting it, or in turning, with a Barthesian perversity, aside to other things – just as Barthelme himself does, when he gives this paragraph a surrealistic hinge *via* the sentence, 'The King of Jordan sits at his ham radio, inviting strangers to the palace', to an account of the narrator's visit to his 'assistant mistress' Azalea:

> I stroke her buttocks, which are perfection, if you can have perfection, under the capitalist system. 'It is better to marry than to burn', St Paul says, but St Paul is largely discredited now, for the toughness of his views does not accord with the experience of advanced industrial societies. I smoke a cigar, to disoblige the cat (p. 124).

The comedy and hence the pleasure of this turns on Barthelme's subtle confusion of religious and political frameworks, for of course it is Marx's and not St Paul's views which have been asserted not to accord with the experience of advanced industrial societies. But Marx is also tough and prophetic, and we are as little inclined to pay attention to him on that account, as to Saint Paul. This is I think because (*inter alia* of course) sex stands here for the contingent and particular, essential to pleasure, which is specific to its erotic object desired for itself, which so effectively averts the gaze from ideological generalizations, which are essentially repetitive. Thus Barthes tells us in *The Pleasure of the Text* that ideology is 'statutorily a language of repetition'[23] and another paragraph of this story begins 'And now the saints come marching in! saint upon saint upon saint, to deliver their message! . . . Alas! It is the same old message' (p.128). Indeed sexual experience brings our relationship with ideology most significantly into 'crisis' (Barthes) as anyone tempted to take St Paul seriously might find to his or her cost. Sexual description in this (and many another) story thus performs a function close to that described in John Berger's *G*:

> Sexuality is by its nature precise; or rather, its aim is precise. Any imprecision registered by any of the five senses tends to block sexual desire. The focus of sexual desire is concentrated and sharp. . . .
>
> In an indeterminate world in fact sexual desire is reinforced by a longing for precision and certainty: beside her my life is arranged. . . .
>
> In a static hierarchical world sexual desire is reinforced by a longing for an alternative certainty: with her I am free. . . .
>
> All generalisations are opposed to sexuality.[24]

[23]Barthes, p. 40.
[24]John Berger, *G* (London, Weidenfeld and Nicolson, 1972), pp. 110f.

Thus in a (static) world in which totalizing ideologies prevail and may need to be resisted, we have the view of sex found in *Women in Love*. In the highly indeterminate, anti-ideological world of the postmodern experimental text, Berger's other generalization applies: hence the peculiar force of the *'prime érotique'* offered to us in the otherwise self-contradicting new novel, which offers a point of apparently stable reference and emotional involvement.[25] Similarly, the particularity and contingency of the sexual description in Barthelme's story affronts the conflict of ideologies within it, and this incongruity is further reinforced by the narrator's peculiar action in smoking a cigar 'to disoblige the cat'. Politics here is happily contaminated by its hidden (metaphorical alliance to comic incident, which takes its place within the story with as little ceremony as the conflicting talk of politics at the dinner table which Barthelme goes on to describe:

> Everyone is talking about capitalism (although some people are talking about the psychology of aging, and some about the human use of human beings, and some about the politics of experience). 'How can you say that?' Azalea shouts, and Marta shouts, 'What about the air?' As a flower moves toward the florist, women move toward men who are no good for them. Self-actualisation is not to be achieved in terms of another person, but you don't know that, when you begin. The negation of the negation is based on a correct reading of the wrong books. (p. 127f.)

But what could a 'correct reading' possibly amount to *here*? Ideology requires a correct reading, that is its deep fault; this type of fiction does not – it escapes ideology. For everything, even the narrator's omniscient comment, is placed *on the same level* within the fiction, and so itself loses authority and becomes a fiction. The writer, like the conversationalist, reduces ideology which requires sustained argument to aphoristic allusion. This is not to say that Barthelme's story could not be seriously thought *about*, from a Marxist point of view, even as it breaks with it as we shall see, and so 'unsettles the reader's historical, cultural and psychological assumptions', as Barthes puts it. This brings to a crisis his relationship with the language of the text, in which we expect consistent narrative, and find apparent contingency, as argued above. For in a Barthelme story (and those of many other writers) the 'usual ordering' of the world is disrupted, and yet we may be tempted to look for a hidden order of things. We may ask for example in what sense these *are*:

The Achievements of Capitalism
   (a) The curtrain wall
   (b) Artificial rain
   (c) Rockefeller Center
   (d) Casals
   (e) Mystification. (p. 126)

[25]Cf. *Claude Simon: Analyse Theorie* (Paris, 10/18, 1975) pp. 226, 231, 239ff., 261ff.

The effect of this on the reader may be the same as that felt by Foucault, when he read a similarly comic and disorienting list in Borges. He tells us that his *Les mots et les choses* first arose:

> out of a passage in Borges, out of the laughter that shattered, as I read the passage, all the familiar landmarks of thought – our thought, the thought that bears the stamp of our age and our geography – breaking up all the ordered surfaces and all the planes with which we are accustomed to tame the wild profusion of existing things and continuing long afterwards to disturb and threaten with collapse our age-old distinction between the Same and the Other. This passage quotes 'a certain Chinese encyclopaedia' in which it is written that 'animals are divided into: (a) belonging to the Emperor, (b) embalmed, (c) tame, (d) sucking pigs, (e) sirens, (f) fabulous, (g) stray dogs, (h) included in the present classification, (i) frenzied, (j) innumerable, (k) drawn with a very fine camelhair brush, (l) *et cetera*, (m) having just broken the water pitcher, (n) that from a long way off look like flies'. In the wonderment of this taxonomy, the thing we apprehend in one great leap, the thing that, by means of the fable, is demonstrated as the exotic charm of another system of thought, is the limitation of our own, the stark impossibility of thinking *that*. But what is it impossible to think, and what kind of impossibility are we faced with here?[26]

Barthelme (and Borges) thus engage in a playful deconstruction of the 'order' of the world: they play with the attempts of ideology to deal with it. And we are also free to play, in making interpretations, none of which in the nature of the case can claim the certainty given by the traditional or modernist text. In so far as the pieces within the game are serious, we are discomfited. It is a serious game, as is the one Abish plays in challenging our stereotypical notions of the German in *How German Is It*, or Apple plays with the American ethic of financial success in *The Oranging of America*.

But in all these cases neither the story, nor ideology, nor our interpretation, can master all the pieces. For underlying this type of writing there is I think a Derridan notion, of our lack of mastery of the metaphorical implications of language, as he argues in his 'White Mythology'[27] and elsewhere. The text will go through a peculiarly indeterminable 'detour of signs' such as he describes in his 'Structure sign and play in the human sciences'.[28] The experimental text of this kind will thus suggest everywhere its own lack of intellectual mastery, quite apart from its tendency to be distracted by the contingent, dreck, or the sexual. It allows its argument to trail off into metaphorical suggestion, as in the list cited. The story is thus disrupted in a number of ways typical of postmodern fiction: by its plotlessness, its insouciance in controlling its own implications (typi-

[26]Michel Foucault, *The Order of Things* (trs. Alan Sheridan, London, Tavistock, 1974), p. xv.
[27]Jacques Derrida, 'White Mythology', *New Literary History* VI; (1974), pp. 5–74.
[28]In R. Macksey and E. Donato, *The Structuralist Controversy* (Baltimore, Johns Hopkins U.P., 1972), pp. 247ff., and in *L'écriture et la différence* (Paris, Seuil, 1967).

cal of surrealism), its willingness to let in the purely or apparently contingent (the King of Jordan and his ham radio) and its jokes. Barthelme cunningly suggests at the beginning of his story, and at its end, that all this may be due to an emotional attitude: in the beginning

> The first thing I did was to make a mistake. I thought I had understood capitalism, but what I had done was assume an attitude – melancholy sadness – toward it. This attitude is not correct. (p. 123)

and in conclusion:

> Smoke, rain, aboulia. What can the concerned citizen do to fight the rise of capitalism, in his own community? Study of the tides of conflict and power in a system in which there is structural inequality is an important task. A knowledge of European intellectual history since 1789 provides a useful background. Information theory offers interesting new possibilities. Passion is helpful, especially those types of passion which are non-licit. Doubt is a necessary precondition to meaningful action. Fear is the great mover, in the end. (p. 128)

But as he suggests elsewhere in an interview, the emotions don't provide consistency any more than the bizarre collection of possibilities above: 'Since we have lived through and experienced the partial failure of many things proposed to us as ideals, there are always mixed feelings – mixed feelings is our condition, our mental set. Not one ideal – mixtures! All of these ideas are useful, but none are absolute.'[29] The elements of the story are never going to be coherently brought together: the concerned citizen and the reader are going to be 'split' as Barthes suggests. Capitalism and the fight against it cannot be understood on straightforward ideological premises, any more than Barthelme's story can. Even my own interpretation is designed to leave the reader free to make his own. The pleasure of this type of experimental text thus depends on a change in our interpretative attitudes (even if we don't accept the ideological scepticism with which it seems to be correlated). It depends upon a willingness to play with ideas in a new way.

This brief analysis of one story is a mere prolegomena to a proper account of the pleasure of the postmodern experimental text. We need to understand much more clearly the relationship between (free) play, and game (which may have implied rules and conventions). Linguistic 'play' indeed, in creation and interpretation (as in, say, Geoffrey Hartman's *Saving the Text*, or Bernard Sharratt's *Reading Relations*), is difficult to define, and its values (freedom from institutional constraints? a flattering complexity for the self-congratulatory reader?) are unclear. And if game also implies convention, what are we to make, say, of the card-playing analogy which underlies a work like Calvino's *The Castle of Crossed Destinies* (1969)? If the conventions here are unclear (despite much work

---

[29]C. Bigsby and H. Ziegler, *The Liberal Tradition and the Radical Imagination* (London, Junction Books, 1981), p. 54.

for example on the new novel) then it is difficult to decide whether the pleasures we get from reflexivity and from self-conscious narration are those of mastering literary conventions (playing the game *well* with the writer) or something else. Perhaps *contra* Barthes and Foucault, we need the hidden figure of the author as the source of these conventions.

Another important field of study is that of the erotic as explicit or hidden within the text, and as a possible model for reading, which will go beyond the Freudian notion of latent fantasy. Most important perhaps is the attempt to find some explanation of the way in which the innovative aesthetic of play which I have outlined (or Barthesian 'bliss') 'contests ideology' as Barthes asserts it to do. This may not depend upon a simple equation of revolution in language with political freedom, but on something rather more straightforward, as in the relationship between humour and politics in Kundera's *The Book of Laughter and Forgetting*. A simple Marcusan account will not do here.

There is a further question too, concerning our toleration of the aesthetic of play in postmodern writing. To what extent will 'we' (that is, readers considered as social groupings) allow the play of the text with matters which we consider to be of independent importance such as the history of the Holocaust? A recently published extract from William Gass's *The Tunnel* raised these problems in an acute form. At this point we may wish to reassert a traditional 'order of things'. But this draws us into the consideration of the function of aesthetic pleasures within society, and that is beyond the scope of my argument here.

Notes on Contributors

Christopher Butler is an Official Student (i.e. Fellow) and Tutor in English at Christ Church, Oxford. His books include *After the Wake: an Essay on the Contemporary Avant Garde* (Oxford, Oxford U.P., 1980) and *Interpretation Deconstruction and Ideology* (Oxford, Oxford U.P., 1984).

John Corner entered higher education as a mature student, first at Ruskin College and then at Cambridge University. He taught at Sunderland Polytechnic until 1980, when he moved to the Department of Communication Studies at Liverpool University. With Jeremy Hawthorn he edited *Communication Studies: an Introductory Reader* (London, Edward Arnold, 1980). He has contributed a number of articles on broadcasting and media analysis to books and journals.

Robert Crosman teaches English, most recently at MIT. He has published articles on Joyce, Milton, Mailer, and on critical theory. His book *Reading Paradise Lost* (Bloomington, Indiana U.P., 1980) won the 1981 Explicator Award. He is currently at work on the politics of critical theory (articles and a book), on an autobiography, and a novel.

Maud Ellmann is a lecturer in the Department of English at the University of Southampton. Her book *Modernist Writing and the Problem of the Subject* is to be published by the Harvester Press in 1984.

Jeremy Hawthorn is Professor of Modern British Literature at the University of Trondheim, Norway. His books include *Identity and Relationship* (London, Lawrence and Wishart, 1973); *Joseph Conrad: Language and Fictional Self-consciousness* (London, Edward Arnold, 1979); and *Multiple Personality and the Disintegration of Literary Character* (London, Edward Arnold, 1983).

P.D. Juhl is Associate Professor in the Department of Germanic Languages and Literatures at Princeton University. He has published a book, *Interpretation: An Essay in the Philosophy of Literary Criticism* (Princeton, Princeton U.P., 1980), and a number of articles on the theory of literature and criticism.

Terry Lovell is a lecturer in sociology at the University of Warwick, where she teaches courses on the sociology of literature and film. Her publications include *Pictures of Reality: Aesthetics, Politics and Pleasure* (London, British Film Institute, 1980), and contributions to Diana Laurenson, ed., *The Sociology of Literature: Applied Studies*, Sociological Review Monograph XXVI (Keele, Staffordshire, Sociological Review, 1978); Denis McQuail, ed., *Sociology of Mass Communications* (London, Penguin, 1972); and to *Screen* and *European Journal of Sociology*.

Colin Mercer, at the time of writing, is Course Team Chairman for the new course on Popular Culture at the Open University. He has edited and contributed to various volumes on the theme of popular culture. He has also written extensively on the work of Antonio Gramsci, on Marxist theory, historiography and popular politics, and is at present writing a book on narrative and pleasure in popular fiction to be published by Routledge and Kegan Paul in 1984/5. He is an editorial board member of *Formations*.

Barbara Hill Rigney is Associate Professor of English at the Ohio State University. Her publications include articles on feminist criticism, and two books: *Madness and Sexual Politics in the Feminist Novel: Studies in Brontë, Woolf, Lessing and Atwood* (Madison, Univ. of Wisconsin Press, 1978; paperback edition 1979), and *Lilith's Daughters: Women and Religion in Contemporary Fiction* (Madison, Univ. of Wisconsin Press, 1980).

R.A. Sharpe is Senior Lecturer in Philosophy at Saint David's University College, Lampeter, University of Wales. He is the author of many articles on various philosophical topics, principally aesthetics but also philosophy of social science, philosophy of mind and action. These have appeared in *Mind, Proceedings of the Aristotelian Society*, and other leading journals. His book *Contemporary Aesthetics: a Philosophical Analysis* (Brighton, Harvester, 1983) was also published in the USA by St Martin's Press. He has held visiting appointments at the University of Michigan, Ann Arbor, and at the University of Queensland.

Iain Wright is a Fellow and Lecturer in English at Queens' College, Cambridge, and has been a Visiting Fellow of the Humanities Research Centre of the Australian National University. His recent publications include essays on Leavis and *Scrutiny*, and on Beckett and poststructuralist criticism. He is presently preparing volumes on E.M. Forster's non-fictional writings and on modern British criticism.

Index

synchronicity, 83–4; *see also* diachronicity; history

texts: and reading, ix; and meaning, xii, 17n, 41; and 'deep reading', 37–8; and deconstruction, 59–71, 89, 93; Barthes and, 86; experimental, 129–39
Thompson, Denys *see* Leavis, F.R.
Times Literary Supplement, The (journal), 72, 85
Todorov, Tzvetan, 115
Tolstoy, Count Lev, *Anna Karenina*, 21
Tovey, Donald Francis, 20
Trotsky, Leon, 9
Tynianov, Juri, 45, 47, 49

utterance, 42, 45, 48–9, 62

Voloshinov, V.N., 48–9, 51, 53, 57; *Freudianism: A Marxist Critique*, 42;

Marxism and the Philosophy of Language, 42

Walker, David H., 117
Walton, Paul *see* David, Howard
Warren, Robert Penn, 3
Waugh, Evelyn, *Brideshead Revisited*, 122
Weimann, Robert, xi, 83, 88
Weldon, Fay, 122
Williams, Raymond, 36; *The Long Revolution*, 28, 29n, 39
Wimsatt, W.K., ix, 1–3
Woolf, Leonard, 72
Woolf, Virginia (*née* Stephen), *A Room of One's Own*, viii, 73–81; *To the Lighthouse*, 73n
Wordsworth, William, 129–30
Working Papers in Cultural Studies (journal), 28
Wright, Iain, ix–x, 82–96
writing, 90; *see also* discourse; utterance

Yorck, Graf, 93

DATE DUE
DATE DE RETOUR
